Essential German
Vocabulary

Lisa Kahlen

Series editor
Rosi McNab

For UK order enquiries: please contact Bookpoint Ltd,
130 Milton Park, Abingdon, Oxon, OX14 4SB.
Telephone: +44 (0) 1235 827720. *Fax:* +44 (0) 1235 400454.
Lines are open 09.00–17.00, Monday to Saturday, with a 24-hour
message answering service. Details about our titles and how to
order are available at www.teachyourself.com

For USA order enquiries: please contact McGraw-Hill Customer
Services, PO Box 545, Blacklick, OH 43004-0545, USA.
Telephone: 1-800-722-4726. *Fax:* 1-614-755-5645.

For Canada order enquiries: please contact McGraw-Hill Ryerson Ltd,
300 Water St, Whitby, Ontario, L1N 9B6, Canada.
Telephone: 905 430 5000. *Fax:* 905 430 5020.

Long renowned as the authoritative source for self-guided learning –
with more than 50 million copies sold worldwide – the *Teach Yourself*
series includes over 500 titles in the fields of languages, crafts, hobbies,
business, computing and education.

British Library Cataloguing in Publication Data: a catalogue record
for this title is available from the British Library.

Library of Congress Catalog Card Number: on file.

First published in UK 2003 as Teach Yourself German Vocabulary
by Hodder Education, 338 Euston Road, London, NW1 3BH.

First published in US 2003 by The McGraw-Hill Companies, Inc.

This edition published 2010.

The *Teach Yourself* name is a registered trade mark of
Hodder Headline.

Typeset by MPS Limited, A Macmillan Company.

Printed in Great Britain for Hodder Education, an Hachette
UK Company, 338 Euston Road, London, NW1 3BH.

The publisher has used its best endeavours to ensure that the URLs
for external websites referred to in this book are correct and active
at the time of going to press. However, the publisher and the author
have no responsibility for the websites and can make no guarantee
that a site will remain live or that the content will remain relevant,
decent or appropriate.

Hodder Headline's policy is to use papers that are natural,
renewable and recyclable products and made from wood grown
in sustainable forests. The logging and manufacturing processes
are expected to conform to the environmental regulations of the
country of origin.

Impression number	10 9 8 7
Year	2016

Contents

Credits

Meet the author

My name is Lisa Kahlen and I have been teaching German to people of all ages in Scotland for the last 20 years, having moved from West Berlin in Germany in 1989, the year that the Berlin Wall came down. It has been an absolute pleasure to have had the opportunity to teach German to so many people and to write books to assist them in their studies, whether they are students learning their very first words in German or advanced learners who are able to converse fluently in the language. My teaching and writing has been aimed at a wide range of students, from children as young as three in German kindergartens and a children's language club in Scotland, to college and university students and adults learning for business or pleasure. I have written a number of German study books, German theatre plays for children, Scottish examination papers, and interactive online learning resources.

My personal tip for learning German is this: adopt the curious and playful approach of a child, and go about it with a sense of humour to make it fun. I hope I have helped my students to do this throughout my many years of teaching German.

I would like to thank Professor Wolf Kahlen (http://www.wolf-kahlen.net/Video/) where his video clip 'Learning German with Russian Bread' gives an artist's humorous view of learning German. I would also like to thank my partner Rob Wilkinson and my son Ernie for their support and patience, and all my students who have been such a great inspiration for my writing. Finally, to all of you who are using this book: Have fun learning German! **Viel Spaß beim Deutsch lernen!**

Lisa Kahlen

Only got a minute?

This book is more than just a list of German words and phrases – it is a key to opening the door to better communication. It is designed to give you the confidence you need to express yourself better in German by increasing your knowledge of current vocabulary, and at the same time showing you how to use the new words you are learning.

The **Introduction** includes some useful learning tips, rules on pronunciation and spelling, and advice on how to use the book to build up your vocabulary much faster. In the **Toolbox** section you will find the most important grammatical rules: the tools you need to speak German. It can be used as an introduction to German grammar and language for beginners or as a reference for students who are more advanced.

The main part of the book is divided into 16 topics. The way the language is organized within the topic areas is a direct result of studies carried out into language learning which show that adults find it easier to remember words if they are put into a context.

As Anglicisms play a more and more important part in the German language, special attention is drawn – in **Insight** boxes – to words which have been taken from the English language and integrated into German, and similarities between English and German words are highlighted. This will help you to build up your vocabulary faster and to communicate in as up-to-date a manner as possible.

In addition, you can listen to and participate in an audio recording via our website: www.teachyourself.com. In the first part of this I explain a method of vocabulary learning and invite you to participate in a vocabulary learning exercise which lasts approximately 30 minutes To see a humorous view of German vocabulary learning, go to the artist Professor Wolf Kahlen's website www.wolf-kahlen.net/Video/

Viel Spaß beim Deutsch lernen!

5 Only got five minutes?

This new version of the book is more than just a list of German words and phrases – it is a key to opening the door to better communication. It is designed to give you the confidence you need to communicate better in German by increasing your knowledge of up-to-date vocabulary including Anglicisms and at the same time showing you how to use the new words you are learning.

The **Introduction** includes some useful learning tips, advice on how to remember new words and on how to use the book to build up your vocabulary much faster. In the **Toolbox** section you will find the most important grammatical rules, providing you with the tools you need to learn more efficiently and to speak German faster. This part of the book is designed to be used for general reference. In order to pronounce newly learned words correctly, you will find in the Toolbox tips on German pronunciation, a guide on how to pronounce vowels, consonants and letter combinations and other tips in connection with spelling. The book is now accompanied by an audio recording, which can be accessed at www.teachyourself.com. In the first part of the recording I explain a method of vocabulary learning and invite you to participate in a vocabulary learning exercise. In the second part of the recording you can listen to and participate in German pronunciation of vowels, consonants and letter combinations.

As German is a much more phonetically consistent language than English – which means that German words are nearly always spelled the way they sound – it is very useful to learn the way vowels, consonants and letter combinations sound, as you will be able to pronounce new words by just looking at the spelling.

The main part of the book, the vocabulary section, is divided into 16 topic areas: personal matters; family; work; education; at home; entertaining, food and drink; in town; in the country; hobbies and sports; clothing; travel; tourism; the body and health; the world; government and society; and the media. The way the language is organized within the topic areas in this book is a direct result of studies carried out into language learning which show that adults find it difficult to learn long lists of words and find it easier to remember words if they are put into a context. The words have been carefully arranged, grouped with other related nouns, verbs, adjectives etc. and useful expressions.

For example, in Unit 1 you learn how to address people correctly. Most older Germans like to be addressed by their title; someone who has gained a medical or academic 'Dr' title in Germany will be pleased if you address him or her with **Herr Doktor** or **Frau Doktor**. You will also learn vocabulary in connection with making arrangements to meet somebody, useful phrases and expressions in connection with meeting people, describing yourself and others, and expressing what you like and dislike. In Unit 1 you will also find a list of words and phrases useful for expressing your opinion, for example **Ich stimme Ihnen zu** *I agree with you*, **Ich schlage vor** *I suggest*, **Das ist völliger Unsinn** *That is complete nonsense*. We look at the difference in usage between **mögen** and **gern(e)** in connection with likes and dislikes. In Unit 1 you will also find a very useful list of verbs which take the dative or accusative (dative = **mir, dir, ihm** etc. **Ich glaube dir** *I believe you*, **Ich glaube ihm** *I believe him*; accusative = **mich, dich, sich** etc. **Ich denke an dich** *I think about you*, **Ich rufe dich an** *I'll phone you*.

The **Don't panic!** section contains useful phrases for beginners as well as more advanced students of German. There are general expressions such as **Vorsicht!** *Pay attention!*, **Passen Sie auf!** *Be careful!*, **Ich habe das nicht mitgekriegt** *I didn't catch what you said*, and some language commonly found on signs, such as **Kein Eingang** *No entry*.

Unit 3 deals with vocabulary in connection with jobs: job titles, work places, related words to do with employment and how these words are connected, such as **Arbeitsplatz** *work place*, **Arbeitskleidung** *work clothes*, **Arbeitsteilung** *division of work*, etc.

It clarifies the word **Entlassung** which stands for two words in English: *dismissal* and *redundancy*. In Units 3 and 4 you will find vocabulary and phrases in connection with writing letters as well as making telephone calls, and language to do with computers.

As Anglicisms play a more and more important part in the German language, special attention is drawn in this new version of the book to words which have been taken from the English language and integrated into German, and similarities between English and German words are highlighted. This will help you to build up your vocabulary faster and to communicate in as up-to-date a manner as possible. You will therefore find in each of the 16 units of this new edition of the book current Anglicisms and similar and easily recognizable words listed in the **Insight** boxes, with each word used in context. This fantastic tool will allow you to increase your vocabulary much faster and to express yourself with greater confidence, knowing which English words have been adopted into the German language.

Special attention is also given in this book to separable verbs or so-called split verbs. They play an important role in the German language. The prefix of the verb has been <u>underlined</u> in this book, e.g. <u>auf</u>stehen *to get up*, <u>an</u>kommen *to arrive*, <u>weg</u>fahren *to leave*, so you can recognize them immediately and remember to split off the prefix when using them in a sentence: **Ich stehe um 6 Uhr auf** *I get up at 6 o'clock*, **Wir kommen um 7 Uhr an** *We will arrive at 7 o'clock*, **Wir fahren heute weg** *We will leave today*.

If you are interested in seeing a humorous view of vocabulary learning by the artist Professor Wolf Kahlen, go to the website http://www.wolf-kahlen.net/Video/. For the audio recording about vocabulary learning and pronunciation exercise, go to www.teachyourself.com

Viel Spaß beim Deutsch lernen!

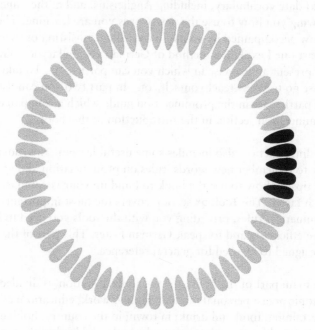

10 Only got ten minutes?

This new version of the book is more than just a list of German words and phrases – it is a key to opening the door to better communication. It is designed to give you the confidence you need to communicate better in German by increasing your knowledge of up-to-date vocabulary, including Anglicisms, and at the same time showing you how to use the new words you are learning. The book is now accompanied by an audio recording consisting of two parts. In part one I explain a method of German vocabulary learning and present an exercise in which you can participate. To take part please go to www.teachyourself.com. In part two you can listen to and participate in the pronunciation guide which accompanies the pronunciation section in the **Introduction** to this book.

The Introduction also includes some useful learning tips, advice on how to remember new words, rules on pronunciation and spelling and tips on how to use the book to build up your vocabulary much faster. The **Toolbox** section covers the most important grammatical rules, providing you with the tools you need to learn more efficiently and to speak German faster. This part of the book is designed to be used for general reference.

The main part of the book, the vocabulary section, is divided into 16 topic areas: personal matters; family; work; education; at home; entertaining, food and drink; in town; in the country; hobbies and sports; clothing; travel; tourism; the body and health; the world; government and society; and the media. The way the language is organized within the topic areas in this book is a direct result of studies carried out into language learning which show that adults find it difficult to learn long lists of words and find it easier to remember words if they are put into a context. The words have been carefully arranged, grouped with other related nouns, verbs, adjectives etc. and useful expressions. For example, in Unit 1 you learn how to address people correctly. Most Germans like to be addressed by their title; someone who has gained a medical or academic 'Dr' title in Germany will be pleased if you address him or her with **Herr Doktor** or **Frau Doktor**. You will learn vocabulary in connection with making arrangements to meet somebody, useful phrases and expressions in connection with meeting people, describing yourself and others and expressing what you like and dislike. In this first unit you will also find a list of words and phrases useful for expressing your opinion, e.g. **Ich stimme Ihnen zu** *I agree with you*, **Ich schlage vor** *I suggest*, **Das ist völliger Unsinn** *That is complete nonsense*. We look at the difference in usage between **mögen** and **gern(e)** in connection with likes and dislikes. In Unit 1 you will also find a very useful list of verbs which take the dative or accusative (dative = **mir, dir, ihm** etc. **Ich glaube dir** *I believe you*, **Ich glaube ihm** *I believe him*. Accusative = **mich, dich, sich** etc. **Ich denke an dich** *I think about you*, **Ich rufe dich an** *I'll phone you*). The **Don't panic!** section contains very useful phrases for beginners as well as more advanced students of German. These include general expressions such as **Vorsicht!** *Pay attention!*, **Passen Sie auf!** *Be careful!*, **Ich habe das nicht mitgekriegt** *I didn't catch what you said*, and language commonly found on signs such as **Kein Eingang** *No entry*.

Unit 3, for example, deals with vocabulary in connection with jobs: job titles, work places, related words to do with employment and how these words are connected, such as **Arbeitsplatz** *work place*, **Arbeitskleidung** *work clothes*, **Arbeitsteilung** *division of work*, etc. It clarifies the word **Entlassung** which stands for two words in English: dismissal and redundancy. In Unit 3.4 you will find vocabulary and phrases in connection with writing letters as well as making telephone calls, and language to do with computers.

As Anglicisms play a more and more important part in the German language, special attention is drawn in this new version of the book to words which have been taken from the English language and integrated into German, and similarities between English and German words are highlighted. This will help you to build up your vocabulary faster and to communicate in as up-to-date a manner as possible. In each of the 16 units of this new edition of the book you will therefore find current Anglicisms and similar and easily

recognizable words listed in the **Insight** boxes and used in context in that unit. This is a fantastic tool as it will allow you to increase your vocabulary much faster and express yourself with greater confidence, knowing which English words have been adopted into the German language.

Special attention is also given to separable verbs or so-called split verbs. They play an important role in the German language. In this book the prefix of the verb has been <u>underlined</u>, e.g. **<u>auf</u>stehen** *to get up*, **<u>an</u>kommen** *to arrive*, **<u>weg</u>fahren** *to leave*, so you can recognize them immediately and remember to split off the prefix when using them in a sentence: **Ich stehe um 6 Uhr auf** *I get up at 6 o'clock*, **Wir kommen um 7 Uhr an.** *We will arrive at 7 o'clock*, **Wir fahren heute weg** *We will leave today*.

As German is a much more phonetically consistent language than English, which means that German words are nearly always spelled the way they sound, it is very useful to learn the way vowels, consonants and letter combinations sound, as you will then be able to pronounce new words by just looking at the spelling. In order to pronounce newly learned words correctly, you will find in the **Introduction** tips on German pronunciation, a guide on how to pronounce vowels, consonants and letter combinations, and other advice in connection with spelling. You can listen to and participate in this pronunciation guide by going to www.teachyourself.com. You can find it in part two of the recording.

Summary of the Toolbox

In order to use vocabulary you need some tools to put these words into sentences. If you are a beginner, you can use this section to get to know the basics of the German language and to build sentences. If you have learned German before, use the **Toolbox** to revise what you have learned, but I am sure you will also find many new useful tips and explanations.

First we cover the nouns. All German nouns are written with a capital letter and are therefore easily recognized. In German all nouns are either masculine (**der**), feminine (**die**), or neuter (**das**). Although there is no logic to whether a noun is masculine, feminine or neuter, there are some ways to help you remember the gender of a noun. These tips are listed in the **Toolbox** section.

In the article section we explain the basics of German articles. It covers how articles change depending on the function they have in a sentence.

The articles **der, die, das** can change depending on whether the noun is being used as:

▶ the subject in a sentence (nominative)
▶ the direct object (accusative)
▶ the indirect object (dative)

In Unit 1 of the book you will find an extensive list of verbs which take the dative or the accusative.

Pronouns are very important to learn and they are covered in the **Toolbox**, including tips such as:

Remember that there are three words for 'you' in German:

du (informal)
Sie (formal, singular and plural)
ihr (informal, plural)

You should say **Sie** to people over the age of 16, apart from relatives or friends.

We also look at prepositions. After certain prepositions the article changes, e.g. **bis, durch, für, gegen, ohne, um, wider,** which are followed by the accusative. If you are a beginner and this is too complex for you, don't worry! In fact there are many jokes in

Germany about gender and prepositions, as even some German native speakers get it wrong.

Apart from learning verbs, which we need in order to form sentences, it is important to learn the conjugation of verbs and how they work. This is explained as follows:

In German the verb consists of the stem + the ending – **en** or **n** or **ern**.

flieg**en**, fahr**en**
lächel**n**, sammel**n**
wand**ern**, klett**ern**

Pay attention to regular verbs.

In German, the ending of the verb changes for each person.

ich: the verb ends in **e**: **ich wohne**
du: it ends in **st**: **du wohnst**
er/sie/es: it ends in **t**: **er/sie/es wohnt**
wir: it ends in **en**: **wir wohnen**
ihr: it ends in **t**: **ihr wohnt**
sie: it ends in **en**: **sie wohnen**

German has irregular verbs, just as English does, and they have to be learned by heart. The two most important irregular verbs are **haben** *to have* and **sein** *to be*. At the end of the book you will find a useful list of common irregular verbs.

The German language has many separable verbs. They are made up of two parts: a prefix – for example **ab-**, **an-** or **zurück-** – and the infinitive of a verb – for example **fahren** *to drive* or **kommen** *to come*. Examples of separable verbs with these prefixes are **ankommen** *to arrive*, **abfahren** *to leave*, and **zurückkommen** *to come back*. These verbs are very important, and can cause many learners 'a bit of a headache'! We therefore pay special attention to them by underlining prefixes in separable verbs throughout the book, e.g **<u>auf</u>stehen**,

anfangen, **wegfahren**. Because they are underlined you can spot them and easily recognize them as separable.

Some verbs in German need to include a reflexive pronoun for their meaning to be complete, e.g. **ich wasche mich** *I wash myself*. They are called reflexive verbs. German has many more reflexive verbs than English, e.g. 'to sit down' in German is reflexive: **ich setze mich** (lit. 'I sit myself').

To form simple sentences in the **present tense** you have to remember the most important rule: The verb *always* comes second in the main part of the sentence.

In order to talk about the past, we shall be looking at the perfect tense which comprises the past participle and the verb **haben** or **sein**. It is useful to remember that approximately 70% of all verbs take haben and 30% take sein. Another useful guideline is that verbs expressing movement take **sein**:

Ich habe ein Buch gelesen. *I read a book.* **Ich bin nach Hannover gefahren.** *I went to Hanover.*

The future tense is nice and easy to learn:

You can form the future tense with the auxiliary verb **werden** and the infinitive: **Ich werde dich besuchen.** *I am going to visit you.*

You can also use the present tense, as long as you indicate when you are going to do something: **Am Montag besuche ich dich.** *On Monday I am going to visit you.*

To form **negative expressions** you use **kein** or **nicht**, but you have to follow a grammatical rule:

Ich mag kein Fleisch. *I don't like meat.* Use **kein** in front of a noun.

Ich rauche nicht. *I don't smoke.* Use **nicht** with a verb.

We also look at other negative expressions such as: **nichts** *nothing*, **niemand** *nobody*, **noch nie** *never*.

There are two forms of **questions**: 1) asking questions using a question word, e.g. **was** *what*, **wann** *when*, and 2) interrogative questions.

In the first type the question word comes first, followed by the verb, followed by the subject.

Wo wohnen Sie? *Where do you live?*

In the other type you simply invert the pronoun and verb. Start with the verb: **Sprechen Sie Deutsch?** *Do you speak German?* (lit. *Speak you German?*)

We also look at the **conditional,** which is used to translate *would* in English. The conditional always includes a condition, whether this is expressed or not, for example:

Ich würde gerne in die Schweiz fahren (wenn ich genug Geld und Zeit hätte). *I would like to go to Switzerland (if I had enough money and time).*

Adjectives are also covered. An adjective describes a noun or a pronoun. When an adjective is used *after* the noun, the adjective does not change, e.g. **Das Wetter ist schlecht** *The weather is bad*. It also does not change after a pronoun (**er** *he*, **sie** *she*, es *it*): **Es ist schlecht** *It is bad*. It does however change if it comes before the noun: **Das schlechte Wetter. Ich kaufe einen neuen Computer.**

The **comparative** is made by adding **-er** to the base form of the adjective, e.g. **klein** *small*, **kleiner** *smaller*, **weit** *wide*, **weiter** *wider*.

Er ist kleiner als sein Bruder. *He is smaller than his brother.*

The **superlative** is made by adding **am** and the ending **-(e)sten: am größten** *tallest*, **am kleinsten** *smallest*.

Er ist am kleinsten. *He is the smallest.*

Colours and sizes are included in the context of shopping for clothes. There are reminders, e.g., to write all English two-word colour adjectives as one word: **dunkelgrün** *dark green.*

In English most **adverbs** are made by adding *-ly* to an adjective: *quick – quickly. I don't drive quickly.* German adverbs are the same as the adjective: **Ich fahre nicht schnell.**

In order to make arrangements to meet somebody you will need to know **numbers, times, days** and **dates.** Points to remember include: **sechs** but **sechzehn** (the **s** has been dropped), **sieben** but **siebzehn** (the **en** has been dropped). There are two words for Saturday in Germany: **Samstag** and **Sonnabend.**

Expressions of time are also very useful to learn. Remember: **heute Nachmittag** *this afternoon*, **heute früh** *this morning*, **morgen früh** *tomorrow morning*, **gestern Vormittag** *yesterday morning*. **Morgen** has two meanings: *tomorrow* and *morning*. **Guten Morgen** *Good morning*, **Montag morgen** *Monday morning.*

Morgen fahren wir nach München. *Tomorrow we are going to Munich.*

To arrange a time to meet somebody you will need to know how Germans tell the time, which is a bit different from in English. Careful: **Halb zehn** is *half past nine* in English. So in other words 9.30 is expressed in German as half an hour before ten, while in English it is half an hour after nine. Also remember: There is only one word in German for clock and watch – **die Uhr.** *My watch is broken* **Meine Uhr ist kaputt.** Germans also use the same word Uhr for telling the time, e.g. **Es ist 5 Uhr.** *It is 5 o'clock.*

Expressions of quantity, and **weights and measures,** are very useful to know, whether you need them for shopping, measuring things, understanding the weather report or describing how much milk or sugar you want in your tea.

Knowing how to **be polite, give orders** or **request something** in a foreign language is very important. We therefore give you expressions you can use to communicate with confidence in various situations, e.g. those including the word **bitte: Hier, bitte!** *Here you are!* **Bitte, bitte** *You're welcome*, **bitte** *please*.

Apart from the pronunciation guide there is a section on **German spelling**. As mentioned above, German is a much more phonetically consistent language than English, which means that German words are nearly always spelled the way they sound.

Although **Hochdeutsch** *High German* is the language spoken or understood throughout Germany; there are many dialects spoken in and around the 16 **Länder** *states* in Germany. Many consider the best **Hochdeutsch** to be that spoken in and around Hanover in the north of Germany.

German has many long nouns called **compound nouns.** Don't be put off by them; they are simply a combination of more than one word. When reading a long word for the first time, try to split it up and take a little breath in between elements. **Kindergarten = Kinder + garten.** In this book we look at these compound words and use them to build up your vocabulary.

Finally, if you are interested in seeing a humorous artist's view of vocabulary learning, go to the website http://www.wolf-kahlen.net/Video/ by Professor Wolf Kahlen.

Viel Spaß beim Deutsch lernen!

Introduction

Did you know that German is the second most spoken language in Europe, with over 100 million speakers? And in the USA, approximately 1.5 million people speak German. For native English speakers, learning German vocabulary, when done systematically, can be fun as there are many similarities with their own language.

There have been many studies carried out into the way we learn vocabulary. The Swiss, who are generally acknowledged as experts in multi-language learning, are also leaders in the understanding of the processes of language acquisition and some of their findings may be of interest to people wanting to broaden their vocabulary.

> 'Studies have shown that the most successful way [of learning vocabulary] is when the student is able to relate the new word to a concept and to integrate it into a conceptual system.'
>
> (Wokusch, 1997)

This means that the most successful way of learning vocabulary is to put the new language into a context. It is for this reason that the vocabulary in this book has been given in context rather than, as in a dictionary, in alphabetical order. The words have been chosen as the words most likely to be useful or of interest to the learner.

Throughout the book I will give you tips on how to make learning German words and expressions easier and more interesting. As Anglicisms play a more and more important part in the German language, special attention is drawn in this new edition of the book to words which have been taken from the English language and integrated into German, by listing or highlighting Anglicisms or similarities between English and German words in each chapter. This will help you to build up your vocabulary faster and to ensure that you communicate in as up-to-date a manner as possible.

The book is now accompanied by two audio recordings, which can be accessed at www.teachyourself.com. In the first recording I explain a method of vocabulary learning and invite you to participate in a vocabulary learning exercise which lasts approximately 30 minutes. In the second recording you can listen to and participate in German pronunciation of vowels, consonants and letter combinations. This will enable you to read and pronounce newly learned words from the book.

How this book works

This book is more than just a list of words – it is a key to opening the door to better communication. It is designed to give you the confidence you need to communicate better in German by increasing your knowledge of up-to-date vocabulary and at the same time showing you how to use the new words you are learning.

The first part of the book includes some useful learning tips, rules on pronunciation and shortcuts to look out for when learning new words. The toolbox provides you with the tools you need to speak a language. It includes basic information about the structure of the language and useful tips, including how to address people, how to ask questions, how to talk about what you have done and what you are going to do, useful expressions and shortcuts to language learning. This part of the book is designed to be used for general reference.

The main part of the book is divided into topic areas: personal matters, family, work, education etc. Most adults complain that they find it very difficult to learn vocabulary and wish they had learnt it when they were younger. What they don't realize is that they are still trying to learn vocabulary in the same way as they did when they were children. The way the language is organized within the topic areas in this book is a direct result of studies carried out into language learning which show that adults find it difficult to learn long lists of words and find it easier to remember words if they are put into a context. The words have been carefully arranged, grouped with other related words, nouns, verbs, adjectives etc. and useful expressions with up-to-date notes about language fashions where relevant, so that the new language can be used immediately.

Make learning vocabulary more interesting

▶ First decide which topic you are going to look at today.
▶ Look at the words which are similar/same or Anglicism at first.
▶ See how many words you know already and tick them off.
▶ Choose which new words you want to learn – don't try to do too many at once but learn a certain amount each day.
▶ Count them so you know how many you are going to try to learn.
▶ Say them out loud; you could even record yourself saying them and listen to your recording while driving, on a bus or lying on the beach, or whatever you do when you don't have to think about other things.
▶ Learn some words before falling asleep. You might even start dreaming in German! See how many words you have remembered when you wake up the next day.

Tips to remember new words

▶ Learn words in a context. Build a sentence with each new word you learn.
▶ Look at words which are similar in English and German such as to **finden** *find*, **schwimmen** *swim*, **Vater** *father*, **kommen** *to come*. Remember the words which are nearly the same: **Haus** *house*, **Garten** *garden*.
▶ List Anglicisms such as **sorry**, **relaxen** and **der Computer**. You will be astonished how many words you know already by doing that. Tips on this are given throughout the units of this book. Look out for the **Insight** boxes which focus on the same or similar words in English and German.
▶ Look out for words which are the same in English and in German but may have a different pronunciation,

e.g. die Inflation, die Imagination, die Butter, England. If you are not sure about the pronunciation of German vowels go to the pronunciation guide in the Toolbox or the audio recording at www.teachyourself.com

▶ Try to associate words with pictures or situations, e.g. try to imagine a picture of a rose when you say the word rosa *pink*.

▶ See if you can split the word into bits, some of which you know already: **Sommerferien = Sommer** (*summer*) + **Ferien** (*holidays*) = *summer holidays*.

▶ Look for words related to ones you know already:

▶ **Tag** (*day*), **täglich** (*daily*); **die Tageszeitung** (*daily paper*), **tagsüber** (*during the day*); **Sonne** (*the sun*), **sonnig** (*sunny*), **der Sonnenuntergang** (*sunset*), **Sonnenaufgang** (*sunrise*), **Sonntag** (*Sunday*).

▶ Learn the value of typical beginnings and endings used to alter the meaning of words, e.g. **un; in; ehrlich/unehrlich** (*honest/dishonest*); **abhängig/unabhängig** (*dependent/independent*); **möglich/unmöglich** (*possible/impossible*).

Spelling tips

These don't always work but they may help!

▶ If a word begins with *th* in English, this often appears as a **d** in German: *Thursday*, **Donnerstag**; *to think*, **denken**; *thirsty*, **durstig**; *thanks*, **danke**.

▶ If a word begins with *p* in English, it is often **pf** in German: *pan*, **Pfanne**; *pipe*, **Pfeife**; *plaster*, **Pflaster**; *to pick*, **pflücken**.

▶ Where you see a word with the letter *k* in the middle, try replacing this with **ch**: *make*, **machen**; *cake*, **Kuchen**; *cook*, **kochen**; *weekly*, **wöchentlich**.

▶ Look out for words beginning with **im-, in-, re-, sub-** or **dis-** in German and begin the same in English. Words beginning with **des-** in German begin with **dis-** in English: **Immunität**, *immunity*; **inadäquat**, *inadequate*; **immateriell**, *immaterial*; **interessant**, *interesting*; **inflexibel**, *inflexible*; **Inflation**, *inflation*; **realistisch**, *real*; **reagieren**, *to react*; **reduzieren**, *to reduce*; **Substanz**, *substance*; **subventionieren**, *to subsidize*;

Diskothek, *discotheque*; **disharmonieren**, *to be discordant*; **diskret**, *discreet*; **Desinfektion**, *disinfection*; **Desaster**, *disaster*.

▶ Many words which end in *-able* in English end in *-abel* in German: *acceptable*, **akzeptabel**; *comfortable*, **komfortabel**; *miserable*, **miserabel**.

▶ German ending *-ig* cognates with *-y* in English: *thirsty*, **durstig**; *hungry*, **hungrig**; *gawky*, **spindlig**.

▶ German ending *-sieren* cognates with *-ize* in English: **kritisieren**, *criticize*; **fantasieren**, *fantasize*; **modernisieren**, *modernize*.

Write words down

▶ Copy a list of the most important words onto A4 paper with a broad felt tip and stick it on the wall so that you can study it when doing some household jobs (such as washing up or ironing), shaving or putting on make-up.

▶ For names of objects around the house, you could write the word on a sticky label and attach it to the actual object.

▶ Copy lists of words in German and English in two columns. First, say each word out loud, then cover up one column and try to remember each word in the other column. This is a very old but effective method of learning.

▶ Do something else for half an hour and then come back and see how many you can still remember. Choose between three and five words each day, write them on a sticker and carry this sticker around with you all day, looking at it from time to time.

▶ Write down the first letter of each new word and put a dot for each missing letter, cover up the word and see if you can complete the word.

▶ Pick a few words you find difficult to remember: write each one down with the letters jumbled up; leave them for a while, then later try to unscramble each one.

▶ In your list, mark the difficult words: ask someone else to test you on the ones you have marked.

▶ Transfer words you can't remember onto a free software package such as quizlet.com and do fun exercises with these words until you remember them.

Shortcuts: looking for patterns

Certain letter patterns reveal important facts about the type of word you are trying to learn:

▶ Most nouns in German ending in -o, -tum, -ment, -eum, -ium, -um and -ett are neuter: **das Auto, das Radio, das Inferno, das Altertum, das Instrument, das Museum, das Delirium, das Duett.**

▶ Nouns in German ending in -age, -e, -ei, -heit, -keit, -schaft, -ie, -in, -ion, -tät, -ung are feminine: **die Garage, die Rose, die Malerei, die Frechheit, die Einsamkeit, die Eigenschaft, die Energie, die Medizin, die Infektion, die Universität, die Unterhaltung.**

▶ Most nouns in German ending in -el, -en, -er, -ig, -ich and -ling are masculine: **der Opel, der Wagen, der Teller, der Honig, der Kranich, der Feigling.**

You saw earlier in the introduction how other endings can convert one word into another; if you know the basic word, it is easy to work out the converted word. Similarly, some German words can be converted by adding a syllable at the beginning, and most work the same as in English, as follows:

ent-	= -de-/dis-	**entmachten** (*deprive*); **entdecken** (*discover*); **enträtseln** (*to decipher*)
ent-	= un-	**entladen** (*unload*); **entfalten** (*to unfold*)

The following syllables added to the beginning of a word can cause it to have the opposite or negative meaning:

un-	= un-	**freundlich** (*friendly*), **unfreundlich** (*unfriendly*); **angenehm** (*pleasant*), **unangenehm** (*unpleasant*)
miss-	= mis-/dis-	**verstehen** (*to understand*), **missverstehen** (*misunderstand*); **das Missgeschick** (*misfortune*); **Missachtung** (*disregard*); **missbilligen** (*to disapprove*)

ver-	= *for-*	**bieten** (*to offer*), **verbieten** (*forbid*); **geben** (*to give*), **vergeben** (*to forgive*)
in-	= *in-*	**tolerant, intolerant; diskret** (*discreet*), **indiskret** (*indiscreet*), **Insolvenz** (*insolvency*)
des-	= *dis-*	**informiert** (*informed*), **desinformiert** (*disinformed*); **Solvenz** (*solvency*)

Pronunciation

Insight

Learning the alphabet is very useful. There will be many situations in which you may have to spell your name, addresses, e-mail address, or other words. You might have to spell at the reception of a hotel, when booking a restaurant, to fill in forms or over the phone and in many other contexts.

The good news is that German is a much more phonetically consistent language than English, which means that German words are nearly always spelled the way they sound. I recommend learning the way letters and letter combinations sound and you will be able to pronounce new words by just looking at the way they are spelled.

To listen to the sounds and to do some pronunciation practice, go to www.teachyourself.com

The alphabet

a	*ah*	j	*yot*	r	*err*
b	*beh*	k	*kah*	s	*ess*
c	*tseh*	l	*ell*	t	*teh*
d	*deh*	m	*em*	u	*oo*
e	*eh*	n	*en*	v	*fow*
f	*eff*	o	*oh*	w	*veh*
g	*geh*	p	*peh*	x	*iks*
h	*hah*	q	*kuh*	y	*ueppsilon*
i	*ee*			z	*tsett*

To listen to the pronunciation of the alphabet go to
www.teachyourself.com

Transcript of pronunciation exercise

1 Vowels

First of all let's look at the pronunciation of vowels. German vowels
a/o/i/e/u are pronounced *long* or *short* depending on the consonants
that follow. They are pronounced short if they are followed by two or
more consonants, for example when the vowel **a** is followed by l and
t in the word **alt,** or by l and d in the word **Geld.** Say aloud: **Geld, alt.**

They are pronounced long if they are followed by one consonant or
by *h*, e.g. **der Tag.** The a is followed by the consonant **g**: Der Tag.
Say: **Der Tag.**

The same applies for the Umlaut **ü.**

Der Bus (which is the bus) or **das Jahr** (*the year*).

So say: **Bus, Jahr.**

Other words with a long **u**: du, tun, gut

The u is short in words like **Hund, und** and **Butter.**

Can you hear the difference?

Let's now look at the pronunciation of the individual German vowels.

a (ah) sounds like English *spa*, *father* or *hard*. This is a long sound
in German: **Familie, Name, Tag, haben.** Please repeat: **Familie,
Name, Tag, haben.**

Now let's look at the short **a.** Short **a** sounds like English
cut, *hut*, *sample*. In German the short **a** is found in **Ampel**

traffic light, **wann** *when*, **Apfel** *apple*. Say out loud: **Ampel, wann, Apfel**.

Long **e** or **eh** is found in **Tee** *tea*, **sehen** *to see*, **Regen** *rain*. Say: **Tee, sehen, Regen**.

Short **e** is as in the English word *met*. In German this is found in **Bett** *bed*, **nett** *nice*. Repeat: **Bett, nett**.

The German vowel **e** at the end of a word is pronounced in the same way: **Tage** *days*, **Woche** *week*, **ich wohne** *I live*. Say aloud: **Tage, Woche, Ich wohne**.

Next let's look at the German vowel **i**.

There is long **i** (ee) as in English *feet*, *leave*, *here*. In German the word for *love* is **Liebe**; the word for *knee* is **Knie**; *how* in German is **wie**. Please say out loud: **Liebe, Knie, wie**.

There is short **i** as in English *fish* and *is*. In German this is found in **Kind** *child*, **du bist** *you are*, **der Tisch** *the table*. Say out loud: **Kind, bist, Tisch**.

o can be long as in English *so*, *no*, *go*. In German the word for *son* is **Sohn**, for *cathedral* **Dom**, *to live* is **wohnen**. Say: **Sohn, Dom, wohnen**.

o can be short as in English *soft* and *hot*. In German *often* is **oft**, *however* is **doch**, and *tomorrow* is **morgen**. Repeat: **oft, doch, morgen**.

Long **u** is as in English *you*, *June* and *shoe*. In German the word for addressing a friend is **du**, *the watch is* **Uhr**, and the word for *good* is **gut**. Repeat: **du, Uhr, gut**.

Short **u** sounds like English *foot*. In German: **Hund, und, Butter**.

Note that the letter **e** is always pronounced at the end of the word, e.g. **Name, Schule, ich gehe.**

Umlauts:

The vowels **a, o, u** sound different when they have dots (called Umlauts) over them: **ä, ö, ü.** They are best practised within a word. You might have heard them in names like **Müller** and **Jörg,** and in the word **Mädchen.**

ä is similar to English *Kate, spare, men* or *air.* In German: **Käse** for *cheese,* **spät** for *late,* **Mädchen** for *girl.* Say out loud: **Käse, spät, Mädchen.**

ü (ew) doesn't have an equivalent in English. The best way to learn it is to listen to the sound in words and practise the pronunciation. You might already be able to pronounce **fünf, Müller, Jürgen, München.**

ö (ur) doesn't have an equivalent in English either but is a bit like English *sir* with rounded lips. Try these: **Köln, Jörg, können.**

Two vowels together:

au is pronounced *ow* as in English *how* or *house.* The word for *lift* is **Aufzug,** *pigeons* are **Tauben,** and a *woman* is a **Frau.** You try: **Aufzug, Tauben, Frau.**

äu sounds like *boy* in English: **Mäuse** *mice,* **Gebäude** *building.* Say: **Mäuse, Gebäude.**

eu sounds a bit like *foil.* In German: **Freunde, Deutsch, neun.**
ie sounds like English *here:* **Bier, Brief, Liebe.**
ei sounds like English *eye:* **frei, drei, mein, Ei.**

2 Consonants
Now let's look at the pronunciation of consonants. Most consonants are easy to pronounce for English learners.

The consonants **b, d, g** are pronounced the same as in English at the beginning of the word: English *bed* is **Bett**, *blue* is **blau**, *date* is **Datum**, *to go* is **gehen**. B for **Bett**, b for **blau**, d for **Datum**, g for **gehen**.

Note: The consonants **t, k** and **p** must be pronounced at the end of the word: **nicht, kaputt, krank, schlank, schlapp**. At the end of a word **b** is pronounced **p**: **Kalb**; and **d** is pronounced **t**: **Hand, Wand**.

c is not often used on its own apart from in foreign words: **Café, Camping**. It is more often found in combination: **ch** sounds like **ck**: **Chaos, Charakter**.

ch after **a, au, o** and **u** is pronounced like the Scottish word *loch*: **Dach, Bach, Strauch, Loch, doch, Buch, suchen**. After **e, ei, eu, i, ä, äu, ü, ch** sounds softer. **Teich, euch, ich, euch, Dächer, Bräuche**.

g is the same as in English when preceding a vowel: **Wege, sagen**. When it is at the end of a syllable **g** is pronounced like a **k**: **weggehen**.

h: you don't pronounce the **h** after a vowel, it just shows you that the vowel is pronounced long: **ge hen, fe hlen, So hn, wo hnen, Sa hne**.

j at the beginning of a word is pronounced as **y** in English: **Jugend, Januar**.

k: pronounce the **k** at the beginning and the end of a word: **krank, Kneipe**.

l: the pronunciation is much lighter than English **l**: **gelb** *yellow*, **leben** *to live*.

r before a vowel is pronounced by gargling slightly or spoken gutturally: **Rad fahren, regnen**. With another consonant or a single **r** at the end of the word (**lieber, wieder**) it is, however, much weaker and is pronounced like the **r** in English here.

s is pronounced in two different ways: as in English *house*, before consonants and at the ends of words: **das, Haus**; as in English *busy*, when it precedes a vowel: **Rose, Saft** *juice*.

sch is pronounced like English *sh* in *sheep*: **schön** *nice*, **Fisch** *fish*
th: in German this is pronounced t: **Theorie, Theologie**
v sounds like English *for, from*: in German **VW, Verkehr**
w sounds like English v *very*: **wohnen, Wein**
ss, ß are pronounced s, ss

Insight

Always pronounce the **e** at the end of a word: **Dose, Rose, Hose**. And always pronounce the **k** at the beginning of a word: **Kneipe, Kirsche, Kuh**.

Insight

The letter **ß** stands for **ss**. New spelling rules were introduced in 1998. The **ß** (Eszett) is now only used after long vowels: **Straße, Gruß, Grüße, Fuß, Füße**.

Ss is used after a short vowel: **Fluss, dass, Fass**.

Don't worry too much about the choice of either **ß** or **ss** as even some people in Germany are still confused about it. You will also find the **ß** used in the old way in some books.

The same word but different pronunciation:

isolation	**Isolation**
depression	**Depression**
ambition	**Ambition**
progression	**Progression**
information	**Information**
blind	**blind**
butter	**Butter**

tiger	**Tiger**
tunnel	**Tunnel**
Berlin	**Berlin**
London	**London**

Insight

In German all nouns, names, cities, countries are written with a capital letter. You also write **Sie** (formal for *you*) and **Du** (informal) with capital letters when writing letters.

3 German intonation
The voice rises towards a comma and towards the end of a question but falls towards the end of a statement.

To sum up, once you are familiar with all these rules, German spelling and pronunciation are very reliable. Of course you won't learn them overnight. Listen to the recording (www.teachyourself.com) and practise the pronunciation. The best way to learn is of course to listen to native German speakers as often as possible. Here are some ideas as to how you can make recordings of natural spoken German:

▶ If you are in Germany, try recording from the local radio, or even people speaking, though you ought to ask their permission first!
▶ In some parts of the UK, you can sometimes pick up German radio: try playing around with your tuner, and if you find a German radio station, try to record some German.
▶ If you have German friends, ask them to make recordings for you, perhaps sending you messages with their family news, or giving their views on topics of interest to you.
▶ If you have satellite TV, see if you can also receive German television, and if not, talk to your local TV shop to ask if it is worth re-tuning your satellite equipment.
▶ If you have access to the internet, try to find German radio broadcasts via radio station websites.
▶ Once you have some recordings, listen to them as often as possible, and try to repeat what you hear, imitating the sounds and repeating short chunks of German. You might try writing

out small sections, saying them out loud and comparing your version with the original.

▶ If you have German friends, try recording short messages on CDs; then send them to your friends and ask them to comment on and correct your pronunciation.

▶ When speaking to German people, ask them to correct your pronunciation when possible.

Toolbox

Nouns – gender and plurals

German nouns are very easy to spot: they always begin with a capital letter. Nouns are either masculine (m), feminine (f) or neuter (n). This is called the gender of a noun.

	m	f	n
Singular	der	die	das
Plural	die	die	die

There is often no logic as to whether a noun is masculine, feminine or neuter, so it's best to learn a new word plus its gender: don't just learn **Termin**, learn **der Termin**.

Tips on recognizing gender

You can recognize a feminine gender in most nationalities and occupations by the ending -in:

Engländer (m)	Engländerin (f)
Schotte (m)	Schottin (f)
Makler (m)	Maklerin (f)
Busfahrer (m)	Busfahrerin (f)

There are a few exceptions:

Deutsche (f)
Angestellte (f)

Masculine nouns (der): all days, months, and seasons are masculine:

der Montag   **der Dienstag**
der Januar   **der Februar**
der Frühling   **der Sommer**

All names for cars and long-distance trains are masculine:

der BMW, der Mercedes, der VW
der IC, der Euro-City, der InterCity Express

All names for lakes are masculine (as the word for lake **der See**):

der Tegernsee
der Bodensee
der Wannsee

Usually, names of alcoholic drinks are masculine:

der Vodka, der Schnaps, der Wein (exception: **das Bier**)

Neuter nouns (das): names of hotels, cafés and theatres: **das Hotel zum Hang, das Hotel Kranz, das Hilton Hotel**. Names of colours: **das Rot, das Gelb**. Most metals: **das Kupfer, das Aluminium**.

Most tree names are feminine: **die Fichte, die Tanne, die Buche**, but: **der Ahorn**.

Most flowers and fruits are feminine: **die Osterglocke, die Nelke, die Rose, die Kirsche, die Banane, die Zitrone**, but: **der Apfel**.

Nouns which end in -age, -e, -ei, -heit, -keit, -schaft, -ie, -in, -ion, -tät or -ung are almost always feminine: **die Garage, die Tankstelle, die Malerei, die Frechheit, die Einsamkeit, die Eigenschaft, die Energie, die Medizin, die Infektion, die Universität, die Schaltung.**

Nouns which end in -el, -en, -er, -ig, -ich or -ling are usually masculine: **der Apfel, der Magen, der Gärtner, der Honig, der Kranich, der Feigling.**

Nouns which end in -tum, -ment, -eum, -ium, -um or -ett are usually neuter: **das Altertum, das Instrument, das Museum, das Delirium, das Duett.**

Remember: the last word of a compound word determines the gender.

der Ferienort
die Ferien + der Ort = der Ferienort
die Autobahn
das Auto + die Bahn = die Autobahn

Insight

Every time you learn a new noun learn it with both the article and the plural form. It is easier to memorize.

Plural noun endings as indicated in this book:

(-)	**der Hamster, die Hamster**	(no change)
(¨)	**die Mutter, die Mütter**	(Umlaut)
(e)	**der Schuh, die Schuhe**	(ending e)
(¨e)	**der Gast, die Gäste**	(Umlaut + e)
(er)	**das Schild, die Schilder**	(ending er)
(¨er)	**das Fass, die Fässer**	(Umlaut + er)
(n)	**die Farbe, die Farben**	(ending n)
(en)	**die Frau, die Frauen**	(ending en)
(s)	**das Radio, die Radios**	(ending s)

The plural of most feminine German nouns is created by adding -en or -n: **die Schule, die Schulen; die Fahrkarte, die Fahrkarten.**

Nouns that add -s in the plural are mainly of foreign origin or are words that end in a vowel: **der Job, die Jobs; das Hobby, die Hobbies; das Auto, die Autos; die Oma, die Omas.**

Some plural forms are identical to the singular: **der Wagen, die Wagen; der Ellbogen, die Ellbogen; der Computer, die Computer.**

Pronouns

Nominative (subject)

Singular		Plural	
I	**ich**	*we*	**wir**
you	**du**	*you*	**ihr**
he	**er**	*they*	**sie**
she	**sie**	*you*	**Sie** (formal)
it	**es**		

Other cases

Pronouns in German change according to their function in the sentence, just as they do in English, when I changes to me, she to her, etc.:

<u>I</u> *went by train to London. My friends took* <u>me</u> *home in their car.*

<u>She</u> *really enjoys reading. I saw* <u>her</u> *in the library.*

Singular				Plural			
Acc (object*)		dat (indirect object*)		acc (object*)		dat (indirect object*)	
me	**mich**	*(to) me*	**mir**	*us*	**uns**	*(to) us*	**uns**
you	**dich**	*(to) you*	**dir**	*you*	**euch**	*(to) you*	**euch**
him	**ihn**	*(to) him*	**ihm**				
her	**sie**	*(to) her*	**ihr**	*them*	**sie**	*(to) them*	**ihnen**
it	**es**	*(to) it*	**ihm**				
				you (formal)	**Sie**	*(to) you*	**Ihnen**

*and after certain prepositions.

Articles/determiners

Definite article: *the*

The word for *the* is **der** (m), **die** (f), **das** (n) or **die** (pl) in the nominative. **Der** changes in the accusative to **den** (m). All articles change in the dative: **dem** (m), **der** (f), **dem** (n), **den** (pl).

	Singular			Plural
	m	f	n	
nom	**der** Mann	**die** Frau	**das** Kind	**die** Männer
acc	**den** Mann	**die** Frau	**das** Kind	**die** Männer
dat	**dem** Mann	**der** Frau	**dem** Kind	**den** Männern

The genitive is **des Mannes, der Frau, des Kindes, der Männer.**

Nominative
The woman lives in Berlin.
('The woman' is the subject of the sentence, and therefore in the nominative.)

Die Frau wohnt in Berlin.

Accusative
Can you see the man who is working in the street?
('The man' is the direct object of the sentence, and therefore in the accusative.)

Siehst du **den** Mann, der in der Straße arbeitet?

Dative
Give the book to the child!
('The child' is the indirect object of the sentence, and therefore in the dative.)

Geben Sie das Buch **dem** Kind!

Give the books to the children!
('The children' is the indirect object of the sentence, and therefore in the dative.)

Geben Sie die Bücher **den** Kindern!

Prepositions
The articles (*the, a* etc.) also change after prepositions: see the Toolbox entry on prepositions.

Indefinite article: *a/an*, and possessive adjectives

The word for *a/an* is **ein/eine/einen/einem**; for my: **mein/meine/meinen/meinem**.

Singular			Plural
	f	m	n	
my	**meine** Tante	**mein** Onkel	**mein** Kind	**meine** Kinder
your	**deine** Tante	**dein** Onkel	**dein** Kind	**deine** Kinder
his	**seine** Tante	**sein** Onkel	**sein** Kind	**seine** Kinder
her	**ihre** Tante	**ihr** Onkel	**ihr** Kind	**ihre** Kinder
our	**unsere** Tante	**unser** Onkel	**unser** Kind	**unsere** Kinder
your	**eure** Tante	**euer** Onkel	**euer** Kind	**eure** Kinder
your	**Ihre** Tante	**Ihr** Onkel	**Ihr** Kind	**Ihre** Kinder

Meine Landkarte ist verschwunden. *My map has disappeared.*
Mein Radio ist kaputt. *My radio is broken.*
Mein Auto ist sehr alt. *My car is very old.*
Seine Tante wohnt in Köln. *His aunt lives in Cologne.*
Sein Onkel kommt aus Leipzig. *His uncle comes from Leipzig.*
Ihr Enkelkind lebt in Hamburg. *Her grandchild lives in Hamburg.*

Remember: her = ihr/e; Ihr/e with a capital letter is your (formal).

Example: Ich gebe **ihr** ihre Tasche. *I give her her handbag.*
Ich möchte gerne **Ihre** Tochter treffen. *I would like to meet your daughter.*

A/ein, *my*/mein, *your*/dein, *his*/sein, *her*/ihr, *your*/euer, *our*/unser, *no*, *any*/kein.

Singular			Plural
	m	f	n	
nom	**ein** Bruder	**eine** Schwester	**ein** Baby	**keine** Kinder
acc	**einen** Bruder	**eine** Schwester	**ein** Baby	**keine** Kinder
dat	**einem** Bruder	**einer** Schwester	**einem** Baby	**keinen** Kindern
gen	**eines** Bruders	**einer** Schwester	**eines** Babys	**keiner** Kinder

Ein Bruder von mir studiert zur Zeit in Frankfurt.
One of my brothers is studying in Frankfurt at present.

Ich habe **einen** Bruder und eine Schwester.
I have a brother and a sister.

Lass uns in **ein** schönes Restaurant gehen.
Let us go to a nice restaurant.

In German there is also a word for '*not a*' (see **Negative expressions**).

This/these

	Singular			Plural
	m	f	n	
nom	**dieser** Mantel	**diese** Jacke	**dieses** Kleid	**diese** Schuhe
acc	**diesen** Mantel	**diese** Jacke	**dieses** Kleid	**diese** Schuhe
dat	**diesem** Mantel	**dieser** Jacke	**diesem** Kleid	**diesen** Schuhen

Nominative
Dieser Mantel steht ihr gut.
Diese Jacke steht ihr gut.
Dieses Kleid steht ihr gut.
Diese Schuhe stehen ihr gut.

Accusative
Ich trage **diesen** Mantel gerne.
Ich trage **diese** Jacke gerne.
Ich trage **dieses** Kleid gerne.
Ich trage **diese** Schuhe gerne.

Dative
Zu **diesem** Mantel trage ich einen Hut.
Zu **dieser** Jacke trage ich einen Hut.
Zu **diesem** Kleid trage ich einen Hut.
Zu **diesen** Schuhen trage ich Hosen.

Prepositions

The article changes when it is used after certain prepositions, e.g. **bis, durch, für, gegen, ohne, um, wider** are followed by *the accusative*:

Das Buch ist für **den** Studenten. *The book is for the student.*
Das Auto fuhr gegen **den** Baum. *The car crashed into the tree.*
Fahren Sie durch **den** Tunnel. *Drive through the tunnel.*

The preposition **entlang** (*along*) also changes the article to the *accusative*, but it follows the noun:

Ich fuhr den Kurfürstendamm entlang *I drove along the Kurfürstendamm.*

The following prepositions are *always* followed by the dative: **aus, außer, bei, gegenüber, mit, nach, seit, von, zu**:

Ich hole das Buch aus **dem** Auto. *I get the book from the car.*
Sie hat außer **der** Schwester keine Verwandten. *She does not have any relatives apart from her sister.*
Er wohnt bei **seiner** Tante. *He lives with his aunt.*
Wir fahren mit **dem** Bus. *We are going by bus.*
Nach **dem** Theater sollten wir in eine Kneipe gehen. *After the theatre we should go to a pub.*
Seit **dem** Unfall auf der Autobahn fahre ich langsamer. *Since the accident on the motorway, I drive more slowly.*
Sie hat den Stadtplan von **einer** Tankstelle. *She got the street map from a petrol station.*
Ich gehe zu **dem** kleinen Laden um die Ecke. *I go to the small shop around the corner.*

For examples of prepositions following verbs, and of prepositions taking the dative or the accusative, depending on whether they indicate motion or position, see Unit 1.

Verbs

Infinitives and present tense

There is one way of expressing the present tense in German, while in English there are three:

I *live in* ...	ich lebe in ...
I *am living in* ...	ich lebe in ...
I *do live in* ...	ich lebe in ...

In English the infinitive of a verb is always preceded by 'to' (*to go/to eat*). In German the verb consists of the stem + the ending -en:

wohn	+ en	= wohnen
kauf	+ en	= kaufen
fahr	+ en	= fahren

A few others end in **-ern** or **-n**:

kümm	+ ern	= kümmern
fütt	+ ern	= füttern

For regular verbs in the present tense the following endings are added to the stem:

ich ends in	e	ich wohne in Berlin
du	st	du wohnst in Berlin
er	t	er wohnt in Berlin
sie	t	sie wohnt in Berlin
es	t	es wohnt in Berlin
wir	en	wir wohnen in Berlin
ihr	t	ihr wohnt in Berlin
sie	en	sie wohnen in Berlin
Sie	en	Sie wohnen in Berlin

Word order

Rule 1

The most important rule in a German sentence is: The verb *always*
comes second.

Most sentences begin with the subject, followed by the verb.

Ich **fahre** nach Berlin. Ich **fahre** jedes Jahr nach Berlin.

Rule 2
Time, manner, place

In longer sentences the word order is usually:

subject,	verb,	time,	manner,	place
Ich	fahre	jetzt	mit dem Auto	nach Edinburg.

Expressions of *time* describe when something is done/happens –
jetzt *now*, **heute** *today*.

Ich wohne **jetzt** in Glasgow. *I am now living in Glasgow.*
Ich arbeite **heute** im Büro. *I am working in the office today.*

Expressions of *manner* describes how something is done/happens:
schnell *quickly*, **mit dem Zug** *by train*.

Ich fahre heute **mit dem Zug** nach London. *I am going today by train to London.*

Es passiert **sehr schnell**. *It happens very quickly.*

Expressions of place describe where something is done/happens: **in Berlin** *in Berlin*, **auf dem Land** *in the country*.

Ich wohne im Moment mit meiner Familie **auf dem Land**. *At the moment I'm living with my family in the country.*

Rule 3
Inverted word order

If you begin the sentence with something other than the subject the verb must still come first followed by the subject.

Heute lerne ich deutsche Grammatik. *Today I am going to learn German grammar.*

Auxiliary verbs *to have* and *to be*

> **Insight**
>
> Useful verbs to learn: *to have*, **haben** and *to be*, **sein**. You will use them constantly, so learn them by heart from the beginning.

to be	sein
I am	**ich bin**
you are	**du bist**
he is	**er ist**
she is	**sie ist**
it is	**es ist**
we are	**wir sind**
you are	**ihr seid**
they are	**sie sind**
you are	**Sie sind**

to have	haben
I have	ich habe
you have	du hast
he has	er hat
she has	sie hat
it has	es hat
we have	wir haben
you have	ihr habt
they have	sie haben
you have	Sie haben

Some commonly used verbs are: **arbeiten, gehen, fahren, kaufen, machen** and **spielen**:

	to work	to go	to drive	to buy	to make/do	to play
ich	arbeite	gehe	fahre	kaufe	mache	spiele
du	arbeitest	gehst	fährst	kaufst	machst	spielst
er/sie/es	arbeitet	geht	fährt	kauft	macht	spielt
wir	arbeiten	gehen	fahren	kaufen	machen	spielen
ihr	arbeitet	geht	fahrt	kauft	macht	spielt
sie	arbeiten	gehen	fahren	kaufen	machen	spielen
Sie	arbeiten	gehen	fahren	kaufen	machen	spielen

	to know	to know	to eat	to see	to be called
ich	weiß	kenne	esse	sehe	heiße
du	weißt	kennst	isst	siehst	heißt
er/sie/es	weiß	kennt	isst	sieht	heißt
wir	wissen	kennen	essen	sehen	heißen
ihr	wisst	kennt	esst	seht	heißt
sie	wissen	kennen	essen	sehen	heißen
Sie	wissen	kennen	essen	sehen	heißen

Here are some more commonly used verbs:

to *answer*	antworten, ich antworte
to *arrive*	<u>an</u>kommen, ich komme <u>an</u>
to *ask*	fragen, ich frage
to *be able to*	können, ich kann
to *bring/fetch*	bringen, ich bringe
to *call (phone)*	<u>an</u>rufen, ich rufe <u>an</u>
to *cancel*	<u>ab</u>sagen, ich sage <u>ab</u>
to *drive*	fahren, ich fahre
to *find*	finden, ich finde
to *forget*	vergessen, ich vergesse
to *go in*	<u>rein</u>gehen, ich gehe <u>rein</u>
to *go out*	<u>raus</u>gehen, ich gehe <u>raus</u>
to *have to*	müssen, ich muss
to *know (somebody)*	kennen, ich kenne
to *know how to*	wissen, ich weiß
to *leave*	verlassen, ich verlasse
to *look for*	suchen, ich suche
to *need*	brauchen, ich brauche
to *pay*	bezahlen, ich bezahle
to *reserve*	reservieren, ich reserviere
to *see*	sehen, ich sehe
to *study*	studieren, ich studiere
to *take*	nehmen, ich nehme
to *want/would like to*	möchten, ich möchte
to *write*	schreiben, ich schreibe

Separable verbs

German separable verbs are similar to English verbs such as
to get <u>up</u>, to go <u>out</u>, to sit <u>down</u>, but there are many more in

German and the structure of a sentence with a separable verb is different.

Separable verbs are made up of two parts: a prefix, for example **ab-, an-** or **auf-,** and the infinitive of a verb. In the infinitive form the prefix is attached to the front of the verb: <u>ab</u>fahren *to depart*, <u>an</u>kommen *to arrive*, <u>auf</u>stehen *to get up*.

Insight

Some prefixes can be translated literally, e.g. **aus** *out*, **zurück** *back*, **auf** *up*. A good way to learn separable verbs is as follows: take the infinitive of a verb such as **gehen** *to go* and add prefixes, e.g **aus** *out* = <u>**aus**</u>**gehen** *to go out*, **zurück** *back* = <u>**zurück**</u>**gehen** *to go back*, **rein** *in* = <u>**rein**</u>**gehen** *to go in*, raus *out* = <u>**raus**</u>**gehen** *to go out*. As separable verbs are so important in the German language you will find the prefixes of all such verbs in this book underlined, so you can spot them immediately and be able to separate them correctly. Look out for them throughout the book.

Word order with separable verbs
The structure of a sentence with separable verbs is different from in English. In English the preposition comes straight after the verb; in German it goes to the end of the sentence.

I get <u>up</u> at 8 o'clock. **Ich stehe um 8 Uhr <u>auf</u>.**
I get <u>up</u> every morning at 8 o'clock. **Ich stehe jeden Morgen um 8 Uhr <u>auf</u>.**
I go <u>out</u> with my friends at the weekend. **Ich gehe am Wochenende mit meinen Freunden <u>aus</u>.**

Insight

When you read a sentence in German make sure that you go to the end of it to see if there is a prefix, as the meaning of the whole sentence could change. Compare the following sentences: Ich ziehe am Montag **um**. *I am going to move house on Monday.*

(Contd)

Ich ziehe mich schnell **an**. *I am getting dressed quickly.* Ich ziehe die Kinder gut **auf**. *I bring up the children well.*

The same applies when listening to German speakers. Don't interrupt a German speaker in the middle of a sentence when he or she is using a separable verb, otherwise you might never find out what he/she wanted to say!

Talking about the past

In spoken German, the perfect tense is generally used instead of the imperfect. The perfect tense comprises the auxiliary verb **haben** or **sein** and the *past participle*:

Ich habe ein Buch gelesen. *I read a book.*
Ich habe in Deutschland gewohnt. *I lived in Germany.*
Ich bin nach London geflogen. *I flew to London.*
Ich bin ins Kino gegangen. *I went to the cinema.*

Verbs with *haben*

Insight
Remember: approximately 70% of all verbs take **haben** (*to have*). Only 30% take **sein** (*to be*).

The following common verbs form the perfect tense with **haben**:

to achieve erreichen: *I achieved my goal.* Ich habe mein Ziel erreicht.
to answer beantworten: *I answered the question.* Ich habe die Frage beantwortet.
to ask fragen: *I asked for the bill.* Ich habe nach der Rechnung gefragt.
to attend <u>teil</u>nehmen: *I attended the meeting.* Ich habe an der Besprechung <u>teil</u>genommen.
to buy kaufen: *I bought a new car.* Ich habe ein neues Auto gekauft.

to complete vervollständigen: *I completed the puzzle.* Ich habe das Puzzle vervollständigt.

to do tun: *I did that.* Ich habe das getan.

to drink trinken: *I drank too much coffee.* Ich habe zu viel Kaffee getrunken.

to eat essen: *I did not eat anything.* Ich habe nichts gegessen.

to hear hören: *I heard a loud noise.* Ich habe ein lautes Geräusch gehört.

to listen to zuhören: *I listened to the announcement.* Ich habe der Ansage zugehört.

to read lesen: *I read an interesting book.* Ich habe ein interessantes Buch gelesen.

to say sagen: *I did not say anything.* Ich habe nichts gesagt.

to sleep schlafen: *I slept until 8 o'clock.* Ich habe bis 8 Uhr geschlafen.

to take nehmen: *I took the next train.* Ich habe den nächsten Zug genommen.

to talk sprechen: *I talked to him briefly.* Ich habe kurz mit ihm gesprochen.

to think denken: *I thought about him.* Ich habe an ihn gedacht.

to write schreiben: *I wrote him an email.* Ich habe ihm eine E-Mail geschrieben.

Verbs with *sein*

Insight

Remember: All verbs of motion take **sein** (*to be*). Try to learn the most common such as:

to go **gehen,** *to drive/travel/go* **fahren,** *to fly* **fliegen,** *to swim* **schwimmen,** *to come* **kommen,** *to jog* **joggen.**

Wir sind mit dem Auto nach Berlin **gefahren.** *We took the car to Berlin.*

Wir sind in die Stadt **gegangen.** *We went into town.*

Wir sind nach Sylt **geflogen.** *We flew to Sylt.*

Er ist 10 Bahnen **geschwommen.** *He swam 10 lengths.*

Sie ist gestern Abend in die Kneipe **gekommen.** *She came to the pub last night.*

Verbs expressing a change of state of mind:

Ich bin <u>auf</u>gewacht	*I woke up*
Er ist gestorben	*He died*
Ich bin <u>ein</u>geschlafen	*I fell asleep*

Reflexive verbs

There are very few reflexive verbs in English; one of them is the
verb to introduce yourself – *I introduce myself*: Ich stelle **mich**
vor. In German many verbs are reflexive.

to have a good time sich amüsieren: *I had a good time (lit. I
amused myself) in the cinema.* Ich habe mich im Kino amüsiert.

to film sich filmen: *We filmed ourselves in front of the Brandenburger
Tor.* Wir haben uns vor dem Brandenburger Tor gefilmt.

to get on sich verstehen: *I got on really well with him.* Ich habe
mich mit ihm wirklich gut verstanden.

to hurry sich beeilen: *I hurried to get the bus.* Ich habe mich beeilt
um den Bus zu bekommen.

to introduce sich vorstellen: *He introduced me to his sister.* Er hat
mich seiner Schwester vorgestellt.

to meet sich treffen: *They met at the tourist office.* Sie haben sich
am Verkehrsbüro getroffen.

to meet again sich <u>wieder</u>treffen: *They met again at the train
station.* Sie haben sich am Bahnhof <u>wieder</u>getroffen.

to see again sich <u>wieder</u>sehen: *They saw each other again the next
day.* Sie haben sich am nächsten Tag <u>wieder</u>gesehen.

to shower sich duschen: *I took a shower at 9 o'clock.* Ich habe
mich um 9 Uhr geduscht.

to sit down sich setzen: *I sat down beside my colleague.* Ich habe
mich neben meine Kollegin gesetzt.

If you want to learn more about reflexive verbs go to **Verbs taking
dative or accusative** in Unit 1.

Imperfect tense

You use the imperfect mainly to write a report or talk about an event in a more formal way. Very common in the spoken language, however, are the words: **war** (*was*), **hatte** (*had*), **musste** (*had to*), **konnte** (*was able to*), **wollte** (*wanted to*).

I was:	ich war, du warst, er/sie es war
	wir waren, ihr wart, sie waren, Sie waren
I had:	ich hatte, du hattest, er/sie/es hatte
	wir hatten, ihr hattet, sie hatten, Sie hatten
I had to:	ich musste, du musstest, er/sie/es musste
	wir mussten, ihr musstet, sie mussten, Sie mussten
I could:	ich konnte, du konntest, er/sie/es konnte
	wir konnten, ihr konntet, sie konnten, Sie konnten
I wanted to:	ich wollte, du wolltest, er/sie/es wollte
	wir wollten, ihr wolltet, sie wollten, Sie wollten

Es war ein wunderschöner Urlaub. *It was a wonderful holiday.*
Das Wetter war sehr gut. *The weather was very good.*
Wir hatten einen sehr angenehmen Flug. *We had a very pleasant flight.*
Mussten Sie lange warten? *Did you have to wait long?*
Konnten Sie in dem Zug schlafen? *Were you able to sleep in the train?*

Other verbs in the imperfect:

	flew	*came*	*wrote*	*went*	*learned*	*studied*
ich	flog	kam	schrieb	ging	lern**te**	studier**te**
du	flogst	kamst	schriebst	gingst	lern**test**	studier**test**
er/sie/es	flog	kam	schrieb	ging	lern**te**	studier**te**
wir	flogen	kamen	schrieben	gingen	lern**ten**	studier**ten**
ihr	flogt	kamt	schriebt	gingt	lern**tet**	studier**tet**
sie	flogen	kamen	schrieben	gingen	lern**ten**	studier**ten**
Sie	flogen	kamen	schrieben	gingen	lern**ten**	studier**ten**

Er schlief im Flugzeug. *He slept in the plane.*
Sie gingen mit dem Manager zu einer Besprechung. *They went to a meeting with the manager.*
Ich flog nach Köln. *I flew to Cologne.*
Es war kalt/warm. *It was cold/hot.*
Ich musste zu dem Termin gehen. *I had to go to the appointment.*
Er sprach zu den Zuschauern. *He was talking to the audience.*
Ich sprach mit dem Mann. *I was talking to the man.*

Talking about the future

The future tense is formed with the auxiliary verb **werden** and the *infinitive*:

Ich werde nach Hamburg fliegen. *I am flying to Hamburg.*

Ich werde ein Auto mieten. *I am going to rent a car.*

Wir werden unsere Verwandten besuchen. *We will visit our relatives.*

Insight

There is an easy way of talking about events in the future, as you can use the present tense to indicate when you are going to do something: i.e. *In summer I am (I shall be) going to Switzerland.* **Ich fahre im Sommer in die Schweiz.**

Use the present tense when it is obvious that you are going to do something:

Are you going to take the bus? **Nehmen Sie/nimmst du den Bus?**

I will be taking the bus. **Ich nehme den Bus.**

Useful phrases in the future (both forms):

I will go (in two hours). Ich werde (in zwei Stunden) gehen/ich gehe in zwei Stunden. *Will you be going to the meeting?* Werden Sie zu der Besprechung gehen? *Will you be going to the meeting this afternoon?* Gehen Sie heute Nachmittag zu der Besprechung?

I will be there. Ich werde da sein. *I will be there (tomorrow).* Ich bin (morgen) da.

I will do that. Ich werde es machen. *I will do that today.* Ich mache es (heute).

Will you do it? Werden Sie/Wirst du es es machen? *Will you do it (next week)?* Machen Sie/Machst du es (nächste Woche)?

Will you take the bus? Werden Sie/Wirst du den Bus nehmen? Nehmen Sie/Nimmst du den Bus?

How will you go? Wie werden Sie/wirst du fahren? Wie fahren Sie/fährst du?

When will you arrive? Wann werden Sie/wirst du ankommen? Wann kommen Sie/kommst du an?

When will you leave? Wann fahren Sie/fährst du ab? Wann werden Sie/wirst du abfahren?

What will the weather be like? Wie wird das Wetter sein?

How much will it cost? Was kostet es? Was wird es kosten?

Will it be suitable for children? Wird es für Kinder geeignet sein? Ist es für Kinder geeignet?

What will he do? Was wird er machen? Was macht er (morgen)?

What will he have? Was wird er haben?

What will you take? Was werden Sie/wirst du mitnehmen? Was nehmen Sie/nimmst du mit?

When will it be? Wann wird es sein? Wann ist es?

Is it going to rain (tomorrow)? Wird es regnen? Regnet es morgen?

It will probably rain. Es wird wahrscheinlich regnen. Es regnet wahrscheinlich.

Will there be much traffic? Gibt es viel Verkehr da? Wird es viel Verkehr geben?

Conditional and subjunctive

Conditional

The conditional is formed with the auxiliary verb **würden** plus the infinitive. It corresponds to the English pattern verb plus infinitve.

I would like to go to the park. Ich würde gerne in den Park gehen.
I would appreciate it if you came with me. Ich würde es schätzen, wenn du mit mir kommen würdest.
I would come along. Ich würde <u>mit</u>kommen.
I would go to view the castle. Ich würde das Schloss besichtigen gehen.
It would be Monday. Es würde Montag werden.
I would have it on Friday. Ich würde es am Freitag haben.
I would do that. Ich würde das tun.
He would buy the shoes if they were cheaper. Er würde die Schuhe kaufen, wenn sie billiger wären.
Would you buy this house? Würdest du dieses Haus kaufen?
Would you go there? Würden Sie dorthin gehen?
Would you go with me to the cinema. Würden Sie mit mir ins Kino gehen?

....

Insight

It is very common to use the conditional as a polite request: **würden Sie/würdest du …**:

Würden Sie mir bitte aus dem Mantel helfen! *Would please help me out of my coat!*

Würden Sie mir bitte sagen wie spät es ist! *Would you please tell me what time it is!*

Würdet ihr bitte ruhig sein! *Would you please be quiet!*

Würden Sie das bitte nehmen! *Would you please take that!*

Würden Sie bitte das Formular unterschreiben! *Would you please sign that form!*

Subjunctive

There are two forms of the subjunctive: the general subjunctive and the special subjunctive. The general subjunctive is more common and falls into the following categories: wishes and hopes: **bleib gesund/ bleiben Sie gesund** (*stay healthy*); **mögen Sie glücklich sein** (*may you be happy*); **mögest du gesund werden** (*may you be well again*).

The second form of the subjunctive is used for: if sentences after **als ob** and if sentences after **wenn...** (hypothetical):

Er sah aus, als ob er nichts verstanden hätte. *He looked as if he had not understood a thing.*
Es sieht so aus, als ob es regnen würde. *It looks as if it is going to rain.*
Er tut so, als ob er es könnte. *He pretends that* (lit: *as if*) *he could do that.*
Wenn ich mehr Geld hätte, würde ich eine Weltreise machen. *If I had more money I would travel around the world.*
Wenn ich Sie/du wäre, würde ich das tun. *If I were you I would do that.*
Wenn ich könnte, würde ich es machen. *If I could I would do it.*

Negative expressions

How to say you don't do/don't like something

Insight

Remember: You use **mögen** in connection with a noun:

Ich mag keine Pizza. (*I don't like pizza.*)

But: use **gerne** with a verb: **Ich studiere nicht <u>gerne</u>.** (*I don't like to study*).

Ich tanze nicht gerne. *I don't like to dance.*
Ich mag ... nicht. *I don't like ...*
Ich mag das nicht. *I don't like that.*
Ich ... nicht gerne. *I don't like ...*
Ich singe nicht gerne. *I don't like singing.*

Use kein in front of a noun:

Ich mag kein Fleisch. *I don't like meat.*
Ich esse kein Fleisch. *I don't eat meat.*
Mein Freund hat kein Auto. *My friend doesn't have a car.*
Ich gucke kein Fernsehen. *I don't watch television.*

Use nicht with a verb:

Ich rauche nicht. *I don't smoke.*
Ich tanze nicht. *I don't dance.*
Sie ruft mich nicht an. *She doesn't phone me.*

Nichts = *anything*:

Ich mache nichts. *I don't do anything.*
Ich habe nichts. *I haven't got anything.*
Nichts ist nicht gut genug. *Nothing is not good enough.*

Nobody/anybody:

Ich kenne niemanden. *I don't know anyone.*
Ich habe niemanden gesehen. *I haven't seen anyone.*
Niemand geht in das Geschäft. *No one goes to that shop.*

Noch nie = *never*:

Ich bin noch nie in Leipzig gewesen. *I have never been to Leipzig.*
Er hat noch nie Austern gegessen. *He has never eaten oysters.*
Wir haben den Film noch nie gesehen. *We have never seen the film.*

Noch nicht = *not yet:*

Ich habe mit ihr noch nicht gesprochen. *I have not yet spoken to her.*
Ich habe das Zimmer noch nicht gebucht. *I have not booked the hotel room yet.*
Der Bus ist noch nicht gekommen. *The bus has not arrived yet.*

Immer noch nicht = *still not:*

Er hat den Brief immer noch nicht geschrieben. *He still has not written the letter.*
Der Zug ist immer noch nicht angekommen. *The train has still not arrived.*

Nicht mehr = *any more:*

Ich gehe dort nicht mehr hin. *I don't go there any more.*
Ich werde ihn/sie nicht mehr sehen. *I won't see him/her any more.*
Ich spiele nicht mehr. *I don't play any more.*

Kein = *not any:*

Haben Sie keine Zigaretten mehr? *Don't you have any more cigarettes?*
Hast du/Haben Sie keine? *Haven't you got any?*
Nein, ich habe keine. *No, I haven't.*
Nein, ich konnte keinen Termin bekommen. *No, I couldn't get an appointment.*

Other negatives

Haben Sie keinen Tisch gebucht? *Did you not book a table?*
Nein, sie sind nicht ans Telefon gegangen. *No, they didn't answer the phone.*
Sind Sie nicht zur Bank gekommen? *Didn't you get to the bank?*
Nein, sie war nicht geöffnet. *No, it wasn't open.*
Haben Sie nicht/hast du nicht mit ihm gesprochen? *Didn't you speak to him?*

Nein, ich habe mit ihm noch nicht gesprochen. *No, I haven't spoken to him yet.*
Haben Sie keine Tickets für die Show bekommen? *Didn't you get any tickets for the show?*
Nein, es gab keine. *No, there weren't any left.*
Haben Sie ihren Freund nicht gesehen? *Didn't you see your friend?*
Er war nicht da. *No, he wasn't in.*

Don't ...!:

No entry	kein Eintritt
No exit	kein Ausgang
No admission	kein Zutritt
No smoking	Nichtraucher
No dogs	keine Hunde
No drinking water	kein Trinkwasser
Don't touch	nicht berühren/nicht anfassen
Don't eat it	nicht essen
Don't open the window	Fenster nicht öffnen

Verboten = *is not allowed/permitted:*

to swim	Schwimmen verboten
	Baden verboten
to play ball	Ball spielen verboten
to enter	Eintritt verboten
to smoke	Rauchen verboten
the use of mobile phones	Benutzung von Handys ist verboten
to walk on the ice	Betreten der Eisfläche ist verboten

Interrogative – asking questions

You can ask a question by inverting the pronoun and verb: **Haben Sie** (**Hast du**) ein Auto? *Have you got a new car?*

Do you speak another language?	**Sprechen Sie (Sprichst du) eine andere Sprache?**
Do you drive to Frankfurt?	**Fahren Sie (Fährst du) nach Frankfurt?**
Have you got your key?	**Haben Sie (Hast du) Ihren (deinen) Schlüssel?**
Can you tell me ...?	**Können Sie (Kannst du) mir bitte sagen ...?**
Could you lend me a pen?	**Können Sie mir (Kannst du mir) einen Stift leihen?**
Would you like to come along?	**Würden Sie (Würdest du) gerne mitkommen?**
Would you be able to explain it to me?	**Wären es ihnen (Wäre es dir) möglich es mir zu erklären?**
Are you tired?	**Sind Sie (Bist du) müde?**
Did you go to town?	**Sind Sie (Bist du) in die Stadt gegangen?**
Have you seen him?	**Haben Sie (Hast du) ihn gesehen?**
Did you try the steak?	**Haben Sie (Hast du) das Steak probiert?**
Have you seen the film?	**Haben Sie (Hast du) den Film gesehen?**
Do you smoke?	**Rauchen Sie (Rauchst du)?**
Do you prefer red or white wine?	**Bevorzugen Sie (Bevorzugst du) Rot- oder Weißwein?**
Do you eat fish?	**Essen Sie (Isst du) Fisch?**
Are you taking medication?	**Nehmen Sie (Nimmst du) Medikamente?**
Have you visited her relatives?	**Haben Sie (Hast du) ihre Verwandten besucht?**
Are you in your first year (of study)?	**Studieren Sie (Studierst du) im ersten Jahr?**

Do you regularly go for a swim?	**Gehen Sie (Gehst du) regelmäßig schwimmen?**
Do you need a ticket for this machine?	**Braucht man ein Ticket für diese Maschine?**
Do I need change for the bus?	**Brauche ich Kleingeld für den Bus?**
Do you go along the coast?	**Fahren Sie an der Küste entlang?**

Questions asking for information are introduced by a question word:

Who?	**wer?**	*How?*	**wie?**
When?	**wann?**	*How much?*	**wie viel?**
Where?	**wo?**	*Who/whom?*	**wen?**
Why?	**warum?**	*To whom?*	**wem?**
Why?	**weshalb?**	*From where?*	**woher?**
What?	**was?**	*Whose?*	**wessen?**
Which?	**welche/r/m/s?**	*In which... ?*	**in welchem/r...?**

....

Insight

Be careful not to confuse English *where?* with German **wer?**

where? = **wo?**
who? = **wer?**

....

Who are you?	**Wer sind Sie? Wer bist du?**
Where is Mrs Meier?	**Wo ist Frau Meier?**
How are you?	**Wie geht es Ihnen/Wie geht es dir?**
How much does the street map cost?	**Wie viel kostet der Stadtplan?**
How many visitors are expected?	**Wie viele Besucher werden erwartet?**
How long do we have to wait for the train?	**Wie lange müssen wir auf den Zug warten?**
Who is Mrs Meier?	**Wer ist Frau Meier?**
Who are you supposed to be seeing?	**Wen sollten Sie eigentlich treffen?**
Who gave you permission to do that?	**Wer hat Ihnen/dir die Erlaubnis gegeben, das zu tun?**
Who arranged it for you?	**Wer hat das für Sie/dich arrangiert?**
Who do you think you are?	**Wer glauben Sie, wer Sie sind? Wer glaubst du wer du bist?**

Whose car is it?	**Wessen Auto ist das?**
Whose euros are they?	**Wessen Euros sind das?**
What is wrong/happening?	**Was ist los?**
What is going on?	**Was ist hier los?**
What do you want?	**Was wollen Sie/Was willst du?**
What is the name of your hotel?	**Wie ist der Name Ihres Hotels?**
What kind of conference are you attending?	**Was für eine Konferenz besuchen Sie?**
Which floor are you on?	**In welchem Stock sind Sie?**
Which room are you in?	**In welchem Zimmer sind Sie?**
Which is your place?	**Welcher Platz ist Ihr Platz?**
Which is your car?	**Welches Auto ist Ihr Auto?**
Which is your bag?	**Welche Tasche ist Ihre Tasche?**

The 16 most common questions when abroad:

What is your name?	**Wie ist Ihr/dein Name? Wie heißen Sie/heißt du?**
Where are you from?	**Woher kommen Sie?**
How long are you staying?	**Wie lange sind Sie hier?**
Where are you staying?	**Wo sind Sie <u>unter</u>gebracht?**
Have you got your passport?	**Haben Sie Ihren Personalausweis?**
What do you want?	**Was möchten Sie?/Was möchtest du?**
Do you speak German?	**Sprechen Sie Deutsch?**
Do you like it here?	**Mögen Sie es hier?**
What are you doing here?	**Was machen Sie hier?**
Could you please write it down for me?	**Könnten Sie es bitte für mich aufschreiben?**
Can you spell it please?	**Können Sie es bitte buchstabieren?**
Can you help me?	**Können Sie mir bitte helfen?**
When does the train leave?	**Wann fährt der Zug <u>ab</u>?**
When does the performance start?	**Wann fängt die Vorstellung <u>an</u>?**
When are we going to meet Mr Schmidt?	**Wann treffen wir Herrn Schmidt?**
When are we having dinner?	**Wann essen wir Abendessen?**

Adjectives

An adjective describes a noun or a pronoun. When an adjective is used *after* the noun, the adjective ending does not change, e.g. **Das Wetter ist schlecht.** *The weather is bad.* It also does not change after a prounoun (*he* **er**, *she* **sie**, *it* **es**): **Es ist schlecht.** It is bad. It does however change if it comes before the noun: **Das schlechte Wetter. Ich kaufe einen neuen Computer.**

There are only two different endings for adjectives following the definitive articles, **der, die, das** and **dieser, jener, jeder** and **welcher**. The endings are **-e** and **-en**:

Ich kaufe den neuen Mantel.

Dieser neue Mantel gefällt mir gut.

Welcher blaue Hut passt gut zu dem neuen Mantel?

Die neuen Mäntel gefallen mir gut.

	Singular			*Plural*
	m	*f*	*n*	
nom	**-e**	**-e**	**-e**	**-en**
acc	**-en**	**-e**	**-e**	**-en**
dat	**-en**	**-en**	**-en**	**-en**
gen	**-en**	**-en**	**-en**	**-en**

Adjective endings after the indefinite article, **ein** (*a*), **mein** (*my*),
dein (*your*), etc.:

	Singular			Plural
	m	f	n	
nom	**-er**	**-e**	**-es**	**-en**
acc	**-en**	**-e**	**-es**	**-en**
dat	**-en**	**-en**	**-en**	**-en**
gen	**-en**	**-en**	**-en**	**-en**

Ich kaufe einen groß**en** Stadtplan.
Ein groß**er** Stadtplan ist sehr nützlich.
Ich gebe den groß**en** Stadtplan meiner klein**en** Schwester.
Auf dem Marktplatz gibt es eine neu**e** Eisdiele.
Eine ander**e** alt**e** Eisdiele ist um die Ecke.
Ich gehe gerne in eine groß**e** Eisdiele.
In einer groß**en** Eisdiele gibt es viele verschiedene Eissorten.

Useful words for describing people:

(e.g. **Susanne ist groß**. *Susanne is tall.*)

tall	**groß**	small	**klein**
thin	**dünn**	fat	**dick**
happy	**glücklich**	unhappy	**unglücklich**
quiet	**ruhig**	loud	**laut**
shy	**schüchtern**	self-confident	**selbstbewusst**
relaxed	**entspannt**	stressed	**gestresst**
laid back	**zurückhaltend**	demanding	**fordernd**
self-centred	**ichbezogen**	giving	**hilfsbereit**
selfish	**selbstsüchtig**	selfless	**selbstlos**
egoistic	**egoistisch**	considerate	**rücksichtsvoll**
active	**aktiv**	lazy	**faul**
good looking	**gut aussehend**	ugly	**hässlich**
cheerful	**fröhlich**	depressed	**bedrückt**
intelligent	**intelligent**	stupid	**dumm**
modern	**modern**	conservative	**konservativ**

smart	**gepflegt**	*scruffy*	**ungepflegt**
well-behaved	**artig**	*naughty*	**ungezogen**
erotic	**erotisch**	*prudish*	**prüde**
polite	**höflich**	*rude*	**unhöflich**
self-confident	**selbstbewusst**	*uncertain*	**unsicher**
determined	**entschlossen**	*undecided*	**unentschlossen**
sloaney	**schickimicki**	*casual*	**lässig**
honest	**ehrlich**	*dishonest*	**unehrlich**

Insight

Be careful of false friends! You should not translate sensible by **sensibel** or sympathetic by **sympathisch**.

sympathisch	= *pleasant, likeable*
verständnissvoll	= *sympathetic*
sensible	= *sensitive*
vernünftig	= *sensible*
seriös	= *respectable*
ernsthaft	= *serious*
Ernsthaft?	= *Are you serious?*
Seien Sie/Sei ernst!	= *Be serious!*
Seien Sie/Sei vernünftig!	= *Be sensible!*
Sie ist eine verständnisvolle Person.	= *She is a sympathetic person.*

Insight

Anglicisms are very popular in Germany and more and more people (young and old) are using them.

It may sound a bit funny when you hear an English word being used in a German sentence, but don't be shy: do the same! Listen to German speakers and you might hear sentences such as:

I am totally relaxed.	**Ich bin total relaxed.**
This guy is cool.	**Der Typ ist cool.**
I think that's cool.	**Ich finde das cool.**
Don't be so stressed out.	**Sei nicht so gestresst.**

That's a cool car.	**Das ist ein cooles Auto.**		
My work is heavy at the moment.	**Meine Arbeit ist zur Zeit wirklich heavy.**		
That's powerful.	**Das ist powerful.**		

Some useful words for describing things:

(e.g. **Der Computer ist neu, aber er ist nicht schnell.** *The computer is new but it is not fast.*)

old	**alt**	*new*	**neu**
good	**gut**	*bad*	**schlecht**
cheap	**billig**	*expensive*	**teuer**
fast	**schnell**	*slow*	**langsam**
in good condition	**in Ordnung**	*damaged*	**kaputt**
flimsy	**dünn**	*solid*	**fest**
rough	**rauh**	*smooth*	**glatt**
shiny	**glänzend**	*dull*	**matt**
comfortable	**bequem**	*uncomfortable*	**unbequem**
wide/broad	**breit**	*narrow*	**schmal**
long	**lang**	*short*	**kurz**
thin	**dünn**	*thick*	**dick**
hard	**hart**	*soft*	**weich**
high	**hoch**	*low*	**niedrig**
light	**leicht**	*heavy*	**schwer**
clean	**sauber**	*dirty*	**schmutzig**
heavy	**schwer**	*light*	**leicht**
fragile	**zerbrechlich**	*sturdy*	**stabil**

Comparative and superlative

An example of the comparative is: *He is smaller than his brother.*
Er ist kleiner als sein Bruder.

The comparative is made by adding -er to the base form of the adjective, e.g. *small* **klein**, *smaller* **kleiner**; *wide* **weit**, *wider* **weiter**.

Some adjectives need an Umlaut for the comparative as well as for the superlative: *old* alt, *older* älter, *oldest* am ältesten; *often* oft, *more often* öfter, *most often* am öftesten.

The superlative is made by adding *am* and ending *-(e)sten*: *tallest am* größten, *smallest am* kleinsten:

He is the smallest. Er ist am kleinsten.

bad schlecht	*worse* schlechter	*worst am* schlechtesten
big groß	*bigger* größer	*biggest am* größten
dear teuer	*dearer* teurer	*dearest am* teuersten
easy leicht	*easier* leichter	*easiest am* leichesten
firm fest	*firmer* fester	*firmest am* festesten
good gut	*better* besser	*best am* besten
late spät	*later* später	*latest am* spätesten
little wenig	*less* weniger	*least am* wenigsten
old alt	*older* älter	*oldest am* ältesten
small klein	*smaller* kleiner	*smallest am* kleinsten
tall groß	*taller* größer	*tallest am* größten

But irregular (in German as they *are* in English!):

much viel	*more* mehr	*most am* meisten
good gut	*better* besser	*best am* besten

Colours and sizes

Colours *die Farben*

beige	**beige**
black	**schwarz**
blue	**blau**
brown	**braun**
green	**grün**

grey	grau
golden	gold
lilac	lila
mauve	malvenfarben
natural	naturfarben
orange	orange
pink	rosa
purple	purpur
red	rot
silver	silber
turquoise	türkis
violet	violett
white	weiss
yellow	gelb

Insight

Remember to write all two-word colour adjectives as one word in German: dark green **dunkelgrün**, dark red **dunkelrot**, bright red **knallrot**, pitch black **pechschwarz**, blue-grey **blaugrau**, silver grey **silbergrau**, light blue **hellblau**, light green **hellgrün**.

Also remember: The word for bright in German is **hell: Das Licht ist hell.** (The light is bright.) Watch for false friends! **Hell** in German is not the same as hell in English (which is **die Hölle**).

More colours

salmon pink	lachsrot
khaki	khakifarben
burgundy	burgunderrot
royal blue	königsblau
dark blue	dunkelblau
navy blue	marineblau
pale green	blassgrün
dark green	dunkelgrün
olive green	olivengrün

emerald green	**smaragdgrün**
bottle green	**flaschengrün**
grass green	**grasgrün**
bright red	**hellrot**
scarlet	**scharlachrot**
pale yellow	**blassgelb**
bright yellow	**knallgelb**
emerald	**smaragdfarben**
ruby	**rubinrot**
ruby coloured	**weinrot**
turquoise	**türkis**

Sizes

sehr klein	*very small*	**klein**	*small*
mittelgroß	*medium*	**durchschnittlich**	*average*
groß	*large*	**sehr groß**	*very large*
weit	*wide*	**schmal**	*narrow*
lang	*long*	**kurz**	*short*
zu lang	*too long*	**etwas zu lang**	*a bit too long*
viel zu lang	*far too long*	**viel zu groß/klein**	*far too big/short*

Adverbs

Insight

In English most adverbs are made by adding *-ly* to an adjective: *quick* – quickly. *I don't drive quickly*. In German: **Ich fahre nicht schnell.** Here is the good news: German adverbs are the same as the adjective, and they are therefore easier for you to use.

schnell	*quickly*
langsam	*slowly*
zu schnell	*too fast*
gut	*well*

Kommen Sie schnell!	Come quickly!
Fahren Sie langsam!	Drive slowly!
Sie sind zu schnell gefahren.	You drove too fast.
Das haben Sie gut gemacht.	You did that well.
Das haben Sie gut **ausgesprochen.**	You pronounced that well.
sofort	immediately
total	completely
plötzlich	suddenly
geräuschlos	noiselessly
schmerzhaft	painfully
schmerzlos	painlessly
glücklicherweise	happily
ungefähr	approximately
technisch	technically
traurigerweise	sadly
Die Polizei kommt sofort.	The police are coming immediately.
Ich habe das total vergessen.	I totally forgot about it.
Plötzlich fing es **an** zu regnen.	Suddenly it started to rain.
Glücklicherweise fährt die Fähre alle zwei Stunden.	Luckily the ferry goes every two hours.
sehr	very
wenig	a little
mehr	more
am meisten	most
weniger	less
Wir treffen uns ...:	We meet ...:
selten	rarely
gelegentlich	occasionally
regelmäßig	regularly
manchmal	sometimes
oft	often
sehr oft	very often
bald	soon
nie	never
Wir haben uns schon einmal getroffen.	We have met already.
schon einmal	already

never	**noch nie**
We never met before.	**Wir haben uns noch nie getroffen.**
We met briefly.	**Wir haben uns kurz getroffen.**
fast, faster, fastest	**schnell, schneller, am schnellsten**
well, better, best	**gut, besser, am besten**
badly, worse, worst	**schlecht, schlechter, am schlechtesten**
then	**dann**
now	**jetzt**
afterwards	**nachher**
previously	**vorher**
earlier	**früher**
later	**später**
before the meal	**vor dem Essen**
after the meal	**nach dem Essen**
in order to go to ...	**um nach ... zu gehen ...**
in order to read ...	**um das zu lesen ...**
while he was here	**während er hier war**
during the meeting	**während der Besprechung**

Sentences with *in order to*

Um nach Dresden zu fahren, müssen wir den Zug um 8 Uhr nehmen.
In order to go to Dresden we have to catch the train at 8 o'clock.

Um rechtzeitig <u>an</u>zukommen, sollten wir jetzt gehen.
In order to arrive in time we should leave now.

Impersonal expressions

all	**alles**
that is all.	**das ist alles.**
all inclusive	**alles inklusive**
every	**jede/r**

every half hour	jede halbe Stunde
every moment	jeden Moment
none	kein/e
none of us	keiner von uns

Numbers, times, days and dates

Cardinal numbers

0 null	10 zehn	20 zwanzig
1 eins	11 elf	21 einundzwanzig
2 zwei	12 zwölf	22 zweiundzwanzig
3 drei	13 dreizehn	30 dreißig
4 vier	14 vierzehn	40 vierzig
5 fünf	15 fünfzehn	50 fünfzig
6 sechs	16 sechzehn	60 sechzig
7 sieben	17 siebzehn	70 siebzig
8 acht	18 achtzehn	80 achtzig
9 neun	19 neunzehn	90 neunzig

....
Insight
Remember: **sechs** but **sechzehn**,
           sieben but **siebzehn**,
           dreißig but **zwanzig, vierzig** etc.
....

Bigger useful numbers:

100 einhundert	1000 eintausend
101 einhundert(und)eins	2000 zweitausend
102 einhundert(und)zwei	2010 zweitausend(und)zehn
110 einhundert(und)zehn	5000 fünftausend
150 einhundert(und)fünfzig	10 000 zehntausend
200 zweihundert	a million eine Million
300 dreihundert	a billion eine Billion
500 fünfhundert	

Ordinal numbers

first	**erste**	*fourth*	**vierte**
second	**zweite**	*fifth*	**fünfte**
third	**dritte**	*tenth*	**zehnte**
21st	**einundzwanzigste**		

Some fractions

half   **halb**   *quarter*   **ein Viertel**

Dates

the century	**das Jahrhundert**
1993	**neunzehnhundertdreiundneunzig**
1994	**neunzehnhundertvierundneunzig**
the 20th century	**das zwanzigste Jahrhundert**
the 21st century	**das einundzwanzigste Jahrhundert**
2002	**zweitausend(und)zwei**
2003	**zweitausend(und)drei**
2020	**zweitausend(und)zwanzig**
the 22nd century	**das zweiundzwanzigste Jahrhundert**
the millennium	**das Millenium**
the 1990s	**die neunziger Jahre**
the year 2003	**das Jahr zweitausend(und)drei**
the year 2010	**das Jahr zweitausend(und)zehn**
next year	**nächstes Jahr**
last year	**letztes Jahr**
the year before last	**das vorletzte Jahr**
the coming year	**das kommende Jahr**

Days and months

Monday	**Montag**	*Friday*	**Freitag**
Tuesday	**Dienstag**	*Saturday*	**Samstag/Sonnabend**
Wednesday	**Mittwoch**	*Sunday*	**Sonntag**
Thursday	**Donnerstag**		

January	**Januar**	*July*	**July**
February	**Februar**	*August*	**August**
March	**März**	*September*	**September**
April	**April**	*October*	**Oktober**
May	**Mai**	*November*	**November**
June	**Juni**	*December*	**Dezember**

Expressions of time

second	**die Sekunde**
minute	**die Minute**
hour	**die Stunde**
day	**der Tag**
week	**die Woche**
month	**der Monat**
year	**das Jahr**
yesterday	**gestern**
the day before yesterday	**vorgestern**
today	**heute**
tomorrow	**morgen**
the day after tomorrow	**übermorgen**
morning	**der Morgen**
afternoon	**der Nachmittag**
evening	**der Abend**
night	**die Nacht**
tonight	**heute Abend**

(Contd)

Guten Morgen *Good morning.* **Montag morgen** *Monday morning.*

Morgen fahren wir nach München. *Tomorrow we are going to Munich.*

....

The seasons

spring	**der Frühling/das Frühjahr**
summer	**der Sommer**
autumn	**der Herbst**
winter	**der Winter**

The clock

Es ist:		
	9.20	neun Uhr zwanzig
	7.10	sieben Uhr zehn
	11.30	elf Uhr dreißig
	12.45	zwölf Uhr fünfundvierzig
	20.35	zwanzig Uhr fünfunddreißig
	21.45	einundzwanzig Uhr fünfundvierzig

Note: You use the 24-hour clock for offical time giving, train/plane leaving times, etc. Otherwise, when asking somebody for the time or making arrangements when to meet, use:

9.00 a.m.	**neun Uhr**
9.15	**viertel nach neun**
9.20	**zwanzig nach neun**
9.30	**halb zehn**
9.31	**neun Uhr einundreißig**
9.40	**zwanzig vor zehn**
9.45	**viertel vor zehn**
past	**nach**
to	**vor**
a quarter	**viertel**
half	**halb**

half hour	**die halbe Stunde**
quarter hour	**die Viertelstunde**
three quarters of an hour	**eine Dreiviertelstunde**
midnight	**Mitternacht**
midday	**Mittag**
sunrise	**der Sonnenaufgang**
sunset	**der Sonnenuntergang**

alarm clock	**der Wecker**
wristwatch	**die Armbanduhr**
clock on a tower	**die Turmuhr**
wall clock	**die Wanduhr**
church clock	**die Kirchenuhr**
cuckoo clock	**die Kuckucksuhr**

Can you give me the time?	**Können Sie mir sagen, wie spät es ist?**
Can you wake me up at ...?	**Können Sie mich um ... Uhr wecken?**
We could meet at 6 o'clock.	**Wir könnten uns um 6 Uhr treffen.**
Do we want to meet at half seven?	**Wollen wir uns um halb acht treffen?**
It is late.	**Es ist spät.**
It is early.	**Es ist früh.**
It is too late.	**Es ist zu spät.**
We could meet a bit later	**Wir könnten uns etwas spatter treffen.**
How about a bit later?	**Wie wäre es mit etwas später?**
My watch does not work any more.	**Meine Uhr geht nicht mehr.**
My watch is fast/slow.	**Meine Uhr geht vor/nach.**

Quantity

how heavy?	**wie schwer?**
weight	**das Gewicht**
to weigh	**wiegen**
height	**die Höhe**
to measure	**messen**
length	**die Länge**
content	**der Inhalt**
volume	**das Volumen**
to fit in	**reinpassen**

Weights and measures

how much?	**wie viel?**
kilo	**das Kilo**
half a kilo	**ein halbes Kilo**
500 grams	**500 Gramm**
a pound	**ein Pfund**
a litre	**ein Liter**
a metre	**ein Meter**

a centimetre	**ein Zentimeter**
a kilometre	**ein Kilometer**
a pair	**ein Paar**
a dozen	**ein Dutzend**
a slice of	**eine Scheibe**
a bit more	**etwas mehr**
a bit less	**etwas weniger**
how hot?	**wie warm?**
how cold?	**wie kalt?**
temperature	**die Temperatur**
above	**über**
below	**unter**
minus	**minus**
degree Celsius	**Grad Celsius**
how fast?	**wie schnell?**
distance	**die Distanz(en), die Entfernung(en)**
speed	**die Geschwindigkeit(en)**
kilometre per hour	**der Kilometer pro Stunde**
mile	**die Meile(n)**
to drive	**fahren**
how fast	**wie schnell**
slowly	**langsam**
too fast	**zu schnell**
too slowly	**zu langsam**
bottle	**die Flasche (n)**
jar	**das Glas ("er)**
tin	**die Dose (n)**
box	**die Schachtel (n)**
pot	**der Topf ("e)**
coffee pot	**die Kaffeekanne (n)**
package	**die Verpackung (en)**
lots of	**viele ...**
little	**wenig ...**
more of	**mehr ...**
full	**voll**
empty	**leer**
some honey	**ein bisschen Honig**

lots of sugar	**ganz viel Zucker**
hardly any salt	**kaum Salz**
just a bit of milk	**nur ein bisschen Milch**
just a drop	**nur ein Tropfen**

Exclamations, giving orders and being polite

Expressions such as **Entschuldigen Sie (bitte)** (*excuse me please*) or Entschuldigung (*sorry*) as well as **danke** and **bitte** are used the same way as in the UK.

But various other meanings of the word **bitte** also occur: when passing something on to somebody it is polite and necessary to say: **hier bitte** or **bitte** or **bitte schön** or **bitte sehr**. All these expressions have a similar meaning to *here you are* but are much politer.

The reply is then **danke** (*thanks*), **ich danke Ihnen** (*thank you*) **ich danke dir, danke schön, vielen Dank** (*many thanks/thanks a lot*). You are welcome = **gern geschehen**.

Apart from please the word **bitte** has also other meanings:

it's a pleasure	**bitte bitte**
sure!	**aber bitte**
it is nothing!	**bitte keine Ursache**
help yourself!	**bitte nur zu**
there you are!	**na bitte**
not at all!	**aber ich bitte dich/Sie!**
I would be glad if you would …	**ich bitte darum …**

Other expressions with **bitte**:

I would like to ask you.	**Ich möchte Sie/dich bitten.**
I would like to ask you for something.	**Ich möchte Sie um etwas bitten.**
You can ask me for anything.	**Sie können mich um alles bitten.**

Don't ask me for anything.	**Fragen Sie mich bitte um nichts.**
May I asked you for your name?	**Darf ich Sie um Ihren Namen bitten?**
don't please	**bitte nicht**
(used in a shop as an invitation to you to say what you want)	**bitte schön**
thanks	**danke**
many thanks	**vielen Dank**
thank you	**danke sehr**
thank you	**danke schön**
thank you very much	**herzlichen Dank**
to thank	**danken**
to be grateful	**dankbar sein**
to thank for	**sich bedanken für**
Help!	**Hilfe**
Fire!	**Feuer**
Cheers!	**Prost/zum Wohl**
Wait!	**Warten Sie!**
Stop!	**Stop! Anhalten!**
Listen!	**Hören Sie mal! Hör mal!**
Look! ⎱	**Schauen Sie mal! Schau mal!**
Look! ⎰ Have a look	**Sehen Sie/Sieh mal!**
Look! ⎰	**Gucken Sie/guck mal!**
Pass me a knife please.	**Reichen Sie (Reich) mir bitte ein Messer.**
Fetch a glass.	**Holen Sie sich (Hol) dir ein Glas.**
Take the chocolates.	**Nehmen Sie (Nimm) die Schokolade.**
Bring me my bag.	**Bringen Sie (Bring) mir meine Tasche.**
Order a beer for me.	**Bestellen Sie (Bestell) mir ein Bier.**
Pay for me please.	**Bezahlen Sie (Bezahl) für mich bitte.**
Write it down please.	**Schreiben Sie (Schreib) es bitte auf.**
Spell it please.	**Buchstabieren Sie (Buchstabier) es bitte.**
Repeat that please.	**Wiederholen Sie (Wiederhol) das bitte.**
Say it again please.	**Sagen Sie (Sag) es noch einmal.**
Try it again.	**Probieren Sie (Probier) es noch einmal.**
Check it again.	**Überprüfen Sie (Überprüf) es noch mal.**

Dialogue

A	Ich lade Sie ein.	*I invite you.*
B	Oh, vielen Dank.	*Many thanks.*
A	Gern geschehen.	*It's a pleasure.*

Excuse me.	**Pardon. Entschuldigung.**
I'm sorry.	**Es tut mir Leid.**
Sorry.	**Das tut mir Leid.**
Excuse me.	**Entschuldigen Sie bitte.**
I didn't mean it.	**Ich wollte das nicht.**
I did not know that.	**Das wusste ich nicht.**
I did not understand that.	**Ich habe das nicht verstanden.**
Sorry I'm late.	**Tut mir Leid für die Verspätung.**

When somebody tells you something bad has happened to him/her you respond with: **Das tut mir Leid.**

Dialects, idiomatic language, standard German and word building

There are three categories into which the German language can be divided. **Dialekt/Mundart** (*dialect*), **Umgangssprache** (*idiomatic language, local usage*) and **Hochdeutsch** (*High German/standard German*). **Hochdeutsch** is grammatically correct, free of accent and taught in all schools.

Umgangssprache is often just a few words and expressions of the city or area which are different. You can pick them up easily after a while.

There are, however, various dialects in Germany, Austria and Switzerland and local people speak this dialect. Among them are **Bayrisch, Hessisch, Sächsisch, Friesisch, Plattdeutsch, Schwäbisch** and, in Switzerland, **Schweizerdeutsch**, which again changes from area to area (*Kanton*).

A dialect has its own words, the meaning of which might not be so clear to people speaking a different dialect.

Insight
Don't worry about dialects too much. If you are spending time in a region where a dialect is spoken, you will get used to it and pick it up. You can use **Hochdeutsch** which you will probably have learnt at school, university or in a German class. This will be understood throughout Germany, and people will make an effort to speak **Hochdeutsch** to you in response.

Compound nouns

Insight
German has many long words, but don't worry about them: they are just a combination of more than one word. When reading a long word for the first time, try to split it up and take a little breath in between the elements. You might also find that you see a familiar word within it.

Examples:

Schwarzwälderkirschtorte
Schwarz/wälder/kirsch/torte
schwarz *black*
die Wälder *forest*
die Kirsche *cherry*
die Torte *tart*
= *black forest cherry tart (Black Forest gateau)*

Note: The letter e has been dropped in **Kirsche**.

der Kindergeburtstagskuchen
Kinder/geburtstags/kuchen

die Kinder *children*
der Geburtstag *birthday*
der Kuchen *cake*
= *children's birthday cake*

Note: An **s** has been added on **Geburtstag** so that it can be pronounced more easily.

Word building

Insight

Word building is another good way to build up your vocabulary and give structure to your sentences. Look out for examples throughout the book.

Examples:	
verstehen	*to understand*
das Verstehen	*understanding*
Ich verstehe Sie.	*I understand you.*
Ich verstehe Sie nicht.	*I don't understand you.*
Ich verstehe Sie nicht ganz.	*I don't quite understand.*
Ich verstehe Sie, wenn sie langsam sprechen.	*I understand when you speak slowly.*
Verstehen Sie mich?	*Do you understand me?*
Haben Sie mich verstanden?	*Did you understand me?*

Anglo-German vocabulary

Insight

As Anglicisms play a very important part in modern German, you will find them listed in context in each of the 16 units of this book. This will allow you to build up your vocabulary much faster and communicate more fluently, by knowing which English words have been adopted into the German language.

Many English words and terms have been adopted into German, not only in the field of computer technology, marketing jargon and the media but also in everyday language. English vocabulary is being used more and more. English verbs are taken and 'made German' by adding the German verb ending **-en**, e.g. *to mail* **mailen**, *to relax* **relaxen**. Young people in particular use a lot of Anglicisms. For example, instead of using the expression **Entschuldigung** you will hear *Sorry*.

Examples of German sentences containing English words and expressions:

That's cool.	**Das ist <u>cool</u>.**
I like my job.	**Mein Job gefällt mir gut.**
That was a good joke.	**Das war ein guter <u>Joke</u>.**
We are going to a party tomorrow.	**Wir gehen morgen zu einer <u>Party</u>.**
That's a good song.	**Das ist ein guter <u>Song</u>.**
I am really happy.	**Ich bin total <u>happy</u>.**
Hi!	**<u>Hi!</u>**
You should relax again.	**Du solltest mal wieder <u>relaxen</u>.**
Sale	**<u>Sale</u>**
<u>Don't worry, be happy!</u>	

Examples of verbs

relaxen	*to relax*
surfen	*surf (internet)*
babysitten	*to do baby sitting*
downloaden	*to download*
mailen	*to send an email*
joggen	*to jog*
kidnappen	*to kidnap*
launchen	*to launch*
mergen	*to merge*
saven	*to save*

Examples of nouns

der Actionfilm	das Poster
Wellness	Firstclass
die Beachparty	Fitness Center
die Boxershorts	Lastminute-Flight
das Picknick	die Leggings
der Lifestyle	der Loser
der Computer	die Lovestory
der Export	der Nightclub
der Fanclub	

Insight

As an English speaker you will be surprised how much Anglo-German vocabulary you already know. Think of the words used in English which are actually German such as: autobahn, bratwurst, Fahrenheit, rucksack, wunderbar.
In addition, the two languages have many identical or similar words called cognates such as: *name* **Name**, *address* **Adresse**, *bus* **Bus**, *December* **Dezember**, to name a few.

Look out for more Anglo-German vocabulary and similar or the same words in English and German throughout the book. They are listed in each unit.

Summary

This is a summary of the most **important points** made in the Toolbox section. If you are not sure about any of the points, go back and look at them again.

Nouns

▶ All German nouns are written with a capital letter and are therefore easily recognized.

▶ In German all nouns are either masculine (**der**), feminine (**die**) or neuter (**das**). Although there is no logic to whether a noun is masculine, feminine or neuter, there are some ways to help you remember the gender of a noun.

The article or cases

Der/die/das can change depending on whether the noun is being used as:

▶ The subject in a sentence (nominative)
▶ The direct object (accusative)
▶ The indirect object (dative)

Pronouns

Remember: There are three words for you in German –

du (informal, singular)
Sie (formal, singular and plural)
ihr (informal, plural)

You should say **Sie** to people over the age of 16, apart from relatives or friends.

Prepositions

After certain prepositions the article changes, e.g. **bis, durch, für, gegen, ohne, um, wider** are followed by the accusative.

Other prepositions are followed by the dative.

Verbs

In German the verb consists of the stem + the ending: **-en, -n** or **-ern**.
flieg<u>en</u>, fahr<u>en</u>,
lächel<u>n</u>, sammel<u>n</u>
wand<u>ern</u>, klett<u>ern</u>

Regular verbs:

In German, the endings of the verb change for each person.

ich	the verbs ends in e	Ich wohne
du	verb ends in st	du wohnst
er/sie/es	ends in t	er/sie/es wohnt
wir	ends in en	wir wohnen
ihr	ends in t	ihr wohnt
sie	ends in en	sie wohnen

Irregular verbs:

These verbs have to be learnt by heart. The two most important irregular verbs are *to have* **haben** and *to be* **sein**.

Separable verbs:

The German language has many separable verbs. They are made up of two parts: a prefix – for example **ab-, an-** or **zurück-** – and the infinitive of a verb, e.g. **fahren** or **kommen**. Separable verbs: **ankommen** to arrive, **abfahren** to leave, **zurückkommen** to come back. The prefixes of these verbs are underlined throughout this book so that you can recognize them immediately.

Reflexive verbs:

Some verbs in German need a reflexive pronoun for their meaning to be complete.

I wash myself **Ich wasche mich.** These verbs are called reflexive verbs.

Structure of sentences in the present tense:

The most important rule is: The verb always comes second in the main part of the sentence.

Talking about the past
The perfect tense comprises the past participle and the verb **haben** or **sein**.

Around 70% of all verbs take haben; around 30% take **sein**.

Ich <u>habe</u> ein Buch gelesen.
Ich <u>bin</u> nach Hannover gefahren.

Future tense
You can form the future tense with the auxiliary verb **werden**
and the infinitive: **Ich werde dich besuchen.** *I am going to*
visit you.

Or: you can use the present tense if you indicate when you are
going to do something:

On Monday I am going to visit you. **Am Montag besuche**
ich dich.

Negative expressions
Use kein in front of a noun: **Ich mag kein Fleisch.** *I don't like meat.*

Use **nicht** with a verb: **Ich rauche nicht.** *I don't smoke.*

Nichts *nothing/not anything*, **niemand** *nobody/not anybody*,
noch nie *never*, **immer noch nicht** *still not*, **nicht mehr** *not any*
more.

Asking questions using a question word
Questions asking for information are introduced by a question
word: *who* **wer**, *when* **wann** etc.

The question word comes first, followed by the verb, followed by
the subject.

Wo wohnen Sie? *Where do you live?*

Interrogative – asking questions
You can ask a question by inverting the pronoun and verb:
Sprechen Sie Deutsch? *Do you speak German?*

Conditional
The conditional always includes a condition, whether this is expressed or not, for example:

Ich würde gerne in die Schweiz fahren (wenn ich genug Geld und Zeit hätte). *I would like to Switzerland (if I had enough time and money). The conditional is used to translate would in English.*

Adjectives
An adjective describes a noun or a pronoun. When an adjective is used after the noun, the adjective ending does not change, e.g. **Das Wetter ist schlecht.** The weather is bad. It also does not change after a pronoun (er *he*, sie *she*, es *it*). **Es ist schlecht.** It is bad. It does however change if it goes before the noun.

Das schlechte Wetter. Ich kaufe einen neuen Computer.

Comparative and superlative
The comparative is made by adding -er to the base form of the adjective, e.g. *small* **klein**, *smaller* **kleiner**, *wide* **weit**, *wider* **weiter**.

Er ist kleiner als sein Bruder. He is smaller than his brother.

The superlative is made by adding am and ending -(e)sten: *tallest* **am größten**, *smallest* **am kleinsten**.

Er ist am kleinsten. *He is the smallest.*

Colours
Remember: Write all two-word colour adjectives as one word: *dark green* **dunkelgrün**.

Adverbs
In English most adverbs are made by adding *-ly* to an adjective: *quick – quickly. I don't drive quickly.*

German adverbs are the same as the adjective: **Ich fahre nicht schnell.**

Numbers, times, days and dates

Remember: **sechs** but **sechzehn** (the s has been dropped); **sieben** but **siebzehn** (the en has been dropped).

There are two words for Saturday in Germany: **Samstag** and **Sonnabend**.

Expressions of time

These are very useful to learn. Remember: **heute Nachmittag** *this afternoon*, **heute früh** *this morning*, **morgen früh** tomorrow *morning*, **gestern Vormittag** *yesterday morning*. **Morgen** has two meanings: *tomorrow* and *morning*. **Guten Morgen** *Good morning*. **Montag morgen** *Monday morning*.

Morgen fahren wir nach München. *Tomorrow we are going to Munich.*

The clock

Remember: **halb zehn** is *9.30*, **halb vier** is *3.30*, **halb elf** is *10.30*.

Also remember: The same word is used for clock and watch in German: **die Uhr. Meine Uhr ist kaputt.** (*My watch is broken.*) **Es ist 5 Uhr.** (*It is 5 o'clock.*)

German spelling

The good news is that German is a much more phonetically consistent language than English, which means that German words are nearly always spelt the way they sound. I recommend learning the way letters and letter combinations sound and you will be able to pronounce new words by just looking at the way they are spelt. Remember: go to www.teachyourself.com to do some pronunciation practice.

German vocabulary and dialects

High German **Hochdeutsch** is the language spoken or understood throughout Germany but there are many dialects spoken in Germany depending on the region. Many people consider the best

Hochdeutsch to be that spoken in and around Hanover in the north of Germany.

Compound nouns

German has many long nouns. Don't worry about them too much; they are just a combination of more than one word. When reading a long word for the first time try to split it up and take a little breath in between the elements. You might also find that you see a familiar word within the long word.

Anglicisms

As Anglicisms play a very important part in modern German, you will find in each of the 16 units of this Anglicisms and same or similar words in English and German listed in context. This will allow you to build up your vocabulary much faster and communicate more fluently by knowing which English words have been adopted into the German language.

1

Personal matters

1.1 Titles, greetings, introducing yourself and others and making arrangements

Core vocabulary

Insight

It would be worthwhile initially to take some time to familiarize yourself with the following words in connection with greetings and introducing yourself, as they are either Anglicisms or words which are similar in English and German. This will help you to build up your vocabulary faster. By being aware of which Anglicisms are used you will be able to communicate in as up-to-date a manner as possible.

Doctor **der Doktor/die Doktorin**, *professor* **der Professor/die Professorin**, *hello* **hallo**, *bye* **bye**, *hi* **hi** (these last three are used a lot by young people), *morning* **der Morgen**, *night* **die Nacht**, *my* **mein**, *colleague* **der Kollege/die Kollegin**, *widowed* **verwitwet**, *single* **single**, *daughter* **Tochter**, *son* **Sohn**, *name* **Name**.

Titles

Mr	**Herr**
Mrs	**Frau**
Miss	**Fräulein**
Dr	**Dr. Doktor/in**
Prof	**Prof. Professor/in**
Earl	**Graf/Gräfin**
Baron/ess	**Baron/in**

Insight

Fräulein is an old-fashioned word and is hardly used any more. Most women prefer to be called **Frau** instead of **Fräulein** regardless of their marital status. **Fräulein** is only used to indicate marital status.

Addressing somebody with their title is important in Germany. If someone has a doctorial title (medical or academic) it is usual to address them as Herr Doktor/Frau Doktor with or without the surname: **Guten Tag, Herr Doktor; Guten Tag, Herr Doktor Meier; Guten Tag, Frau Doktor Meier.**

▶ At present both female and male titles can be used for female job titles, academic or medical professions: **Frau Rechtsanwältin** (+ surname), **Frau Rechtsanwalt** (+ surname). **Guten Tag, Frau Rechtsanwältin** (Meier), **Guten Tag, Frau Rechtsanwalt.**

Professor:	**Herr Professor** (+ surname),
Frau	**Professor/in** (+ surname).
Doctor (medical or academic):	**Herr Doktor, Frau Doktor/Frau Doktorin.**
Judge:	**Herr Richter/Frau Richter/in.**
Mayor:	**Herr/Frau Bürgermeister/in.**
Member of parliament:	**Frau Abgeordnete/Herr Abgeordneter.**

When addressing nobility **Herr** or **Frau** is dropped: **Guten Tag Baronin Meier, Guten Tag Graf Meier.**

Greetings

The most common greetings are:

Hello	**hallo**
Good morning	**guten Morgen**
Good afternoon	**guten Nachmittag**
Good evening	**guten Abend**
Good night	**gute Nacht**
Goodbye	**auf Wiedersehen**
Goodbye (on the phone)	**auf Wiederhören**
Bye	**tschüss**
Hi	**hi**

Introducing yourself

my	**mein**
your (formal)	**Ihr**
your (informal)	**dein**
name	**der Name**
is	**ist**

to be called	**heißen**
how/what	**wie**

Introducing someone
I would like to introduce you to ...: Ich möchte Ihnen gerne ...
<u>vor</u>stellen

Mrs Meier	**Frau Meier**
Mr Meier	**Herrn Meier**
my husband/son	**meinen Mann/Sohn**
my wife/daughter	**meine Frau/Tochter**
my colleague	**meinen Kollegen Herrn Meier/meine Kollegin Frau Meier/Herrn Professor Dr Schmidt**
Are you Mrs ...?	**Sind Sie Frau ...?**
Mr ...?	**Sind Sie Herr ...?**
Mr Schmidt's (female) colleague?	**Sind Sie die Kollegin von Herrn Schmidt?**

Useful phrases to introduce yourself and others

I would like to introduce myself.	**Ich möchte mich vorstellen.**
My name is Mrs. Klein.	**Mein Name ist Frau Klein.**
My name is Mr. Braun.	**Mein Name ist Herr Braun.**
This is (my husband/wife/friend).	**Das ist mein(e) Mann/Frau/ Freund/Freundin.**
Do you know each other?	**Kennen Sie sich schon?**
Yes, we do.	**Ja, wir kennen uns.**
No, we don't know each other.	**Nein, wir kennen uns nicht.**

Insight

A nice reply after having been introduced to someone, or having introduced yourself to someone, is:

Freut mich Sie kennen zu lernen. *Pleased to meet you.*

or (informal): **Freut mich dich kennen zu lernen**

or an even shorter form: **Freut mich.**

Remember to answer with: **Freut mich auch**. *(I am pleased too.)*

The older generation tend to use the word **Angenehm** instead.

For example:

> **Guten Tag. Mein Name ist Lisa Kahlen. Wie heißen Sie?**
> **Mein Name ist Rob Wilkinson.**
> **Freut mich Sie kennenzulernen.**
> **Freut mich auch.**

I am ...	**Ich bin ...**
single	**ledig/single**
married	**verheiratet**
divorced	**geschieden**
separated	**getrennt**
widowed	**verwitwet**
engaged	**verlobt**

Making arrangements

What shall we do this evening?	**Was wollen wir heute Abend machen?**
May I invite you to a ...?	**Kann ich Sie zu ... ein̲laden?**
May I invite you for a coffee.	**Kann ich Sie/dich zu einem Kaffee ein̲laden.**
What would you like to do?	**Was möchten Sie gerne tun?**
Where would you like to go?	**Wohin möchten Sie gehen?**
I would like to go to ...	**Ich möchte gerne in ... gehen.**
bar	**in eine Bar**
nightclub	**in einen Nachtclub**
restaurant	**in ein Restaurant**
theatre	**ins Theater**
cinema	**ins Kino**
disco	**in eine Diskothek**
club	**in einen Club**
play	**in ein Theaterstück**
musical	**in ein Musical**

but:

I would like to go to a concert.	**Ich möchte gerne auf ein Konzert gehen.**

I would like to see a comedy.	**Ich möchte gerne eine Komödie sehen.**
When shall we meet?	**Wann sollen wir uns treffen?**
I don't mind.	**Mir ist das gleich.**
At 9 o'clock.	**Um 9 Uhr.**
That's fine with me.	**Das passt mir gut.**
I will pick you up.	**Ich werde Sie (dich) abholen.**
Great!	**Prima!**
to arrange a meeting	**ein Treffen vereinbaren**
to book a table	**einen Tisch buchen**
to go out	**ausgehen**
to watch a film	**einen Film ansehen**

Useful phrases

Excuse me.	**Entschuldigen Sie bitte/ Entschuldige.**
Pardon?	**Entschuldigung? Wie bitte?**
I don't understand.	**Ich verstehe das nicht.**
I didn't catch that.	**Ich habe das nicht ganz verstanden.**
Can you speak more slowly?	**Könnten Sie/kannst du etwas langsamer sprechen?**
How do you say ... in German?	**Wie sagt man ... auf Deutsch?**
I apologize.	**Entschuldigung.**
I'm sorry.	**Es tut mir Leid.**
I beg your pardon.	**Entschuldigung.**
I didn't mean it.	**Ich habe das nicht so gemeint.**
Forgive me.	**Verzeihung.**
Sorry, it was my fault.	**Entschuldigung, es war mein Fehler.**
It was your fault.	**Es war Ihr/dein Fehler.**
Thank you very much.	**Vielen Dank/danke/danke schön/danke sehr.**
I enjoyed it very much.	**Ich habe es sehr genossen.**
I had a lovely time.	**Ich hatte eine wunderbare Zeit.**
We must do it again some time.	**Wir sollten das irgendwann noch einmal machen.**

I will see you again tomorrow.	**Ich sehe Sie (dich) morgen wieder.**
I would like to see you again.	**Ich würde Sie (dich) gerne wiedersehen.**
It's a pleasure.	**Gerne.**
Have a good time!	**Viel Spaß!**
Have a safe journey.	**Kommen Sie/komm gut nach Hause.**
Good luck.	**Viel Glück.**
All the best.	**Alles Gute.**
Happy birthday!	**Herzlichen Glückwunsch zum Geburtstag!**
Merry Christmas!	**Frohe Weihnachten!**
Congratulations!	**Herzlichen Glückwunsch!**
Happy New Year!	**Frohes Neues Jahr!**

Insight

In Germany you would expect a real answer to the question **Wie geht es Ihnen?** while in Britain the question is often responded to with more of an echo.

Asking someone you would address with **Sie**: A: **Wie geht es Ihnen?** *How are you?*

B: **Mir geht es gut, danke und Ihnen?** *I'm fine, thanks, and you?*
A: **Mir geht es sehr gut, danke.** *I am very well, thanks.*

Asking a friend or relative:

A: **Wie geht es Dir?** *How are you?*
B: **Mir geht es super, und dir?** *I am great, and you?*
A: **Mir geht es nicht so gut.** *I am not so well.*
B: **Das tut mir Leid.** *I'm sorry about that.*

You may find it easier to use the short form for **Wie geht es dir(Ihnen)?** which is: **Wie geht's?**

The same applies to the answer: Short form: **Gut, danke.**
Fine, thanks.

Try to practise various answers instead of just answering
gut *fine*. There may be days when you are feeling fine/great/
wonderful and others when you are feeling not very well/
tired, so it's a good idea to learn several expressions.

I'm fine too.	**Mir geht es auch gut.**
very good	**sehr gut**
excellent	**ausgezeichnet**
fantastic	**fantastisch**
really good	**wirklich gut**
wonderful	**wunderbar**
I'm not so well today.	**Mir geht es heute nicht so gut.**
I'm a bit tired today.	**Ich bin heute etwas müde.**
I feel really bad.	**Mir geht es wirklich schlecht.**
I feel absolutely terrible.	**Mir geht es total schlecht.**
I feel sick. (physically)	**Mir ist übel.**
I'm ill.	**Ich bin krank.**

Other expressions

see you soon	**bis dann**
see you later	**bis später**
have a nice weekend	**schönes Wochenende**
enjoy the rest of the day/evening	**schönen Tag/Abend noch**
take care	**mach's gut** (informal)**/machen Sie es gut** (formal)

Useful verbs

to introduce	**sich <u>vor</u>stellen**
to introduce somebody	**jemanden <u>vor</u>stellen**
to meet somebody	**jemanden treffen**
to get to know somebody	**jemanden kennen lernen**
to meet up with	**sich treffen mit**
to recognize	**erkennen**
to greet somebody	**jemanden grüßen/begrüßen**

Extras

welcoming of the guests	**die Begrüßung der Gäste**
introduction (can also mean imagination or the performance)	**die Vorstellung**
to introduce somebody	**jemanden <u>vor</u>stellen**
to introduce (or imagine)	**sich <u>vor</u>stellen**
please introduce yourself	**stellen Sie sich bitte vor**
the meeting	**das Treffen**
to meet	**sich treffen**
meeting place	**der Treffpunkt**
to arrange a meeting	**ein Treffen vereinbaren**
to cancel a meeting	**ein Treffen <u>ab</u>sagen**
to turn up to a meeting	**zu einem Treffen erscheinen**

Other meanings of the verb sich <u>vor</u>stellen

Guess what, I'm flying to Berlin too!	**Stellen Sie sich <u>vor</u>, ich fliege auch nach Berlin.**
I imagined your brother exactly like that.	**Ich habe mir Ihren Bruder genauso <u>vor</u>gestellt.**

Typical German expressions

Have fun!	**Viel Spaß!**
Have a good journey.	**Ich wünsche Ihnen eine gute Reise.**
Bon appetit! (Have a good meal!)	**Mahlzeit!**
Good luck!	**Viel Glück!**
Every success!	**Viel Erfolg!**

Have a good journey!	**Gute Reise!**
(used when people leave by car, bicycle etc.)	**Gute Fahrt!**
Come on in! Welcome! (lit.: heartily welcome!)	**Herzlich willkommen!**
Get home safely!	**Kommen Sie gut nach Hause!**

1.2 Where are you from?

Core vocabulary

···

Insight

Many names of countries and nationalities are very similar or the same in German and English. Try to learn those first, then find the ones which are different.

···

Where do you come from? *Woher kommen Sie?*

I come from ...	**Ich komme aus ...**
I am ...	**Ich bin ...**
I speak ...	**Ich spreche ...**

Austria	**Österreich**	**Österreicher/in**	**Österreichisch**
Belgium	**Belgien**	**Belgier/in**	**Flämisch, Französisch**
England	**England**	**Engländer/in**	**Englisch**
Finland	**Finnland**	**Finne/in**	**Finnisch**
France	**Frankreich**	**Franzose/in**	**Französisch**
Germany	**Deutschland**	**Deutsche/r**	**Deutsch**
Greece	**Griechenland**	**Grieche/in**	**Griechisch**
Ireland	**Irland**	**Ire, Irin**	**Irisch, Gälisch, Englisch**
Italy	**Italien**	**Italiener/in**	**Italienisch**
Scotland	**Schottland**	**Schotte/in**	**Schottisch**
Spain	**Spanien**	**Spanier/in**	**Spanisch**
Switzerland	**die Schweiz**	**Schweizer/in**	**Deutsch, Französisch, Italienisch**

Turkey	die Türkei	Türke/in	Türkisch
Wales	Wales	Waliser/in	Walisisch
Bosnia	Bosnien	Bosnier/in	Serbisch
Croatia	Kroatien	Kroate/in	Kroatisch
Denmark	Dänemark	Däne/in	Dänisch
Hungary	Ungarn	Ungar/in	Ungarisch
Latvia	Lettland	Lette/Lettin	Lettisch
Lithuania	Litauen	Litauer/in	Litauisch
Norway	Norwegen	Norweger/in	Norwegisch
Poland	Polen	Pole/in	Polnisch
Romania	Rumänien	Rumäne/in	Rumänisch
Russia	Russland	Russe/Russin	Russisch
Sweden	Schweden	Schwede/in	Schwedisch

More countries/continents

Africa	**Afrika**	India	**Indien**
America	**Amerika**	Iran	**Iran**
Australia	**Australien**	Iraq	**Irak**
China	**China**	New Zealand	**Neuseeland**
Europe	**Europa**	USA	**USA**
Japan	**Japan**		

Useful phrases

Do you speak English?	**Sprechen Sie Englisch?**
Yes, I speak some English.	**Ja, ich spreche etwas/ein wenig/ein bisschen Englisch.**
What languages do you speak?	**Welche Sprachen sprechen Sie?**
I speak Spanish, German, Italian.	**Ich spreche Deutsch, Spanisch, Italienisch.**
What nationality are you?	**Was ist Ihre Nationalität/ Staatsangehörigkeit?**
Where were you born?	**Wo sind Sie geboren?**
I was born ...	**Ich bin in ... geboren**
I live ...	**Ich lebe/wohne ...**
in the north/south/east/west	**im Norden, Süden, Osten, Westen**
near the sea	**in der Nähe vom Meer**
on the coast	**an der Küste**
in the mountains	**in den Bergen**
in the city	**in der Stadt**
in a village	**auf dem Dorf**
in the suburbs	**am Stadtrand**
in the country	**auf dem Land**

Useful verbs

to live	**leben**	*I live*	**ich lebe**
to live	**wohnen**	*I live*	**ich wohne**
to speak	**sprechen**	*I speak*	**ich spreche**
to be born	**geboren sein**	*I was born in ...*	**ich bin in ... geboren**

Insight

Did you notice the similarity of words such as: **Englisch** *English*, **leben** *to live*, **Spanisch** *Spanish*, **Nationalität** *nationality*, **Norden** *north*, **Süden** *south*, **Osten** *east*, **Westen** *west*, **Küste** *coast*, **sprechen** *speak*?

Athens	**Athen**	Hesse	**Hessen**
Baltic Sea	**Ostsee**	Lower Saxony	**Niedersachsen**
Bavaria	**Bayern**	North Sea	**Nordsee**
Bavarian Forest	**Bayrischer Wald**	Nuremberg	**Nürnberg**
Black Forest	**Schwarzwald**	Munich	**München**
Brussels	**Brüssel**	Moselle	**Mosel**
Brunswick	**Braunschweig**	Moscow	**Moskau**
Cologne	**Köln**	Rhine	**Rhein**
Lake Constance	**Bodensee**	Saxony	**Sachsen**
Hanover	**Hannover**	Thuringia	**Thüringen**

1.3 Personal appearance

man **der Mann**, teenager **der Teenager**, baby **das Baby**, blue **blau**, long **lang**, hair **das Haar**, blond **blond**, green **grün**, brown **braun**, normal **normal**, person **die Person**, character **der Charakter**, relative **relativ**, attractive **attraktiv**, fit **fit**, puberty **die Pubertät**, midlife crisis **Midlifecrisis**, friendly **freundlich**, loud **laut**, nervous **nervös**, reserved **reserviert**.

Insight

Some words in English and German look the same but have a different meaning. These are called **'false friends'**.

It would be worth spending some time learning them. In this section of the book you will come across the following false friends:

bad **Bad**. English *bad* = German **schlecht**, while **das Bad** in German is the *bathroom*.

a relative **relativ**. A relative is **ein Verwandter** in German, but the adjective *relative* = **relativ** in German.

sensible **sensibel**; *sensible* is **vernünftig** in German. **Sensibel** in German is English *sensitive*.

brave **brav**. English *brave* is **tapfer/mutig**, but **brav** in German is well *behaved*.

decent **dezent**. *Decent* is **anständig/ordentlich**, while German **dezent** is *discreet, unobtrusive*.

extravagant **extravagant**; *extravagant* is **verschwenderisch/ übertrieben**, while *flamboyant/stylish* is **extravagant** in German.

familiar (well known) **familär**; *familiar/well* known is **bekannt/ vertraut**, while German **familiär** is *informal/family related*. German **familiar** also means *colloquial*.

English *fast* **fast** in German. English *fast* is **schnell** but **fast** in German means *almost*.

gross **groß**; *gross* in English is **plump**, and German **groß** means *tall*.

Core vocabulary

Could you perhaps describe yourself?	**Können Sie sich eventuell beschreiben?**
What are you like?	**Wie sehen Sie/siehst du aus?**
What does he/she look like?	**Wie sieht er/sie aus?**
He/she is a ...	**Er/sie ist ein/e ...**

man	**Mann**	*woman*	**Frau**
girl	**Mädchen**	*boy*	**Junge**
teenager	**Teenager**	*child*	**Kind**
baby	**Baby**	*adult*	**Erwachsener**
youth	**Jugendlicher**		

Use the following grid to describe yourself and someone you know well:

I am **ich bin**	*relatively* **relativ**	*tall* **groß**
Are you ... **Sind Sie**	*very* **sehr**	*small* **klein?**
He/She is **Er/sie ist**	*average* **durchschnittlich**	*tall* **groß**

I am **Ich bin**	*relatively* **relativ**	*tall* **groß**
	very **sehr**	*small* **klein**
	rather **eher**	*slim* **dünn**
	average **durchschnittlich**	*well built* **vollschlank**

I have **ich habe**	**long lange**	*blonde hair* **blonde Haare**
He has **er hat**	**short kurze**	*brown hair* **braune Haare**
She has **sie hat**	*medium length* **mittellange**	*dark hair* **dunkle Haare**
I have **Ich habe**	*blue* brown** **blaue, braune** *green** **grüne**	*eyes* **Augen**

*For more colours see the Toolbox.

looks	**das Aussehen**
to look like	**aussehen**
I look ...	**Ich sehe ... aus.**
He looks attractive	**Er sieht attraktiv aus**
person, character	**der Typ**
He is a great person.	**Er ist ein super Typ.**
He seems to be well balanced.	**Er scheint ausgeglichen zu sein.**
He seems to be very friendly.	**Er scheint sehr freundlich zu sein.**
He seems to be very balanced.	**Er wirkt sehr ausgeglichen.**
likeable	**sympathisch**

person, character	die Person, der Charakter		
She is an extremely likeable/ unlikeable person.	Sie ist eine ausgesprochen sympathische/ unsympathische Person.		
The woman looks really cool.	Die Frau sieht total cool aus.		
She has a strong/weak personality.	Sie ist eine starke/schwache Persönlichkeit.		
He is good looking.	Er ist gut aussehend.		

attractive	**attraktiv**	unattractive	**unattraktiv**
fashionable	**modisch**	unfashionable	**altmodisch**
interesting	**interessant**	uninteresting	**uninteressant**
fit	**sportlich**	unfit	**unsportlich**
good looking	**gut aussehend**	ugly	**hässlich**
neat	**gepflegt**	untidy	**ungepflegt**
smart	**schick**	scruffy	**heruntergekommen**
ordinary	**ordinär**	different	**ungewöhnlich**
tall	**groß**	short	**klein**
underweight	**untergewichtig**	overweight	**übergewichtig**
well built	**vollschlank**	slim	**schlank**
anorexic	**magersüchtig**	obese	**fettleibig**
right handed	**Rechtshänder**	left handed	**Linkshänder**
short sighted	**kurzsichtig**	long sighted	**weitsichtig**
agoraphobic	**agoraphobisch**	claustrophobic	**klaustrophobisch**

Useful phrases

How much do you weigh?	**Wie viel wiegen Sie/wiegst du?**
I weigh 75 kg.	**Ich wiege 75 kg.**
How tall are you?	**Wie groß sind Sie/bist du?**
I am 1.59 m.	**Ich bin 1,59 (Meter).**

Useful verbs

to look like someone	**wie jemand <u>aus</u>sehen**
I look like ...	**Ich sehe <u>aus</u> wie ...**
to put on weight	**zunehmen**
I am putting on weight	**Ich nehme <u>zu</u>**

to lose weight	**abnehmen**
I am losing weight	**Ich nehme ab**
to get fit	**fit werden**
I am getting fit	**Ich werde fit**

Extras

He/she is	**Er/sie ist**
in puberty	**in der Pubertät**
in his/her teens	**im Teenager-Alter**
an adolescence	**im Jugendalter**
mid-twenty	**Mitte zwanzig**
middle aged	**mittleren Alters**
having a midlife crisis	**in der Midlifecrisis**
in the menopause	**in den Wechseljahren**
of a certain age	**in einem gewissen Alter**
old age	**im hohen Alter**
age of retirement	**im Rentenalter**

1.4 What sort of person are you?

Core vocabulary

I am **Ich bin**	shy/talkative **schüchtern/redselig**
Are you **Sind Sie/bist du**	happy/unhappy **glücklich/unglücklich?**
He is **Er ist**	friendly/unfriendly **freundlich/unfreundlich**
She is **Sie ist**	good/helpful **gut/hilfsbereit**

Character and feelings

hard working	**fleißig**	lazy	**faul**
interesting	**interessant**	uninteresting	**uninteressant**
nice	**nett**	nasty	**böse**
quiet	**ruhig**	loud	**laut**
reliable	**zuverlässig**	unreliable	**unzuverlässig**
funny	**lustig**	serious	**ernst**

crazy, mad	verrückt	boring	langweilig
strange, odd	merkwürdig	normal	normal
considerate	rücksichtsvoll	inconsiderate	rücksichtslos
capable	fähig	useless	unfähig
confident	selbstbewusst	nervous	nervös
generous	großzügig	mean	geizig
helpful	hilfsbereit	unhelpful	nicht hilfsbereit
odd	merkwürdig	normal	normal
polite	höflich	rude	unhöflich
practical	praktisch	impractical	unpraktisch
reliable	zuverlässig	unreliable	unzuverlässig
relaxed	entspannt/ relaxt	uptight	angespannt
sensitive	sensibel	unfeeling	unsensibel
serious	ernst	frivolous	leichtsinnig
sincere	aufrichtig	insincere	unaufrichtig
strong willed	willensstark	weak	willensschwach
reserved	verschlossen/ reserviert	receptive	aufgeschlossen
stubborn	stur	open minded	aufgeschlossen
courageous	mutig	frightened	furchtsam

The five senses

sight	das Sehvermögen	to see	sehen	I see	ich sehe
hearing	das Gehör	to hear	hören	I hear	ich höre
taste	der Geschmack	to taste	schmecken	I taste	ich schmecke
smell	der Geruch	to smell	riechen	I smell	ich rieche
touch	das Gefühl	to touch	fühlen	I touch	ich fühle

Useful phrases

He/She has ...	Er/Sie hat ...
a sense of humour	einen Sinn für Humor
plenty of willpower	eine starke Willenskraft
a kind heart	ein offenes Herz
a weakness for ...	eine Schwäche für ...
a good imagination	eine gute Vorstellungskraft

Useful verbs

to be bored	**gelangweilt sein**
I am bored	**Ich bin gelangweilt**
to be interested in ...	**sich interessieren für ...**
I am interested in ...	**ich interessiere mich für ...**
to be worried about ...	**sich Sorgen machen um/wegen ...**
I am worried about ...	**Ich mache mir Sorgen um/wegen ...**

Insight

Look out for false friends here!

interested in ≠ **interessant; interessant** = *interesting*
If you said **Ich bin interessant,** that would mean: *I am an interesting person.*
I am interested in translates as: **Ich interessiere mich für ...**
Ich interessiere mich für Sprachen. *I am interested in languages.*
Er ist sehr interessant. *He is a very interesting person.*

Extras

to be worried about	**besorgt sein um**
to be scared of	**Angst haben vor**
to have a weakness for	**eine Schwäche haben für**
to feel an affection for	**eine Sympathie haben für**

1.5 My things

Insight

The following vocabulary items are either Anglicisms or similar words in English and German. This will help you to build up your vocabulary faster. By being aware which Anglicisms are in current use, you will be able to communicate in as up-to-date a manner as possible.

cheque book **das Scheckbuch,** *credit card* **die Kreditkarte,** *passport* **der Pass;** *computer* **der Computer,** *mouse* **die Maus,** *laptop* **der Laptop,** *scanner* **der Scanner,** *DVD* **die DVD,** *CD* **die CD,** *camera* **die Kamera,** *video* **das Video,** *digital* **digital,** *film* **der Film,** *photo* **das Foto.**

Many words in connection with Information Technology (IT) are similar or the same in both languages. For more on those words, see Unit 3.

Core vocabulary

bag	**die Tasche (n)**
briefcase	**die Aktentasche (n)**
cheque book	**das Scheckbuch ("er)**
credit card	**die Kreditkarte (n)**
diary	**der Terminkalender (-)**
driving licence	**der Führerschein (e)**
glasses/sunglasses	**die Brille/die Sonnenbrille (n)**
keys	**die Schlüssel**
notebook	**der Notizblock ("e)**
notepaper	**das Briefpapier (-)**
passport	**der Pass/der Personalausweis (e)**
pencil	**der Bleistift (e)**
purse	**der Geldbeutel (-)**
wallet	**die Brieftasche (n)**
watch	**die Uhr (en)**

The word for *your*, *his* and *her* usually follows the same pattern as the word for *my*. See the section on possessive adjectives in the Toolbox.

On my desk: my ...

computer	**mein Computer**
disk	**meine Diskette**
fax	**mein Fax**
hard drive	**meine Festplatte**
mobile	**mein Handy**

mouse	**meine Maus**
laptop	**mein Laptop**
phone	**mein Telefon**
printer	**mein Drucker**
scanner	**mein Scanner**

Insight

Did you notice that a mobile phone is called **das Handy** (with English pronunciation)? This is an example of how English-sounding words are sometimes adopted into the German language but mean something different.

At home: my ...

DVD	**mein DVD-Spieler**
CD player	**mein CD-Spieler**
discs	**meine Disketten**
camera	**meine Kamera, mein Fotoapparat**
video camera	**meine Videokamera**
digital camera	**meine Digitalkamera**
film	**mein Film**
photos	**meine Fotos**

My friends

girlfriend (f)	**meine Freundin**
boyfriend (m)	**mein Freund**
female friends	**meine Freundinnen**
male friends	**meine Freunde**
colleagues	**meine Kollegen**
boss	**mein Chef**
fellow student	**mein Studienfreund**

Here are a few expressions used in colloquial German:

all my stuff	**mein ganzes Zeug**
all my papers	**meine ganzen Unterlagen**
my bumf	**mein Papierkram**
all this stuff	**dieser ganze Kram**

all this junk	**dieses ganze Gerümpel**
bookcase	**das Bücherregal**

Useful phrases

Have you got a ...?	**Haben Sie ein/e/en ...?**
I have lost my ...	**Ich habe mein/e/n ... verloren**
I can't find my ...	**Ich kann mein/e/n ... nicht finden**
Have you seen my ...?	**Haben Sie/Hast du mein/e/n ... gesehen?**

Insight

Have a look at the following verbs. These English verbs are similar to German or have been 'made German' by adding the letters -en at the end of the English verb.

to mail **mailen**, *to send* **senden**, *to find* **finden**, *to fax* **faxen**, *to save* **saven**, *to scan* **scannen**

Other useful verbs

to forget	**vergessen**
to lose/mislay	**verlieren/verlegen**
to print out	**<u>aus</u>drucken**
to reduce	**verkleinern**
to enlarge	**vergrößern**

1.6 I think, I feel

to like	**mögen**	liking	**die Zuneigung**	I like	**ich mag**
to love	**lieben**	love	**die Liebe**	I love	**ich liebe**
to prefer	**<u>vor</u>ziehen**	preference	**die Vorliebe**	I prefer	**ich ziehe <u>vor</u>**
to dislike	**nicht mögen**	dislike	**die Abneigung**	I dislike	**ich mag ... nicht**
to hate	**hassen**	hate	**der Hass**	I hate	**ich hasse**

Core vocabulary

To indicate that you like something or like doing something, you use **mögen** and **gerne**.

I like pizza.	**Ich mag Pizza.**
I like jazz music.	**Ich mag Jazzmusik.**
We like sport.	**Wir mögen Sport.**
He liked the film.	**Er hat den Film gemocht.**
They liked our presentation.	**Sie mochten unseren Vortrag/ unsere Präsentation.**

The verb **mögen: ich mag, du magst, er/sie/es mag, wir mögen, ihr mögt, sie mögen, Sie mögen.**

To say *to like doing something*, you use **etwas gerne tun**. Simply add **gerne** and the *verb* to indicate that you like doing it:

I dance.	**Ich tanze.**
I like dancing.	**Ich tanze gerne.**
I like reading.	**Ich lese gerne.**
She likes studying.	**Sie studiert gerne.**
He liked talking.	**Er hat gerne geredet.**

| We liked to dance. | **Wir haben gerne getanzt.** |
| She liked jogging. | **Sie joggte gerne.** |

Insight

In German the verb **lieben** to love is used more in connection with a person and not so much with things. You use **mögen** for things, and **lieben** for people.

to love **lieben**: I love **ich liebe**, love **die Liebe**, to love **sich lieben**, to make love **Liebe machen/sich lieben**.

I love my house. **Ich mag mein Haus.**
I love my children. **Ich liebe meine Kinder.**
They made love. **Sie machten Liebe/Sie liebten sich.**

There are two ways of expressing to prefer: you can use either **vorziehen** or **etwas lieber tun**: lieber in connection with a verb:

| I prefer to walk. | **Ich gehe lieber.** |
| I prefer to drive. | **Ich fahre lieber.** |

You can also use **lieber** in connection with a noun:

| I prefer listening to classical music. | **Ich höre lieber klassische Musik.** |
| She prefers going to the opera. | **Sie geht lieber in die Oper.** |

Remember: <u>vor</u>ziehen is more formal than lieber. It is a separable verb:

I prefer tennis.	**Ich ziehe Tennis <u>vor</u>.**
He prefers to go on his own.	**Er zieht es <u>vor</u>, alleine zu gehen.**
Do you prefer taking the train?	**Ziehen Sie es <u>vor</u>, den Zug zu nehmen?**
to dislike	**nicht mögen**
I don't like that.	**Ich mag das nicht.**
She does not like to fly.	**Sie fliegt nicht gerne.**
to hate	**hassen**
You should not hate him.	**Sie sollten ihn nicht hassen.**
I don't hate anything.	**Ich hasse nichts.**
Do you hate the rain?	**Hassen Sie den Regen?**

to believe	glauben	belief	der Glaube	I believe	ich glaube
to feel	fühlen	feeling	das Gefühl	I feel	ich fühle
to think	denken	thought	der Gedanke	I think	ich denke
to worry	sich sorgen	worry	die Sorge mich	I worry	ich sorge mich
to advise somebody	jemandem raten	advice	der Rat	I advise you	Ich rate Ihnen/dir
to encourage	ermutigen	encouragement	die Ermutigung	I encourage you	ich ermutige Sie/dich
to exaggerate	übertreiben	exaggeration	die Übertreibung	I am exaggerating	ich übertreibe
to joke	einen Witz machen	joke	der Witz	I am joking	ich mache einen Witz
to lie	lügen	lie	die Lüge	I am lying	ich lüge
to promise	versprechen	promise	das Versprechen	I promise	ich verspreche

Verbs taking dative or accusative

Insight

A small number of verbs are followed by the dative, and others by the accusative. In English you say: *I give the book to* him, which is the dative; in other words you say *him* instead of *he*. The same applies in German, but the German language has many verbs which either take the accusative (**mich, dich,** etc.) or dative (**mir, dir,** etc.). Do you know the expression **Wie geht es Ihnen?** *How are you?* Or asking a child, friend or relative, **Wie geht's dir?** Probably without realizing it, you have just used the dative.

Don't worry too much if you can't remember if a verb takes the dative or accusative. There are some German native speakers who also have problems getting the **dir** and **dich** and **Sie** und **Ihnen** right. On the other hand it is a good idea to memorize some of the verbs, in order to get it right.

It is useful to learn the personal pronouns in the list below or use it as a reference.

	nominative	accusative	dative
singular			
I	**ich**	**mich**	**mir**
you	**du**	**dich**	**dir**
you (formal)	**Sie**	**Sie**	**Ihnen**
he	**er**	**ihn**	**ihm**
she	**sie**	**sie**	**ihr**
it	**es**	**es**	**ihm**
plural			
we	**wir**	**uns**	**uns**
you	**ihr**	**euch**	**euch**
you (formal)	**Sie**	**Sie**	**Ihnen**
they	**sie**	**sie**	**ihnen**

Common verbs which take the dative

	glauben *(to believe)*
I believe him/her	**ich glaube ihm/ihr**
	danken *(to thank)*
I thank him for the flowers.	**Ich danke ihm für die Blumen.**
	gefallen *(to please)*
I like the dress (lit. The dress pleases me).	**Das Kleid gefällt mir.**
	vertrauen *(to trust)*
I trust him/her.	**Ich vertraue ihm/ihr.**

Other examples of verbs taking the dative

jemandem etwas raten (*to advise*) Ich rate ihm/ihrmehr Sport zu treiben *I advise him/her to do more sport.*

jemandem etwas versprechen (*to promise*) Ich verspreche meiner Sekretärin eine Gehaltserhöhung. *I promise my secretary a pay rise.*

Verbs which take the accusative

Many reflexive verbs are followed by the accusative, because the pronoun is the direct object:

sich waschen (*to wash*) Ich wasche mich. *I wash myself.*

sich <u>hin</u>setzen (*to sit down*) Kann ich mich hier hinsetzen?
 Can I sit down here?
sich verlaufen (*to get lost*) Ich habe mich verlaufen. *I got lost.*
sich <u>um</u>ziehen (*to get changed*) Sie zieht sich um. *She gets changed.*
sich freuen auf (*to look forward to*) Ich freue mich auf mein Essen.
 I am looking forward to my food.
sich verlassen auf (*to rely on*) Ich kann mich auf ihn verlassen.
 I can rely on him.

Other examples of verbs taking the accusative

<u>an</u>rufen (*to phone*) Ich rufe dich <u>an</u>. *I phone you.*
fotografieren (*to take pictures*) Ich fotografiere meine Tante. *I take
 a picture of my aunt.*
<u>ab</u>holen (*to collect*) Ich hole Sie am Bahnhof <u>ab</u>. *I collect you at the
 train station.*
<u>wieder</u>sehen (*to see again*) Ich sehe dich bald <u>wieder</u>. *I'll see you
 again soon.*
besuchen (*to visit*) Ich besuche meinen Enkel in Berlin. *I visit my
 grandson in Berlin.*
<u>ein</u>laden (*to invite*) Ich lade Sie gerne zu einem Kaffee <u>ein</u>. *I would
 like to invite you for a coffee.*
suchen (*to look for*) Ich suche die Hauptstraße. *I am looking for
 the Hauptstrasse.*
jemanden mögen (*to like somebody/something*) Ich mag ihn. *I like
 him.*
jemanden lieben (*to love somebody/something*) Ich liebe sie. *I love
 her.*
jemanden <u>vor</u>ziehen (*to prefer somebody/something*) Ich ziehe ihn
 <u>vor</u>. *I prefer him.*
an jemanden denken (*to think about somebody/something*) Ich
 denke an ihn. *I am thinking about him.*
sich Sorgen machen über (*to worry about somebody/something*)
 Ich mache mir Sorgen über meinen Vater. *I am worried about my
 father.*
jemanden ermutigen (*to encourage somebody*) Ich ermutige meinen
 Sohn mit dem Rauchen <u>auf</u>zuhören. *I encourage my son to stop
 smoking.*

Witze machen über (*to make jokes about something/somebody*)
Ich mache einen Witz über Politiker. *I am making a joke about
politicians.*
hassen (*to hate*) Ich hasse es. *I hate it.*

Examples of verbs and prepositions taking the accusative

denken **an** *to think about* Ich denke an dich. *I'm thinking
about you.*
erinnern **an** *to remind* Du erinnerst mich an deine Schwester.
You remind me of your sister.
glauben **an** *to believe in* Ich glaube an den Frieden. *I believe
in peace.*
stolz sein **auf** *to be proud of* Ich bin stolz auf dich. *I am proud
of you.*
sich freuen **auf** *to look forward to* Ich freue mich auf unseren
Urlaub. *I am looking forward to our holiday.*
sich bedanken **für** *to thank for* Ich bedanke mich für den Brief.
I thank you for the letter.
sich interessieren **für** *to be interested in* Ich interessiere mich für
moderne Kunst. *I am interested in modern art.*

Examples of verbs with prepositions taking the dative

beginnen **mit** *to start with* Ich beginne mit meinem Reitunterricht.
I'm starting my horse riding classes.
<u>auf</u>hören **mit** *to stop with* Ich höre mit dem Rauchen <u>auf</u>. *I stop
smoking.*
träumen **von** *to dream of* Ich träume von ihm. *I dream of him.*
sich erholen **von** *to recover from* Ich erhole mich von meiner
Operation. *I recover from my operation.*
enttäuscht sein **von** (*to be disappointed*) Ich bin von ihr/ihm
enttäuscht. *I am disappointed in her/him.*
überzeugt sein **von** (*to be convinced/to be sure of*) Sie ist sehr von
sich überzeugt. *She is very sure of herself.*

Prepositions taking the dative or accusative

dative = no motion accusative = motion

an *at* **An dem** Strand ist es schön. *It is nice on the beach.* (no motion)

Ich gehe **an den** Strand. *I go to the beach.* (motion)

in *in* Ich studiere **in der** Schule. *I study at school.*
Ich gehe **in die** Schule. *I go to school.*

auf *on* Ich lege das Buch **auf den** Tisch. *I put the book on the table.*
Auf dem Tisch liegt ein Buch. *There is a book on the table.*

hinter *behind* Ich fahre das Fahrrad **hinter den** Garten. *I drive the bike behind the garden.*

Das Fahrrad ist **hinter dem** Garten. *The bike is behind the garden.*
neben *next to* Er fährt das Auto neben das Haus. *He drives the car beside the house.*

Das Auto steht **neben dem** Haus. *The car is parked beside the house.*

über *over* Das Flugzeug fliegt **über die** Insel. *The plane is flying over the island.*

Dicke Wolken sind **über der** Insel. *Over the island are heavy clouds.*

Negative and positive emotions

> ## Insight
>
> The following words in connection with emotions are either Anglicisms or similar words in English and German. Learning them will help you to build up your vocabulary faster.
>
> *to be stressed* **gestresst sein**, *to be relaxed* **relaxt sein**, *to be nervous* **nervös sein**, *to be happy* **happy sein**.

| to be disappointed | enttäuscht sein | I am disappointed | Ich bin enttäuscht |
| to be relieved | erleichtert sein | I am relieved | Ich bin erleichtert |

to be depressed	**deprimiert sein**	I am depressed	**Ich bin deprimiert**
to be elated	**begeistert sein**	I am elated	**Ich bin begeistert**
to be stressed	**gestresst sein**	I am stressed	**Ich bin gestresst**
to be relaxed	**relaxt sein**	I am relaxed	**Ich bin relaxed**
to be discouraged	**entmutigt sein**	I am discouraged	**Ich bin entmutigt**
to be encouraged	**ermutigt sein**	I am encouraged	**Ich bin ermutigt**
to be nervous	**nervös sein**	I am nervous	**Ich bin nervös**
to be confident	**zuversichtlich sein**	I am confident	**Ich bin zuversichtlich**
to be worried	**sich Sorgen machen**	I am worried	**Ich mache mir Sorgen**
to be reassured	**beruhigt sein**	I am reassured	**Ich bin beruhigt**
to be sad	**traurig sein**	I am sad	**Ich bin traurig**
to be happy	**fröhlich/happy**	I am happy	**Ich bin fröhlich/ happy**
to be ashamed	**sich schämen**	I am ashamed	**Ich schäme mich**
to be proud	**stolz sein**	I am proud	**Ich bin stolz**
to be unfortunate	**Pech haben**	I am unfortunate	**Ich habe Pech**
to be lucky	**Glück haben**	I am lucky	**Ich habe Glück**

Verbs which are used with another verb

(would like to)	**(möchten)**	I would like to go to the marketplace.	**Ich möchte zum Marktplatz gehen.**
to have to	**müssen**	I must leave.	**Ich muss gehen.**
to be allowed to	**dürfen**	You are not allowed to smoke here.	**Sie dürfen hier nicht rauchen.**
ought to	**sollen**	I ought to stay at home.	**Ich sollte zu Hause bleiben.**

Useful compound words

lieben *to love*	**lieb gewinnen** *to grow fond of*	**lieb haben** *to be fond of*
liebevoll *loving*	**lieblos** *unloving*	**liebenswert** *loveable*
lieblich *lovely*	**liebenswürdigerweise** *kindly*	**die Liebenswürdigkeit** *politeness*
der Gedanke *the thought*	**die Gedankenlosigkeit** *absent-mindedness*	**gedankenlos** *absent minded*
gedankenvoll *thoughtful*	**die Gedankenarmut** *lack of thought*	**gedanklich** *intellectual/imaginary*
der bloße Gedanke an *the mere thought of*	**etwas in Gedanken tun** *to do something distractedly*	
der Mut *the courage*	**den Mut verlieren** *to lose courage/heart*	**wieder Mut bekommen** *to gain confidence*
mutig sein *to be courageous*	**mutlos** *discouraged*	
die Mutlosigkeit *discouragement*	**die Ermutigung** *encouragement*	**ermutigen** *to encourage*

1.7 Expressing an opinion

Useful verbs and phrases

> **Insight**
>
> The following words in connection with expressing an opinion are either Anglicisms or similar words in English and German. Learning them will help you to build up your vocabulary faster.
>
> | | | | |
> |---|---|---|---|
> | *to discuss* | **diskutieren** | *discussion* | **die Diskussion** |
> | *clearly* | **klar** | *normally* | **normalerweise** |
> | *principally* | **prinzipiell** | *pros and cons* | **Pro und Kontra** |
> | *complicated* | **kompliziert** | *subjective* | **subjektiv** |
> | *objective* | **objektiv** | *realistic* | **realistisch** |
> | *logical* | **logisch** | *the sense* | **der Sinn** |
> | *argument* | **das Argument** | | |

to believe	**glauben**	*I believe*	**ich glaube**
to consider something	**etwas in Betracht ziehen**	*I consider*	**ich ziehe ... in Betracht**
to think	**denken**	*I think*	**ich denke**
to express	**ausdrücken**	*I express*	**ich drücke ... aus**
to agree	**zustimmmen**	*I agree*	**ich stimme ... zu**

I agree with you. **Ich stimme Ihnen/dir zu.**

disagree	**nicht zustimmen**	*I don't agree*	**Ich stimme ... nicht zu**

I don't agree with you. **Ich stimme Ihnen/dir nicht zu.**

to argue	**argumentieren**	*I argue*	**Ich argumentiere**

I argue with my brother. **Ich argumentiere mit meinem Bruder.**

to ask	**fragen**	*I ask*	**ich frage**

I would like to ask you something. **Ich möchte Sie/dich etwas fragen.**

to dispute	**sich streiten**	*I dispute*	**Ich streite mich.**
to question	**in Frage stellen**	*I question*	**Ich stelle ... in Frage.**

I question what you are saying. **Ich stelle was Sie sagen/du sagst in Frage.**

to quote	**zitieren**	*I quote*	**ich zitiere**
to request	**bitten**	*I request*	**ich bitte**

I would like to request something. **Ich möchte Sie/dich um etwas bitten.**

to suggest	**vorschlagen**	*I suggest*	**ich schlage vor**
to compare	**vergleichen**	*I compare*	**ich vergleiche**
to differ	**unterscheiden**	*I differ*	**ich unterscheide**
to discuss	**diskutieren**	*I discuss*	**ich diskutiere**
to conclude	**zum Schluss kommen**	*I conclude*	**Ich komme zum Schluss.**

I believe that we should do more for the environment. **Ich glaube, dass man mehr für die Umwelt tun sollte.**

I agree with you completely. **Ich stimme Ihnen total zu.**

That is complete nonsense. **Das ist völliger Unsinn.**

on the one hand	**einerseits**
on the other hand	**andererseits**
first	**erstens**

(Contd)

second	**zweitens**
finally	**schließlich**
actually	**eigentlich**
basically	**grundsätzlich**
clearly	**klar**
consequently	**folglich**
fortunately/unfortunately	**glücklicherweise/unglücklicherweise**
generally	**im Allgemeinen**
honestly	**ehrlich**
mainly	**hauptsächlich**
normally	**normalerweise**
obviously	**offensichtlich**
particularly	**besonders/vor allem**
principally	**prinzipiell**
really	**wirklich**
usually/unusually	**gewöhnlich/ungewöhnlich**
in my/his/her opinion	**meiner/seiner/ihrer Meinung nach**
above all	**vor allem/vor allen Dingen**
although	**obwohl**
as a result	**als Ergebnis**
as well as	**sowohl … als auch …**
however	**jedoch**
in many respects	**in vielen Punkten**
in spite of	**trotz**
instead of	**anstelle**
nevertheless	**desto trotz**
otherwise	**andererseits**
similarly	**ähnlich**
the reason is …	**der Grund dafür ist …**
to tell the truth	**um die Wahrheit zu sagen**
I wish I could agree	**ich wünschte ich könnte zustimmen**
I beg to differ	**ich bin anderer Ansicht**
I mean	**ich meine**
I maintain	**ich behaupte**
for example	**zum Beispiel**
etc.	**usw/und so weiter**
in brief	**kurz dargestellt**
the advantages/ disadvantages are …	**die Vorteile/Nachteile sind …**

the pros and cons	**Pro und Kontra**
the pros and cons	**Für und Wider**
to conclude	**zum Ergebnis kommen**
it is	**es ist**
bad/good	**schlecht/gut**
complicated/easy	**kompliziert/einfach**
better/worse	**besser/schlechter**
nice/not very nice	**schön/nicht sehr schön**
too hard/easy	**zu schwer/leicht**
subjective	**subjektiv**
objective	**objektiv**
it is not	**es ist nicht**
objective	**objektiv**
realistic	**realistisch**
logical	**logisch**
It does not make any sense.	**Es macht keinen Sinn.**
It does not change what you say.	**Das ändert nicht was Sie/du sagen/sagst.**

That is completely incorrect. **Das ist völlig falsch.**
The argument does not convince me. **Das Argument überzeugt mich nicht.**
That is nonsense. **Das ist Unsinn/Quatsch.**
Why do you say that? **Warum sagen Sie das?**
You have to explain that more precisely. **Sie müssen das genauer erklären.**

the argument/the fight **der Streit**
to argue, to quarrel, to squabble, to fight, to take legal action
sich streiten
The children argue the whole day. **Die Kinder streiten sich den ganzen Tag.**

quarrelsome **streitsüchtig**
They are really quarrelsome. **Sie sind richtig streitsüchtig.**
quarrelling **die Streiterei** *squabbler* **der Streithahn**
You are a real squabbler **Du bist ein richtiger Streithahn.**

(Contd)

1.8 I do (I + useful action verbs)

Insight

The following words are either Anglicisms or similar words in English and German. Learning them will help you to build up your vocabulary faster.

to wake up **aufwachen**, to eat **essen**, to drink **trinken**, to laugh **lachen**, to sleep **schlafen**, to relax **relaxen**, to come **kommen**, a trick **der Trick**, phone number **die Telefonnummer**, to go to bed **ins Bett gehen**, to come **kommen**.

Useful verbs

to wake up	**<u>auf</u>wachen**	I wake up	**ich wache auf**
to get up	**<u>auf</u>stehen**	I get up	**ich stehe auf**
to take a shower	**duschen**	I take a shower	**ich dusche**
to get dressed	**sich anziehen**	I get dressed	**ich ziehe mich <u>an</u>**
to eat	**essen**	I eat	**ich esse**
to drink	**trinken**	I drink	**ich trinke**
to work	**arbeiten**	I work	**ich arbeite**
to go to work	**zur Arbeit fahren**	I go to work	**ich fahre zur Arbeit**
to start work	**<u>an</u>fangen zu arbeiten**	I start work	**ich fange <u>an</u> zu arbeiten**
to stop work	**<u>auf</u>hören zu arbeiten**	I stop work	**ich höre <u>auf</u> zu arbeiten**
to interrupt work	**die Arbeit unterbrechen**	I interrupt my work	**ich unterbreche meine Arbeit**
to take a break	**eine Pause machen**	I take a break	**ich mache eine Pause**
to go for a break	**zur Pause gehen**	I go for a break	**ich gehe zur Pause**

to go home	nach Hause gehen	I go home	ich gehe nach Hause
to play	spielen	I play	ich spiele
to watch television	**fern**sehen	I watch television	ich gucke/sehe **fern**
to read	lesen	I read	ich lese
to get washed	sich waschen	I get washed	ich wasche mich
to go to bed	ins Bett gehen	I go to bed	ich gehe ins Bett
to laugh	lachen	I laugh	ich lache
to smile	lächeln	I smile	ich lächele
to giggle	kichern	I giggle	ich kichere
to sleep	schlafen	I sleep	ich schlafe
to dream	träumen	I dream	ich träume
to rush	sich beeilen	I am in a rush	ich muss mich beeilen
to relax	sich **aus**ruhen	I relax	ich ruhe mich **aus**/ ich relaxe

Coming and going verbs

All these verbs take sein in the perfect tense.

to walk	gehen	I walk	ich gehe
to go for a walk	spazieren gehen	I go for a walk	ich gehe spazieren
to run	rennen	I run	ich renne
to ride a bicycle	Fahrrad fahren	I ride a bicycle	ich fahre Fahrrad
to drive	fahren	I drive	ich fahre
to arrive	**an**kommen	I depart	ich fahre **ab**
to enter	eintreten	I leave	ich gehe **raus**
to come	kommen	I go	ich gehe
to go up	hochgehen	I go down	ich gehe runter
to stay	bleiben	I return	ich kehre zurück

Communicating

to speak	sprechen
to repeat something	etwas wiederholen
to talk to someone	mit jemandem sprechen

to whisper to someone	jemandem etwas <u>zu</u>flüstern
to shout at someone	jemanden <u>an</u>schreien
to ask a question	eine Frage stellen
to phone	telefonieren
to ask for something	nach etwas fragen
to respond to a question	eine Frage beantworten
to tell a story	eine Geschichte erzählen
to enjoy yourself	sich amüsieren
to be angry	ärgerlich sein
to have trouble/difficulty	Schwierigkeiten haben
to get depressed	deprimiert sein
to know someone	jemanden kennen
to know something	etwas wissen
to cheat	schummeln
to trick	hereinlegen, übers Ohr legen
to challenge	herausfordern
to compliment	jemandem ein Kompliment machen
to neglect	vernachlässigen

Useful verbs

<u>ein</u>steigen	<u>aus</u>steigen	to get in/get out
<u>rein</u>kommen	<u>raus</u>kommen	to enter/to leave
<u>hoch</u>gehen	<u>runter</u>gehen	to walk up/to walk down
<u>runter</u>kommen	<u>rauf</u>kommen	to come down/to come up
<u>weg</u>gehen	<u>hin</u>gehen	to leave/to go to
<u>weg</u>fahren	<u>hin</u>fahren	to drive away/to drive to
<u>ein</u>schlafen	<u>aus</u>schlafen	to fall asleep/to sleep in/have a lie-in
<u>an</u>schreien	<u>auf</u>schreien	to shout at/to shout out

Expression

Enjoy your evening off work!	Schönen Feierabend!
to celebrate	feiern
the celebration	die feier
end of work	der Feierabend

1.9 Don't panic!

Calm down!	**Beruhigen Sie sich!/Beruhige dich!**
Help!	**Hilfe!**
Be careful!	**Aufpassen!**
Careful!	**Vorsicht!**
Watch out!	**Achtung!**
Stay back!	**Zurückbleiben!**
Down!	**Runter!**
Listen!	**Hören Sie/Hör zu!**
I said no.	**Ich sagte nein.**
No, thanks.	**Nein, danke.**
It is enough.	**Es ist genug.**
Be careful!	**Pass auf!/Passen Sie auf!**
Do you understand me?	**Verstehen Sie mich? Verstehst du mich?**
Can you help me?	**Können Sie mir helfen?**
Do you speak English?	**Sprechen Sie/(Sprichst du) Englisch?**
Can you say it again more slowly?	**Können Sie/(Kannst du) das noch mal langsam sagen?**
I didn't catch what you said.	**Ich habe das nicht mitgekriegt.**
Do you understand?	**Verstehen Sie?/(Verstehst Du?)**
Please can you find someone who speaks English?	**Können Sie/(Kannst du) jemanden finden der Englisch spricht?**
Can you write it down for me, please?	**Können Sie/(Kannst du) es bitte für mich aufschreiben?**
How do you spell it?	**Wie buchstabieren Sie/ (buchstabierst du) das?**
Have you got the phone number for ...?	**Haben Sie/(hast du) die Telefonnummer für ...?**
What do I need to dial first?	**Was muss ich zuerst wählen?**
	(Contd)

What is the code for ...?	**Wie ist die Vorwahl für ...?**
How do I get an outside line?	**Wie bekomme ich ein Außenamt?**

Some useful signs

Fire brigade entrance	**Feuerwehreinfahrt**
Emergency entrance	**Notfallaufnahme**
Danger!	**Achtung!**
Watch out!	**Auf**passen!
Warning!	**Warnung!**
Careful!	**Vorsicht!**
No entrance	**Kein Eingang**

TEST YOURSELF

See how many of the questions you can get right without looking back at the unit.

1 What do you say after someone has introduced him/herself to you?
   a Freundlich.
   b Freut mich.
   c Ich freue mich.

2 How do you reply to the question **Wie geht es Ihnen?**
   a Wie geht's?
   b Mir geht es gut, danke, und Ihnen?
   c Gut, und dir?

3 The expression *How do you say that in German?* can be translated as
   a Wann sagt man auf Deutsch ...?
   b Warum sagt man auf Deutsch ...?
   c Wie sagt man das auf Deutsch?

4 Which expression means *Good luck!* in German?
   a Gute Fahrt!
   b Gute Reise!
   c Viel Glück!

5 Which pair of English/German words means the same?
   a nervous/nervös
   b brave/brav
   c decent/dezent

6 Which pair of words do *not have* the same meaning?
   a baby/Baby
   b teenager/Teenager
   c relative/relativ

7 What is the German word for *boring*?
   a langsam
   b langweilig
   c bohrend

8 How do you say in German *I am interested in*?
   a Ich interessiere mich für
   b Ich bin interessant
   c Interessanter Weise

9 Which of these verbs does not exist in German?
   a *to send* senden
   b *to phone* phonen
   c *to scan* scannen

10 Which of the following verbs is *not* a separable verb?
   a anrufen
   b abfahren
   c bekommen

Answers: 1b; 2b; 3c; 4c; 5a; 6c; 7b; 8a; 9b; 10c

2

Family

2.1 My family

Insight

The following words in connection with the topic of family are either Anglicisms or similar words in English and German. Learning them will help you to build up your vocabulary faster.

family **die Familie,** *mother* **die Mutter,** *father* **der Vater,** *brother* **der Bruder,** *sister* **die Schwester,** *uncle* **der Onkel,** *cousin* **der Cousin,** *partner (male)* **der Partner,** *partner (female)* **die Partnerin,** *friend* **der Freund,** *widow* **die Witwe,** *widower* **der Witwer.**

Look out for false friends! English **relative** ≠ German **relativ.** A *relative* is **ein Verwandter.** The English meaning of the German word **relativ** is *relatively.*

I have got many relatives. **Ich habe viele Verwandte.**
I speak German relatively well. **Ich spreche relativ gut Deutsch.**

Core vocabulary

my family and relatives	**meine Familie und Verwandten**
my mother	**meine Mutter**

my father	**mein Vater**
my parents	**meine Eltern**
my sister	**meine Schwester**
my brother	**mein Bruder**
my step-brother	**mein Stiefbruder**
my step-sister	**meine Stiefschwester**
my twin brother	**mein Zwillingsbruder**
my twin sister	**meine Zwillingsschwester**
my grandmother	**meine Großmutter**
my grandfather	**mein Großvater**
my grandparents	**meine Großeltern**
my uncle	**mein Onkel**
my aunt	**meine Tante**
my cousin	**mein Cousin/meine Cousine**
my great-grandparents	**meine Urgroßeltern**

May I introduce ... This is ... Darf ich ... <u>vor</u>stellen. Das ist ...

my husband	**mein Mann**
my wife	**meine Frau**
my father-in-law	**mein Schwiegervater**
my mother-in-law	**meine Schwiegermutter**
my brother-in-law	**mein Schwager**
my sister-in-law	**meine Schwägerin**
my younger brother	**mein jüngerer Bruder**
my younger sister	**meine jüngere Schwester**
my older brother	**mein älterer Bruder**
my older sister	**meine ältere Schwester**
my grandson	**mein Enkelsohn**
my granddaughter	**meine Enkeltochter**
my partner	**mein Partner/meine Partnerin**
my friend	**mein Freund/meine Freundin**
my boyfriend	**mein Freund**
my girlfriend	**meine Freundin**
my godson	**mein Patensohn**
my goddaughter	**meine Patentochter**
my nephew	**mein Neffe**
my niece	**meine Nichte**

He/she is ... /They are ...	Er/sie ist ... /Sie sind ...
a married couple	**ein verheiratetes Paar**
a couple	**ein Paar**
a married couple	**ein Ehepaar**
a divorced woman	**eine geschiedene Frau**
a divorced man	**ein geschiedener Mann**
widow	**Witwe**
widower	**Witwer**
divorced	**geschieden**
engaged	**verlobt**
married	**verheiratet**
We are just good friends.	**Wir sind nur gute Freunde.**

Insight

Note some further words to do with relationships and families
which are the same or similar in English and German.

to flirt **flirten**, *to kiss* **küssen**, *sex* **der Sex**, *darling* **der Darling**,
baby **das Baby**, *teenager* **der Teenager**, *single* **single**, *kids*
die Kids, *babysitter* **der Babysitter**, *to babysit* **babysitten**,
stepmother **die Stiefmutter**, *kindergarden* **der Kindergarten**,
au pair **das Au-pair**, *bride* **die Braut**, *heterosexual*
heterosexuell, *homosexual* **homosexuell**, *lesbian* **lesbisch**,
old **alt**, *young* **jung**, *adopted* **adoptiert**, *Mum* **die Mami**.

Useful verbs

to like someone	**jemanden mögen**	*I like*	**ich mag**
to flirt	**flirten**	*I flirt*	**ich flirte**
to kiss	**küssen**	*I kiss*	**ich küsse**

to go out with someone	**mit jemandem <u>aus</u>gehen**
I'm going out with ...	**Ich gehe mit ... <u>aus</u>**
to get on with someone	**sich gut verstehen mit**
I get on well with ...	**Ich verstehe mich gut mit ...**
to have a good time	**sich amüsieren**
I'm having a good time	**Ich amüsiere mich**

to have intercourse/sex	Geschlechtsverkehr haben/Sex haben
I'm sleeping with ...	Ich habe Sex mit/ich schlafe mit ...
to get married	heiraten
I'm getting married in June	Ich heirate im Juni.
I am married.	Ich bin verheiratet.
to get on each other's nerves	sich auf die Nerven gehen
He gets on my nerves.	Er geht mir auf die Nerven.
to look after someone	sich um jemanden kümmern
I'm looking after ...	Ich kümmere mich um ...

to quarrel	sich streiten	I'm quarrelling	ich streite mich ...
to separate	sich trennen	I'm separating from ...	ich trenne mich von ...
to divorce	sich scheiden lassen	I'm getting divorced.	Ich lasse mich scheiden.
to fall in love	sich verlieben	I'm in love.	Ich bin verliebt.

Pet names

pet name	der Kosename
darling	Liebling
sweetheart	Herzchen
honey	Süße/r
sweetheart	Schatz
little sweetheart	Schätzchen
little angel	Engelchen
granny	Omi
grandpa	Opi
mum	Mami
dad	Papi

Some related words/expressions

love	die Liebe
to love one another/to make love	sich lieben
We love one another/we make love.	Wir lieben uns.
I love you.	Ich liebe dich.
to fall in love	sich verlieben
I am in love.	Ich bin verliebt.
I fell in love.	Ich habe mich verliebt.

lovers	**die Liebenden**
romantic weekend	**das Liebeswochenende**
love song	**das Liebeslied**
love story	**die Liebesgeschichte**
the worry	**der Kummer**
love sickness	**der Liebeskummer**
She/He is love sick.	**Sie/Er hat Liebeskummer.**
declaration of love	**die Liebeserklärung**
She made him/her a declaration of love.	**Sie machte ihm/ihr eine Liebeserklärung.**
He/She is in love.	**Er/Sie ist verliebt.**
the heart	**das Herz**
sweetheart	**Herzchen**
congratulations	**Herzlichen Glückwunsch**
greetings/very best wishes	**Herzliche Grüße**

2.2 Children

Core vocabulary

baby	**das Baby (ies)**
infant	**der Säugling (e)**
child	**das Kind (er)**
boy	**der Junge (n)**
girl	**das Mädchen (-)**
twin	**der Zwilling**
twins	**die Zwillinge**
teenager	**der Teenager (-)**
adolescent	**der Jugendliche (n)**
pregnancy	**die Schwangerschaft (en)**
birth	**die Geburt (en)**
newborn baby	**das Neugeborene (n)**
nanny	**die Tagesmutter (¨)**
childminder	**die Kinderbetreuerin**
babysitter	**der Babysitter (-)**
midwife	**die Hebamme(n)**
crèche	**die Krippe (n)**

playschool	**der Hort (s)**
baby's bottle	**die Babyflasche (n)**
teat	**der Gummisauger (-)**
dummy	**der Schnuller (-)**
bib	**der Latz ("e)**
baby milk	**die Babymilch**
highchair	**der Hochstuhl ("e)**
nappy	**die Windel (n)**
travel cot	**das Reisebett (en)**
cot	**das Kinderbett (en)**
pram	**der Kinderwagen**
pushchair	**der Buggy (ies)**
toy	**das Spielzeug (e)**
wind/colic	**die Blähungen**
an only child	**ein Einzelkind (er)**
an adopted child	**ein adoptiertes Kind**
an orphan	**ein Waisenkind**
children's playground	**der Kinderspielplatz**
swing	**die Schaukel**
slide	**die Rutsche**
climbing frame	**das Klettergerüst**

Useful verbs

to expect a baby	**ein Baby erwarten**
to breast feed	**stillen**
to burp	**<u>auf</u>stoßen**
to change a nappy	**Windeln wechseln**
to cry	**weinen**
to feed	**füttern**
to give a bottle	**die Flasche geben**
to rock	**schaukeln**
to teethe	**zahnen**
to look after	**<u>auf</u>passen**
to child mind	**auf das Kind <u>auf</u>passen**
to babysit	**babysitten**

Useful words and phrases

I am pregnant	**Ich bin schwanger**
I'm on the pill	**ich nehme die Pille**
It's a boy/girl	**es ist ein Junge/Mädchen**
siblings	**die Geschwister (pl)**
family planning	**die Familienplanung**
a spoilt child	**ein verwöhntes Kind**
I need:	**I ch brauche:**
a cream for a sore bottom	**eine Wundcreme**
sun cream/body lotion	**eine Sonnencreme/Babycreme**
something for wind/ teething	**etwas gegen Blähungen/Zahnen**

Compound words

das Kind	child	**kindlich**	childlike
kindisch	childish	**die Kinder**	children
der Garten		**garden**	
der Kindergarten		**kindergarden**	
die Kindergärtnerin		**child educator**	
der Kinderhot		**afterschool care**	
der Spielplatz		**playground**	
der Kinderspieplatz		**children's playground**	
das Kindermädchen		**au pair**	

2.3 Anniversaries, marriage and death

Core vocabulary

birthday	**der Geburtstag**
engagement	**die Verlobung**
marriage	**die Hochzeit, die Heirat**
death	**der Tod**
the wedding	**die Hochzeit**
church	**die Kirche**

register office	**das Standesamt**
engagement ring	**der Verlobungsring**
wedding invitation	**die Hochzeitseinladung**
wedding day	**der Hochzeitstag**
wedding dress	**das Hochzeitskleid**
wedding ceremony	**die Trauung**
wedding ring	**der Ehering**
wedding certificate	**der Eheschein**
wedding cake	**der Hochzeitskuchen**
bride	**die Braut**
bridegroom	**der Bräutigam**
bridesmaid	**die Brautjungfer**
honeymoon	**die Hochzeitsreise**
married life	**die Ehe**
separation	**die Trennung**
divorce	**die Scheidung**
heterosexual	**heterosexuell**
homosexual	**homosexuell**
lesbian	**lesbisch**
gay	**schwul**
death	**der Tod**
dead	**tot**
funeral	**die Beerdigung**
corpse	**der Körper/die Leiche**
coffin	**der Sarg**
cemetery	**der Friedhof**
burial	**die Beerdigung**
cremation	**die Einäscherung**
grave	**das Grab**
death certificate	**der Totenschein**
will	**das Testament**

Useful phrases

Congratulations!	**Herzlichen Glückwunsch!**
Happy birthday	**Herzlichen Glückwunsch zum Geburtstag!**
Congratulations on your engagement/wedding!	**Herzlichen Glückwunsch zu Ihrer/ Eurer Verlobung/Hochzeit**

We would like to send you our best wishes	**Wir möchten unsere besten Wünsche übermitteln.**
I would like to convey my condolences	**Herzliches Beileid.**

Useful verbs

to get engaged	**sich verloben**
to get married	**heiraten**
to die	**sterben**
to bury	**beerdigen**
to be in mourning	**trauern**
to be single	**single sein**
to propose	**einen Heiratsantrag machen**

Insight

Be aware of the following false friend: English *tot* (short for *toddler*) ≠ **tot**. A *tot* is **ein Knirps** in German. **Tot** in German is *dead* in English.

Note too that it is becoming more and more common to use the English word *kids* instead of **Kinder.** You might hear the following sentence while in Germany: **Alle Kids sind cool.** *All kids are cool.*

TEST YOURSELF

See how many of the questions you can get right without looking back at the unit.

1 What is the English word for **Stiefbruder?**
   a stepbrother
   b brother in law
   c brother

2 The word for *relative* (family member) in German is:
   a relativ
   b Verwandte
   c Realität

3 Which of these means *to be married*?
   a Hochzeit
   b heiraten
   c verheiratet sein

4 Which word means *divorce*?
   a die Hochzeit
   b die Scheidung
   c die Verlobung

5 Which of the following expressions means *to propose*?
   a einen Heiratsantrag machen
   b eine Verlobung absagen
   c einen Streit schlichten

6 Which word means *bridegroom*?
   a Braut
   b Brautjungfer
   c Bräutigam

7 Which of the following verbs is a separable verb?
  a verlieben
  b ausgehen
  c erwarten

8 Which word means *wedding invitation*?
  a Hochzeitskleid
  b Hochzeitsvorbereitungen
  c Hochzeitseinladung

9 Which word means *pregnancy* in German?
  a Kindheit
  b Schwangerschaft
  c Prediger

10 Which word means *girlfriend*?
  a Freunde
  b Freund
  c Freundin

Answers: 1a; 2b; 3c; 4b; 5a; 6c; 7b; 8c; 9b; 10c

3

Work

3.1 Job titles

Core vocabulary

I am a/n...	**Ich bin...**
accountant	**Buchhalter/in**
accountant	**Wirtschaftsprüfer/in**
(external financial adviser)	
actor/actress	**Schauspieler/in**
architect	**Architekt/in**
bricklayer	**Maurer/in**
builder	**Bauarbeiter/in**
businessman/woman	**Geschäftsmann/Geschäftsfrau**
cleaner	**die Putzfrau/mann**
dentist	**Zahnarzt/¨in**
doctor	**Arzt/¨in, Doktor/in**
driver	**Fahrer/in**
electrician	**Elektriker/in**
engineer	**Ingenieur/in**
farmer	**Bauer/Bäuerin**
fireman	**Feuerwehrmann**
housewife/househusband	**Hausfrau/mann**
hairdresser	**Frisör/Frisöse**
journalist	**Journalist/in**
lawyer	**Rechtsanwalt/¨in**
lecturer	**Dozent, Hochschullehrer/in**
mechanic	**Mechaniker/in**
musician	**Musiker/in**
nurse (f/m)	**Krankenpfleger/in**
plumber	**Klempner/in**
policeman	**Polizist/in**
postman	**Postbeamte/in**
receptionist	**Emfangsdame/Emfangschef**
scientist	**Wissenschaftler/in**
secretary	**Sekretär/in**
shop assistant	**Verkäufer/in**
shopkeeper	**Ladenbesitzer/in**
student	**Student/in**
teacher	**Lehrer/in**
waiter/waitress	**Kellner/in, Bediemungh**

worker	**Arbeiter/in**
employer	**Arbeitgeber/in**
civil servant	**Beamte/in**
academic	**Akademiker/in**
business person	**der/die Geschäftsmann/frau**
self-employed person	**Selbstständige/r**
au pair	**Au pair**
chairman/woman	**Vorsitzende/r**
chief executive	**Hauptgeschäftsführer/in**
managing director	**leitende/r Direktor/in**
director	**Direktor/in**
company secretary	**Prokurist/in**
departmental head	**Geschäftsführende/r Abteilungsleiter/in**
manager/manageress	**Geschäftsführer/in Manager/in**
manager of department	**Abteilungsleiter/in**
business consultant	**Geschäftsberater/in**
personal assistant	**persönliche Assistent/in**
employer/employee	**Angestellte/r**
sales representative	**Verkaufsleiter/in**
computer operator	**Computerbildschirmmitarbeiter/in**

Other useful words in connection with work

person on work experience	**Praktikant/in**
trainee	**Auszubildende/r**
full-time job	**die Vollzeitarbeit**
part-time work	**die Teilzeitarbeit**
temporary and casual work	**die befristete Arbeit**
seasonal work	**die Saisonarbeit**
apprenticeship	**die Lehre**
unemployed	**arbeitslos**
to be retired	**in Rente sein**

Useful words and phrases

....

Insight

The following words in connection with employment are either Anglicisms or similar words in English and German.

Learning them will help you to build up your vocabulary faster. Note the German pronunciation, e.g. illegal.

industry **die Industrie**, *media* **die Medien**, *show business* **das Showgeschäft**, *tourism* **der Tourismus**, *to manage* **managen**, *to communicate* **kommunizieren**, *to negotiate* **negoziieren**, *strike* **der Streik**, *to strike* **streiken**, *illegal* **illegal**.

I would like to work in ...	**Ich möchte in ... arbeiten.**
I would like to work in a shoe shop.	**Ich möchte in einem Schuhgeschäft arbeiten.**
I would like to work as a ...	**Ich möchte als ... arbeiten.**
I would like to work as a waitress.	**Ich möchte als Kellnerin arbeiten.**

I work in ... **Ich arbeite ...**   *I work as a ...* **Ich arbeite als ...**

agriculture **in der Landwirtschaft**	*farmer* **Bauer/¨in**
banking **im Bankwesen**	*clerk* **Angestellte/r**
building trade **im Baugewerbe**	*carpenter* **Zimmermann**
catering **in der Gastronomie**	*pub owner* **Gastwirt/in**
civil service **im öffentlichen Dienst**	*civil servant* **Beamte/r**
finance **im Finanzwesen**	*financial adviser* **Finanzberater/in**
the hotel industry **in der Hotelindustrie**	*hotelier* **Hotelier**
insurance **im Versicherungswesen**	*sales agent* **Versicherungsvertreter/in**

I work in ...	**Ich arbeite ...**
leisure	**in der Freizeitindustrie**
manufacturing	**in der Herstellungsindustrie**
medicine	**im medizinischen Bereich**
the media	**im Mediensektor, in den Medien**

the public services	im öffentlichen Verkehrswesen
purchasing	im Einkaufsbereich
retail	im Einzelhandel
service industry	im Dienstleistungsbereich
show business	im Showgeschäft
textiles	in der Textilindustrie
tourism	im Tourismus
transport	im Verkehrswesen
wholesale	im Großhandel

Useful verbs

> **Insight**
> Young people like to use the verb **jobben** instead of **arbeiten**.
> *To manage* is **managen**.

to work/gain a living	arbeiten/jobben/meinen Lebensunterhalt erwerben
to be out of work	ohne festen Arbeitsplatz sein
to be unemployed	arbeitslos sein
to buy/sell	kaufen/verkaufen
to import/export	importieren/exportieren
to manage	managen/leiten
to manufacture	herstellen
to communicate	kommunizieren
to phone	telefonieren/anrufen
to negotiate	verhandeln/negoziieren
to develop	entwickeln
to build	bauen
to sew	nähen
to clean	putzen
to research	forschen

Related words to do with employment

worker/labourer	der Arbeiter (-)
employer	der Arbeitgeber (-)
employee	der Arbeitnehmer(-)
place of employment	der Arbeitsplatz ("e)
vacancies	freie Arbeitsplätze

unemployment	**die Arbeitslosigkeit**
working atmosphere	**die Arbeitsatmosphäre**
working conditions	**die Arbeitsbedingungen**
work clothes	**die Arbeitskleidung**
division of labour	**die Arbeitsteilung**
overworking	**die Arbeitsüberlastung**
after working hours	**nach Arbeitsschluss**
salaried employee	**der Angestellte (n)**
to employ	**<u>an</u>stellen**
to be employed	**angestellt sein**
to work	**arbeiten**
unemployed	**arbeitslos**
willing to work	**arbeitswillig**
unwilling to work	**arbeitsunwillig**
temporary staff	**die Aushilfe (n)**
the German Federal Labour Office	**die Bundesanstalt für Arbeit**
employee	**die/der Beschäftigte (n)**
working conditions	**die/das Beschäftigungs- verhältnis (se)**
to be employed with	**beschäftigt sein bei**

3.2 Where do you work?

Core vocabulary

Insight

The following words in connection with workplaces are either Anglicisms or similar words in English and German. Learning them will help you to build up your vocabulary faster.

bank **die Bank**, *hotel* **das Hotel**, *post office* **die Post**, *restaurant* **das Restaurant**, *studio* **das Studio**, *reception* **die Rezeption**, *administration* **die Administration**, *distribution* **die Distribution**, *export* **der Export**, *import* **der Import**, *manufacture* **die Manufaktur**, *marketing* **das Marketing**, *factory* **die Fabrik**, *canteen* **die Kantine**, *firm* **die Firma**, *workshop* **der Workshop**, *mine* **die Mine**, *school* **die Schule**.

Insight

Look out for the following false friends in connection with workplaces: *garage* ≠ **Garage**. The German word **Garage** is only used for the garage where you park a car. **Eine Tankstelle** is a petrol station.

I work in a ...	**Ich arbeite ...**
bank	**in einer Bank**
factory	**in einer Fabrik**
farm	**auf einem Bauernhof**
garage	**in einer Werkstatt**
hospital	**in einem Krankenhaus**
hotel	**in einem Hotel**
mine	**in einer Mine**
office	**in einem Büro**
post office	**auf einer Post**
railway	**bei der Bahn**
restaurant	**in einem Restaurant**
school	**in einer Schule**
service station	**an einer Tankstelle**
shopping centre	**in einem Einkaufszentrum**
studio	**in einem Studio**
town hall	**in einem Rathaus**
workshop	**in einer Werkstatt/in einem Workshop**

The company

headquarters	**die Hauptgeschäftsstelle**
subsidiary	**die Tochtergesellschaft**
firm	**die Firma/Firmen**
factory	**die Fabrik (en)**
branch	**die Zweigstelle (n)**
the premises	**die Räumlichkeiten**
conference room	**das Konferenzzimmer**
canteen	**die Kantine**
meeting room	**das Besprechungszimmer**
reception	**die Rezeption**
entrance	**der Eingang**

exit	**der Ausgang**
I work ...	**Ich arbeite ...**
in an office	**in einem Büro**
on a building site	**auf einer Baustelle**
in a workshop	**in einer Werkstatt/in einem Workshop**
in a factory	**in einer Fabrik**
outside	**draußen**
I work in the ... department.	**Ich arbeite in der ...abteilung.**
accounts	**Buchhaltungsabteilung**
advertising	**Werbeabteilung**
export/import	**Export-Importabteilung**
legal department	**Rechtsabteilung**
personnel/human resources	**Personalabteilung**

Insight

The last part of a compound noun, in the examples above **-abteilung** *department*, gives you the article, which means in this case all departments have the article **die: die Werbeabteilung, die Schuhabteilung** etc.

Remember, however, to change the article from **die** to **der** after the preposition **in**. **Ich arbeite in <u>der</u> Schuhabteilung/ der Werbeabteilung** etc.

Other areas of work

I am working in ...	**Ich arbeite ...**
information technology	**in der Informationstechnologie**
insurance	**bei einer Versicherung**
manufacture	**in der Manufaktur**
marketing	**im Marketing**
property	**mit Grundstücken**
purchasing	**im Einkauf**
sales	**im Verkauf**
administration	**in der Verwaltung/Administration**
gastronomy	**in der Gastronomie**
distribution	**in der Verteilung/Distribution**

Useful phrases

I would like to speak to Mr/Mrs Braun.	**Ich möchte gerne Frau/Herrn Braun sprechen.**
I have an appointment with Mr/Mrs Braun.	**Ich habe einen Termin mit Herrn/Frau Braun.**
Mr/Mrs Braun is still in a meeting.	**Herr/Frau Braun ist noch in einer Besprechung.**
Do you wish to wait?	**Möchten Sie warten?**
Yes, please.	**Ja gerne.**
Please sit down.	**Bitte nehmen Sie Platz.**
Can I get you a coffee?	**Möchten Sie eine Tasse Kaffee?**

Long German words (compound words)

> **Insight**
>
> There is often one part of a long or compound word that can give you a clue to its meaning or help you to remember it. So don't worry about long words in German; all you have to do is break them up and take a little breath in between the elements. You may start enjoying these long words. You will definitely improve your vocabulary by familiarizing yourself with them.

Arbeitsunfähigkeitsbescheinigung can be broken down as follows:

the work/job	**die Arbeit (n)/der Job**
inability	**die Unfähigkeit**
certificate	**die Bescheinigung (en)**
certificate to prove inability to work	**die Arbeitsunfähigkeits-bescheinigung**

More compound words

the job centre	**das Arbeitsamt**
the work/job	**die Arbeit**
the office/centre	**das Amt (¨er)**
employee	**der/die Angestellte (n)**
job centre employee	**die Arbeitsamtsangestelle**

employment agency	**die Arbeitvermittlung**
to arrange	**vermitteln**
work permit	**die Arbeitserlaubnis**
permission	**die Erlaubnis**
employer: lit.: *somebody who gives work*	**der Arbeitgeber**
to give	**geben**
employee: lit.: *somebody who takes work*	**der Arbeitnehmer**
to take	**nehmen**

Some German compound words are difficult to translate:

ein Arbeitstier
Tier = *animal*

Arbeitstier lit.: '*working animal*'/trans. *an extremely hard-working person.*

He/She is a working animal. **Er/Sie ist ein richtiges Arbeitstier.**

die Arbeitswut
die Wut = *rage*

Ihn/Sie hat die Arbeitswut gepackt   lit.: 'He/She fell into a rage of work'. *He/She turned into an workaholic.*

Useful verbs

infinitive	*present tense*	*past participle*
to buy	**kaufen**	**gekauft**
to manage	**managen/leiten**	**gemanagt/geleitet**
to manufacture	**herstellen**	**hergestellt**
to research	**forschen**	**geforscht**
to sell	**verkaufen**	**verkauft**
to study	**studieren**	**studiert**
to travel	**reisen**	**gereist**
to work	**arbeiten**	**gearbeitet**

3.3 Conditions of employment

Core vocabulary

working conditions	**die Arbeitsbedingungen**
the working day	**der Arbeitstag (e)**
the working week	**die Arbeitswoche**
holidays	**die Ferien (-)/der Urlaub**
annual holiday	**der jährliche Urlaub**
national holidays	**die Feiertage**
pay	**die Bezahlung**
salary	**das Gehalt (¨er)**
income	**das Einkommen (-)**
income tax	**die Einkommenssteuer**
VAT	**die Mehrwehrtssteuer MwSt.**
wages	**der Lohn (¨e)**
applicant	**der/die Bewerber/in (nen)**
application	**die Bewerbung (en)**
application form	**das Bewerbungsformular (e)**
CV	**der Lebenslauf (¨e)/CV**
contract	**der Vertrag (¨e)**
job interview	**das Jobinterview(s)**
full-time job	**die Vollzeitstelle (n)**
part-time job	**die Teilzeitstelle (n)**
job share	**Jobshare/die halbe Stelle**
part time	**die Teilzeitstelle (n)**
office hours	**die Bürostunden**
overtime	**die Überstunden**

flexitime	**die flexiblen Arbeitsstunden**
holiday entitlement	**der Urlaubsanspruch**
sick leave	**die Krankenbeurlaubung (en)**
sick note	**die Krankenbescheinigung(en)/(die Arbeitsunfähigkeitsbescheinigung (en)**
redundancy payment	**die Abfindung (en)**

Typical signs found on the door of a shop or an office:

closed today	**Heute geschlossen**
Mondays closed	**Montags geschlossen**
closed for lunch (lit. lunch break)	**Mittagspause**
back soon	**Bald zurück**
The opening hours are ...	**Die Öffnungszeiten sind ...**
The office hours are ...	**Die Bürostunden sind ...**
Sale/Ausverkauf	**Sale**

More words in connections with shops:

coffee break	**die Kaffeepause (n)**
closing time for shops	**der Ladenschluss**
opening hours for shops	**die Ladenöffnungszeiten**

Insight

There is one word in German to cover both dismissal and redundancy: **die Entlassung. Der Personalchef ist entlassen worden** can mean either that he was dismissed or that he was made redundant.

Same or similar words in English and German: *bankruptcy* **der Bankrott**, *standard of living* **der Lebensstandard**, *meeting* **das Meeting**, *stressful* **stressig**, *motivating* **motivierend**, *organized* **organisiert**.

union	**die Gewerkschaft (en)**
union meeting	**die Gewerkschaftsversammlung (en) Gewerkschaftsmeeting**
strike	**der Streik (s)**
demand	**die Forderung (en)**

bankruptcy	**der Bankrott**
standard of living	**der Lebensstandard**
unemployment rate	**die Arbeitslosenrate (n)**
legal minimum wage	**der Mindestlohn (¨e)**

Useful words and phrases

It is stressful/stimulating/ motivating	**Es ist sehr stressig/stimulierend/ motivierend**
He/she is very efficient	**er/sie ist sehr fähig**
organized/disorganized	**organisiert/unorganisiert**
hard working/lazy	**fleißig/faul**

Useful verbs

to be behind with one's work	**mit der Arbeit hinterher hinken**
to have a deadline	**einen Abgabetermin haben**
to be overworked	**überarbeitet sein**
to be stressed	**gestresst sein**
to be a lot of work	**viel Arbeit machen**
to do a good job	**gründliche Arbeit leisten**
to be successful	**erfolgreich sein**

Insight

Did you notice the following words? *strike* **der Streik,** *stressful* **stressig,** *stress* **der Stress,** *marketing* **das Marketing,** *official* **offiziell,** *contact* **der Kontakt,** *to reduplicate* **reduplizieren,** *examination* **das Exam,** *motivated* **motiviert,** *efficient* **effizent.**

3.4 Writing a letter

Addressing somebody in a formal letter

Ways to start a letter
(best way of writing to a company   **Sehr geehrte Damen und**
  when you don't know a specific   **Herren,**
  name)

(only when you know for sure there are only men)	**Sehr geehrte Herren,**
(only when you know for sure there are only women)	**Sehr geehrte Damen,**
(if you know the person's name) (writing to two different people)	**Sehr geehrte Frau Meier,** **Sehr geehrter Herr Braun,** **Sehr geehrte Frau Schmidt,** **Sehr geehrter Herr Meier,**

Many thanks for …	**Vielen Dank für …**
We received …	**Wir haben … erhalten**
I would like to thank you for …	**Hiermit möchte ich mich recht herzlich bei Ihnen für … bedanken.**
We are writing to ask whether …	**Wir möchten uns erkundigen, ob …**
Regarding your letter of …	**In Bezug auf Ihr Schreiben vom …,**
Regarding our telephone call …	**Bezugnehmend zu unserem Telefonat …**
In reply to …	**Ich beziehe mich auf …**
We regret that …	**Wir bedauern sehr, dass …**
We acknowledge the receipt of … (followed by genitive)	**Wir bestätigen den Erhalt …**

Ways to end a formal letter:

With best wishes/kind regards	**Mit freundlichen Grüßen** **Mit besten Grüßen** **Mit besten Empfehlungen** **Hochachtungsvoll** (very formal)

Please don't hesitate to contact me for further information.	**Ich stehe Ihnen gerne für weitere Informationen zur Verfügung.**
We are looking forward to your early reply.	**Wir freuen uns auf Ihre baldige Antwort.**
I look forward to hearing from you soon.	**Ich würde mich sehr freuen, bald wieder von Ihnen zu hören.**

Hoping to hear from you soon.	**Ich hoffe, bald wieder von Ihnen zu hören.**
and remain yours ...	**... und verbleibe mit freundlichen Grüßen**

Addressing someone in an informal letter

Ways to start/close an informal letter

Dear Susanne,	**Liebe Susanne,**
Dear Stefan,	**Lieber Stefan,**
Love from ...	**Alles Liebe von ...**
All my love and best wishes	**Alles Liebe und Gute**
Best wishes	**Viele Grüße**
Best wishes, your ...	**Grüße, Deine/Dein ...**
I am looking forward to hearing from you soon.	**Ich freue mich, bald wieder von Dir zu hören.**
Your Klaus	**Dein Klaus**
Your Claudia	**Deine Claudia**

Other informal letter endings

Take care.	**Mach's gut.**
See you soon.	**Bis bald.**
Phone me.	**Ruf mal an.**
Write to me again.	**Schreib mal wieder.**

3.5 Using the telephone

Core vocabulary

Insight

The following words in connection with using the telephone are either Anglicisms or similar words in English and German. Learning them will help you to build up your vocabulary faster.

telephone **das Telefon,** *to phone* **telefonieren,** *mobile phone* **das Mobiltelefon/das Handy,** *telephone number* **die**

Telefonnummer, *international* **international**, *battery* **die Batterie**, *to text* **texten**.

Germans also call *a mobile phone* **ein Handy**, which is an example of how English/American-sounding words are adopted, and sometimes don't make sense to a native English speaker.

....

(tele)phone	**das Telefon (e)**
mobile phone	**das Mobiltelefon/das Handy (s)**
receiver	**der Hörer (-)**
extension	**der Apparat (e)**
telephone number	**die Telefonnummer (n)**
directory	**das Telefonbuch ("er)**
local call	**das Ortsgespräch (e)**
long distance call	**das Ferngespräch (e)**
international call	**der internationale Anruf (e)**
answering machine	**der Anrufbeantworter (-)**

Useful words and phrases

Could I speak to Mr/Mrs ...?	**Könnte ich bitte Herrn/Frau ... sprechen?**
Can I have extension ... please?	**Bitte verbinden Sie mich mit Apparat ...?**
Who can help me regarding ...?	**Wer kann mir mit ... helfen?**
Who is calling?	**Wer ist dort bitte?**
Can you tell me what it is about?	**Können Sie mir sagen, worum es sich handelt?**
To whom would you like to speak?	**Mit wem möchten Sie sprechen?**
Speaking!	**Am Apparat!**
Can you wait a moment?	**Können Sie einen Moment warten?**
I am putting you through.	**Ich stelle Sie jetzt durch.**
The line is engaged.	**Der Apparat ist besetzt.**
busy	**besetzt**
free	**frei**
Do you want to hold?	**Möchten Sie warten?**

Would you like to leave a message?	Möchten Sie eine Nachricht hinterlassen?
Can I take your name and number?	Könnte ich bitte Ihren Namen und Ihre Telefonummer haben?
My battery is running low.	Meine Batterie ist leer.
Can you ring back?	Könnten Sie zurückrufen?
Can you text me?	Könnten Sie es mir bitte texten?

Answerphone messages

Hier ist der telefonische Anrufbeantworter Schmidt. Wir sind zur Zeit leider nicht erreichbar, aber wenn Sie eine Nachricht hinterlassen wollen, sprechen Sie bitte nach dem Ton.

This is the telephone answering machine of Mr/Mrs Schmidt. Unfortunately you cannot reach us at present but if you wish to leave a message, please speak after the tone.

Es tut mir Leid, wir sind zur Zeit nicht erreichbar, aber Sie können eine Nachricht hinterlassen.

I am sorry, but we are not available at present, but you may leave a message.

Unsere Öffnungszeiten sind montags bis freitags von 8 Uhr bis 16 Uhr. Sie können uns gerne eine Nachricht hinterlassen, wir rufen Sie umgehend zurück.

Our opening hours are Mondays to Fridays from 8 am to 4 pm. You can leave a message and we will phone you back immediately.

Useful verbs

to phone	**anrufen**
to call	**telefonieren**
to call back	**zurückrufen**

to dial	**wählen**
to put someone through	**durch**stellen/verbinden
to look up a number	**eine Nummer nach**schauen
to leave a message	**eine Nachricht hinter**lassen

3.6 Using the computer

Insight

Many words in connection with information technology are taken from the English/American language. For the English-speaking world it is easy to learn and pronounce these words in German. Many English verbs are 'made German' by adding **-en** or **-ieren** and are therefore very easy to identify and to learn.

The most common useful verbs

to boot	**booten**
to chat	**chatten**
to download	**downloaden**
to edit	**editieren**
to format	**formatieren**
to mail	**mailen**
to mark	**markieren**
to program	**programmieren**
to surf	**surfen**
to scan	**scannen**
to skype	**skypen**
to text	**texten**

German verbs similar to English

to click	**anklicken**
to burn	**brennen**
to double click	**doppelklicken**
to log in	**einloggen**

to type (in)	(ein)tippen
to format	formatieren
to go online	online gehen

Other German verbs

to switch on	<u>an</u>stellen
to recharge	aufladen
to print out	ausdrucken
to print	drucken
to edit	<u>ein</u>fügen/editieren
to download	<u>herunter</u>laden
to start	hochfahren
to delete	löschen
to send	schicken

Useful expressions

to text a message	eine Nachricht texten
to send an email	ein(e) E-Mail schicken
to receive an email	ein(e) E-Mail erhalten

Insight

Note that the word **e-mail** has two genders, **die** or **das**, so you can choose the one you prefer.

Useful nouns in connection with computers

user	Der Benutzer
screen	Der Bildschirm
flat screen	Der flache Bildschirm
CD burner	Der CD Brenner
(data) file	Die Datei
database	Die Datenbank
printer	Der Drucker
window	Das Fenster
background	Der Hintergrund
junk mail	Die Junk Mail

delete button	**Die Löschtaste**
mouse	**Die Maus**
virus scanner	**Der Virenscanner**

Insight

The following words are taken straight from English.
The only difference is that in German they are divided into
masculine (**der**), feminine (**die**) and neuter (**das**). They are
listed here according to gender and it may help you to learn
them that way.

masculine	Der Pin	Die Hardware
Der Browser	Der Pixel	Die **Homepage**
Der Chat	Der Provider	Die Mail
Der Chip	Der Scanner	Die Software
Der Cursor	Der Server	Die Tags (pl)
Der Computer	Der Slot	
Der Desktop	Der USB-Stick	**neuter**
Der Domainname		Das Cookie
Der Joystick	**feminine**	Das Internet
Der Laptop	Die Firewall	Das Popup
Der Monitor	Die Flatrate	Das Mail

TEST YOURSELF

See how many questions you can get right without looking back at the unit.

1 The verb to *download* is translated by
  a hochfahren
  b hochladen
  c herunterladen

2 Match the following job titles.
  1 dentist   **a** Wissenschaftler
  2 scientist   **b** Klempner
  3 plumber   **c** Zahnarzt

3 The word *employee* is translated as:
  a Arbeitgeber
  b Arbeitnehmer
  c Arbeiter

4 The word for *apprenticeship* in German is
  a Approbation
  b Abitur
  c Lehre

5 The word for *unemployed* in German is
  a arbeitslos
  b arbeitswillig
  c angestellt

6 Which verb is *not* separable?
  a zurückrufen
  b telephonieren
  c anrufen

7 Which word means *mobile phone*?
   a Telefon
   b Handy
   c Apparat

8 Which expression means *to receive a message*?
   a eine Nachricht texten
   b eine Nachricht schicken
   c eine Nachricht erhalten

9 Which verb is *not* separable?
   a anklicken
   b einloggen
   c chatten

10 Which noun has a feminine gender (**die**)?
   a Scanner
   b Software
   c Provider

Answers: 1c; 2 (1c, 2a, 3b); 3b; 4c; 5a; 6b; 7b; 8c; 9c; 10b

4

Education

4.1 Primary and secondary education

Core vocabulary

> **Insight**
>
> Be aware of the following false friends:
>
> English *gymnasium (gym)* ≠ German **Gymnasium**. A German **Gymnasium** is a grammar school. A *gymnasium (gym)* is **die Turnhalle** or **das Fitness Center** in German.
>
> *high school* ≠ **Hochschule**. A German **Hochschule** is a university. A *high school* in Germany is **eine Gesamtschule** or **eine Realschule**.

kindergarden/nursery	**Der Kindergarten**
primary school	**Die Grundschule**
secondary modern school (with low qualifications)	**Die Hauptschule**
secondary modern school	**Die Realschule**
secondary modern school	**Die Gesamtschule**
grammar school	**Das Gymnasium**
boarding school/public school	**Das Internat**
independent school	**Die Privatschule**

Insight

There are various schools pupils can go to after primary school depending on their academic ability. The school-leaving certificate in each case is called:

from **Hauptschule: Hauptschulabschluss** (lowest qualification)

from **Realschule: Realschulabschluss** (second lowest qualification)

from **Gesamtschule: Realschulabschluss** or **Abitur**

from **Gymnasium: Abitur** (highest school qualification)

Pupils stay in a **Hauptschule** for five or six years and usually enter an apprenticeship (**Lehre**) after that. They can also study for vocational qualifications at a **Berufsschule**. With a **Realschule** qualification (**Realschulabschluss**) pupils can enter an apprenticeship or go into Further Education (**Fachschulen**). They also have the opportunity to enter a **Gymnasium**. **Gymnasium** concludes with the **Abitur** that awards the **Zeugnis der allgemeinen Hochschulreife** (university entrance qualifications).

There will be some changes to the school system in Berlin from 2010/11: **Haupt-, Real-** and **Gesamtschulen** will be abolished and be replaced by a single school system called **Sekundarstufe**.

Insight

The following words in connection with education are either Anglicisms or similar words in English and German. Learning them will help you to build up your vocabulary faster.

classroom **das Klassenzimmer**, *projector* **der Projektor**, *computer* **der Computer**, *overhead projector* **der Overhead-Projektor**, *toilets* **die Toiletten**, *computer room* **der Computerraum**, *school secretary* **die Schulsekretärin/der Schulsekretär**, *kindergarden* **der Kindergarten**.

headmaster	**Schuldirektor/in**
deputy head	**stellvertretender (e) Direktor/in**
secondary teacher	**Hauptschullehrer/in**
secondary school teacher	**Realschullehrer/in**
grammar school teacher	**Gymnasiallehrer/in**
primary teacher	**Grundschullehrer/in**
pupil	**Schüler/in**
the school secretary	**Schulsekretär/in**
the school caretaker	**der Hausmeister (-)**
lesson	**der Unterricht**
break	**die Pause (n)**
bell	**die Schulglocke/klingel (n)**
end of lesson	**das Ende der Stunde**
term	**das Schuljahr (e)**
halfterm	**das Halbjahr (e)**
holidays	**die Ferien**
timetable	**der Stundenplan (¨e)**

School subjects *die Schulfächer*

Insight

The following words for school subjects are either Anglicisms or similar words in English and German. Learning them will help you to build up your vocabulary faster.

biology	**Biologie**	*Latin*	**Latein**
English	**Englisch**	*music*	**Musik**
Religion	**Religion**	*Philosophy*	**Philosophie**
French	**Französisch**	*Russian*	**Russisch**
chemistry	**Chemie**	*mathematics*	**Mathematik**
Spanish	**Spanisch**	*physics*	**Physik**
IT	**Informatik**		

Other subjects

history	**Geschichte**	*art*	**Kunst**
geography	**Erdkunde**	*PE*	**Sport**
German	**Deutsch**	*social science*	**Sozialwissenschaften**
ethics	**Werte und Normen**		

Other vocabulary in connection with school

building	**das Schulgebäude (-)**
corridor	**der Flur (e)**
science lab	**das Labor (e)**
gym	**die Turnhalle (n)**
library	**die Bücherei (en)**
changing room	**der Umkleideraum (¨e)**
girls'/boys' toilets	**die Toiletten Mädchen/Jungen**
desk	**der Schultisch (e)**
blackboard	**die Tafel (n)**
book	**das Buch (¨er)**
chalk	**die Kreide (-)**
exercise book	**das Schulheft (e)**
pencil case	**die Federmappe (n)**
pen	**der Kuli (s)**
pencil	**der Bleistift (e)**
eraser	**das Radiergummi (s)**
calculator	**der Taschenrechner (-)**
ruler	**das Lineal (e)**
report	**das Zeugnis (e)**
school bag	**die Schultasche (n)**
sports kit	**das Sportzeug (-)**

Useful words and phrases

to do homework	**Hausaufgaben machen**
to get a good mark	**gute Noten bekommen**
to sit an exam	**eine Prüfung machen**
to pass a test	**einen Test bestehen**
to fail	**durchfallen**
to resit	**wiederholen**
a pupil who has to repeat one whole class	**ein Wiederholer**
having to repeat a whole year	**sitzenbleiben**
an intelligent pupil who can miss out one whole school year and goes one class up	**Überspringer**
to miss out one school year	**ein Jahr überspringen**

to copy	**kopieren**
to discuss	**diskutieren**
to read	**lesen**
to speak	**sprechen**
to listen	**hören**
to talk	**sprechen**
to write	**schreiben**
to take notes	**mitschreiben**
to be quiet	**ruhig sein**

Insight

The school grading scale runs from **eins** (the best mark) to **sechs** (**fünf** in Austria) which is a fail. Students who fail several subjects have to repeat a whole year (**das Jahr wiederholen**), also called **sitzenbleiben**, which literally means to *remain sitting*.

4.2 Further and higher education

Insight

The following words in connection with further and higher education are either Anglicisms or similar words in English and German. Learning them will help you to build up your vocabulary faster.

philosophy **die Philosophie**, *psychology* **die Psychologie**, *university* **die Universität**, *faculty* **die Fakultät**, *seminar* **das Seminar**, *professor* **der Professor/die Professorin**, *student* **Student**, *exam* **das Examen**, *student* **der Student/die Studentin**, *dissertation* **die Dissertation**, *diploma* **das Diplom**.

There are various types of colleges, universities and courses:

adult education/evening classes	**die Volkshochschule (n)**
vocational college	**die Berufsschule (n)**
technical college	**die Fachschule (n)**
polytechnic	**die Fachhochschule (n)**
university	**die Universität (en) die Hochschule (n)**
degree	**der Universitätsabschluss (¨e)**
degree course	**der Studiengang (¨e)**
economics	**Wirtschaftswissenschaft (en)**
law	**Rechtswissenschaft (en)**
science	**Naturwissenschaften**
social science	**Sozialwissenschaften**
linguistics	**Sprachwissenschaften**
business management	**Betriebswirtschaftslehre**
dentistry	**Zahnmedizin**

Core vocabulary

lecture	**die Vorlesung (en)**
tutorial	**das Kolloqium**
subject	**das Studienfach (¨er)**
lecturer	**die Lehrkraft (¨e)**
research assistant	**Forschungsassistent/in**
graduate	**Hochschulabsolvent/in (en) (nen)**
undergraduate	**Student/Studentin (en) (nen)**
apprenticeship	**die Lehre (n)**
trainee	**der/die Auszubildende (n)**
examination	**das Examen (-)/die Prüfung (en)**
curriculum	**der Lehrplan (¨e)**
teacher training	**der Lehramtsstudiengang (¨e)**
mark	**die Note (n)**
grade	**die Abschlussnote (n)**
research	**die Forschung (en)**
paper	**das Referat (e)**
report	**der Bericht (e)**

dissertation	**die Dissertation (en)**
PhD	**die Doktorarbeit (en)**
to study for a PhD	**promovieren**
thesis for diploma	**die Diplomarbeit (en)**
to present a paper	**ein Referat halten über**
to do a sandwich course	**theoretischer und praktischer Ausbildungsgang**
to study part-time	**Teilzeitstudium**
to attend an evening class	**einen Abendunterricht besuchen**
to do work experience	**ein Arbeitspraktikum machen**
to miss a deadline	**einen Abgabetermin verpassen**

Useful words and phrases in connection with university

> ## Insight
>
> Look at the compound nouns which are based on the word **Studien** + another noun. Remember not to be worried about long words as they are just a combination of two or three nouns. Take a little breath in between the various parts of the noun, e.g. **Studienabschluss (Studien-abschluss)**. This makes it easier to pronounce and also gives you time to think about the second or third part.

studies	**das Studium/Studien**
first-year student	**der Studienanfänger (-)**
study visit	**der Studienaufenthalt (e)**
completion of studies	**der Studienabschluss (¨e)**
subject at university	**das Studienfach (¨er)**
university, college degree course	**der Studiengang (¨e)**
course regulation	**die Studienordnung (en)**
university/college place	**der Studienplatz(¨e)**
to begin one's studies	**ein Studium aufnehmen/ beginnen**
while he was/is a student	**während seines Studiums ...**
to apply for a degree course	**sich für einen Studiengang bewerben**
registration, matriculation	**die Immatrikulation (en)**
to register	**sich immatrikulieren**

registration office	das Immatrikulationsbüro (s)
registration certificate	die Immatrikulations-bescheinigung (en)
to get one's doctorate	die Doktorwürde verliehen bekommen
to study for a PhD	promovieren
She is still doing her doctorate.	Sie sitzt immer noch an ihrer Doktorarbeit.
He has a doctorate in social science.	Er hat einen Doktortitel in Sozialwissenschaften.
examiner	der/die Prüfer/in (-) (nen)
to pass an exam	eine Prüfung bestehen
to repeat an exam	eine Prüfung wiederholen
to fail an exam	durch eine Prüfung durchfallen
to prepare for an exam	eine Prüfung vorbereiten

Useful verbs

....
Insight

The following verbs are either Anglicisms or similar words in English and German. Learning them will help you to build up your vocabulary faster.

to correct **korrigieren,** to discuss **diskutieren,** to learn **lernen,** to qualify **qualifizieren,** to study **studieren.**
....

to explain	erklären
to register/enrol	einschreiben
to teach	unterrichten
to lecture	lehren
to translate	übersetzen
to understand	verstehen
to do research	Forschung betreiben

TEST YOURSELF

See how many questions you can answer without looking back at the unit.

1 What does the German word **Gymnasium** mean in English?
  a gymnasium
  b grammar school
  c fitness centre

2 What is the German word for *lesson*?
  a lesen
  b Lektion
  c Unterricht

3 What is the German verb *to discuss*?
  a Diskussion
  b diskutieren
  c distanzieren

4 What is *to translate* in German?
  a einüben
  b transferieren
  c übersetzen

5 The word *calculator* is translated as:
  a kalkulieren
  b Taschenrechner
  c Lineal

6 A *primary school* is:
  a eine Grundschule
  b eine Hauptschule
  c eine Realschule

7 The German word for *art* is
   a Architektur
   b Kunst
   c Art

8 *To fail a test* translates as:
   a einfallen
   b auffallen
   c durchfallen

9 A law degree course is known as:
   a Rechtswissenschaft
   b Landwirtschaftlehre
   c Betriebswirtschaftslehre

10 A school report/certificate is:
   a eine Schultasche
   b ein Schulzeugnis
   c eine Schulreportage

Answers: 1b; 2c; 3b; 4c; 5b; 6a; 7b; 8c; 9a; 10b

5

....

At home

5.1 The house

Insight

Adverts in newspapers or on internet sites dealing with
renting and selling houses are full of abbreviations and
therefore not always easy to understand. Familiarize yourself
with the abbreviations if you are intending to buy, sell or rent
a house or flat.

Zu vermieten

U-Näh, 2-Zi.-Whg, Kü.- u Badbenutz. vollmöbl. 600 Eur – inkl. Nebenk.
96m, Kaut. 5.OG, Aufzg, gr. SW-Blk. Verm. Tel: 339281048

near the university	**U-Näh = Universitäts-Nähe**
room(s)	**Zi = Zimmer**
flat	**Whg = Wohnung**
kitchen	**Kü. = Küche**
shared bathroom	**Badbenutz = Benutzung**
fully furnished	**vollmöbl. = vollmöbliert**
rates for gas, electricity	**Nebenk. = die Nebenkosten**
deposit	**Kaut. = Kaution**
upper floor	**OG = Obergeschoss**
lift	**Aufzg = Aufzug**
large	**gr. = großer**
southwest	**SW = Südwest**
balcony	**Blk = Balkon**
landlord	**Verm. = Vermieter**

Zu verkaufen

Exklus. Einfamilienhaus im Landhausstil, ruh.
Lage, am Stadtr.

5-Zi, 2 Bäder, Kamine, Wintergarten, Terr., Whirlpool, Sauna,
699000 Euro + Prov. ca.345qm Wohnfl., Fußbodenheiz.,
Doppelfenst. traumh. gepfl. Garten absolute Ruhiglg.
Immobilienmakler Sauer

Tel. 758493827

exclusive	**exklus. = exklusiv**
quiet	**ruh. = ruhig**
outskirts	**Stadtr. = der Stadtrand**
terrace	**Terr. = die Terrasse**
commission	**Prov. = die Provision**
underfloor heating	**Fußbodenheiz. = Fußbodenheizung**
double glazing	**Doppelfenst. = Doppelfenster**
beautiful	**traumh. = traumhafter**
well looked after	**gepfl. = gepflegt**
quiet position	**Ruhiglg. = Ruhiglage**
estate agent	**Immobilienmakler**
mortgage advisor	**Hypothekenberater**

Core vocabulary

....

Insight

The following words in connection with housing are either
Anglicisms or similar words in English and German. Learning
them will help you to build up your vocabulary faster.

house **das Haus (¨er)**, *apartment* **das Apartment (s)**, *garage*
die Garage (n), *cellar* **der Keller (-)**, *chalet* **das Chalet (s)**,
villa **die Villa (Villen)**, *bungalow* **der Bungalow (s)**, *gas* **das
Gas**, *electricity* **die Elektrizität**, *oil* **das Öl**, *water* **das Wasser**,

(Contd)

telephone **das Telefon (e)**, *insulation* **die Isolierung (en)**, *fire alarm* **der Feueralarm**, *balcony* **der Balkon (e)**, *terrace* **die Terrasse (n)**, *garden* **der Garten**, *farm* **die Farm**.

home	**das Zuhause**
flat	**die Wohnung (en)**
studio flat	**die Apartmentwohnung**
block of flats	**das Wohnhaus (¨er)**
the building	**das Gebäude (-)**
floor/storey	**die Etage (n)/das Geschoss (e)**
ground floor	**das Erdgeschoss**
first floor	**die erste Etage/der erste Stock**
second floor	**die zweite Etage/der zweite Stock**
basement	**das Untergeschoss**
attic	**der Dachboden (¨-)**
stairs	**die Treppen**
lift	**der Lift (e), der Aufzug (¨e), der Fahrstuhl (¨)**
estate agent	**der Makler/in**
advertisement	**die Anzeige (n)**
for sale	**zu verkaufen**
for rent	**zu vermieten**
cottage	**das Landhaus (¨er)**
farm	**das Bauernhaus (¨er)/der Bauernhof (¨e)/die Farm**
council flat	**die Sozialwohnung (en)**
detached house	**das Einfamilienhaus**
semi-detached house	**das Zweifamilienhaus**
terraced house	**das Reihenhaus**
central heating	**die Zentralheizung (en)**
double glazing	**das Doppelfenster**
mains sewerage	**die Hauptabwasseranlage (n)**
septic tank	**der Klärbehälter (-)**
soundproofing	**schallgedämpft**
shutters	**die Fensterläden**
burglar alarm	**der Einbrecheralarm**
outside	**draußen**

roof	**das Dach ("er)**
slates	**die Ziegel**
conservatory	**der Wintergarten (¨)**
gate	**das Tor (e)**
path	**der Weg (e)**
lawn	**der Rasen (-)**
flower bed	**das Blumenbeet (e)**
vegetable garden	**der Gemüsegarten (¨)**
greenhouse	**das Gewächshaus ("er)**
the situation	**die Lage (n)**
view	**die Aussicht (en)**
stone	**der Steine (-)**
brick	**der Ziegelstein (e)**
timber	**das Holz ("er)**
concrete	**der Zement**

Useful words and phrases

It overlooks the lake.	**Es ist mit Blick über den See.**
It has a central location.	**Es ist in einer zentralen Lage.**
close to all services	**in einer zentralen Lage für Einkauf- und Verkehrsmittel**
in the town centre	**im Stadtzentrum**
in the suburbs	**im Außenbezirk**
in the country	**auf dem Land**
to rent	**mieten**
the rent	**die Miete**
tenant	**der/die Mieter/in**
a contract	**ein Vertrag**
a lease	**ein Mietvertrag**
to sign a lease	**einen Mietvertrag abschließen**
to cancel a lease	**einen Mietvertrag auflösen**
to terminate lease	**einen Mietvertrag kündigen**
rented flat	**die Mietwohnung (en)**
block of flats	**das Mietshaus (en)**
increase	**die Erhöhung**
rent increase	**die Mieterhöhung**

to demand a rent increase	eine Mieterhöhung verlangen
tenancy	das Mietverhältnis (se)
arrears	der Rückstand (¨e)
rent arrears	die Mietrückstände
the law	das Recht
rent law	das Mietrecht
to rent a house	ein Haus mieten
to get back the deposit	die Mietkaution zurückerhalten
the landlord	der/die Vermieter/in
letting	die Vermietung
to let	vermieten
rentable	vermietbar
Do you rent rooms?	Vermieten Sie Zimmer?

Useful verbs

to buy	kaufen
to sell	verkaufen
to rent	mieten
to view (a house)	besichtigen
to make an appointment	einen Termin vereinbaren

Insight

Look out for the following false friend. **Die Kaution** ≠ caution. English *caution* is **Vorsicht**. **Die Kaution** means a deposit.

If you are intending to buy or rent somewhere to live in Germany, or purely wish to familiarize yourself with authentic adverts, go to local newspapers online or to German websites such as www.immobilienscout24.de or www.ziegert-immobilien.de. I suggest going to sites in which house descriptions are in German and English which is a great way to improve your German.

5.2 Rooms

Core vocabulary

room	**das Zimmer (-)**
entrance	**der Eingang ("e)**
dining room	**das Esszimmer**
sitting room	**das Wohnzimmer**
bedroom	**das Schlafzimmer**
play room	**das Kinderzimmer**
bathroom	**das Badezimmer**
guest toilet	**die Gästetoilette (n)**
study/office	**das Studienzimmer/das Büro (s)**
shower	**die Dusche (n)**
stairs	**die Treppe (n)**
utility room	**die Vorratskammer (n)**
junk room	**die Abstellkammer (n)**
window	**das Fenster (-)**
radiator	**der Heizkörper (-)**
floor	**der Fußboden (")**
foot	**der Fuß**
attic	**der Dachboden ("-)**
ceiling	**die Decke (n)**
door	**die Tür (en)**
wall	**die Wand ("e)**
window sill	**das Fensterbrett (er)**
heating	**die Heizung**

underfloor heating	die Fußbodenheizung
central heating	die Zentralheizung
double glazing	die Doppelfenster
solar-powered heating	die Solarenergieheizung
lock	das Schloss (¨er)
key	der Schlüssel (-)
plug	der Stecker (-)
socket	die Steckdose (n)
switch	der Schalter (-)
handle	der Griff (e)
fuse box	der Sicherungskasten (¨)
fuse	die Sicherung (en)
fuse wire	das Sicherungskabel (-)
torch	die Taschenlampe (n)
curtains	die Gardinen
blinds	die Rollos
shutters	die Rolläden
carpet	der Teppichboden (¨)
rug	der Läufer (-)
tiles	die Fliesen
flooring	der Bodenbelag (¨e)
wallpaper	die Tapete (n)
paint	die Farbe (n)
paintbrush	der Pinsel (-)
ladder	die Leiter (n)

Useful words and phrases

upstairs	oben
downstairs	unten
on the first floor	im ersten Stock
in the basement	im Erdgeschoss
in the attic	auf dem Boden
Where is the …?	Wo ist …?
How does it work?	Wie geht das?
to turn on/off	aufdrehen/abdrehen
to switch on/off	anschalten/abschalten
The floor has to be cleaned.	Der Fußboden muss gereinigt werden.

5.3 Furniture and room contents

Core vocabulary

Insight

A great way to learn new words in connection with the contents of a house is to put stickers on the items in your house for a few days so that you see them every time you pass. At first familiarize yourself with the words which are the same or similar in German and English. Remember to use the correct German pronunciation for the following words.

sofa **das Sofa**, *couch* **die Couch**, *lamp* **die Lampe**, *bed* **das Bett**, *bath* **das Bad**, *toilet* **die Toilette**, *shampoo* **das Shampoo**, *TV* **das TV**, *video* **das Video**, *radio* **das Radio**, *DVD* **DVD**.

furniture	**die Möbel**
sitting room	**das Wohnzimmer (-)**
armchair	**der Sessel (-)**
settee	**das Sofa (s)**
three-piece suite	**die Sitzgarnitur (en)**
coffee table	**der Wohnzimmertisch (e)**
bookcase	**das Bücherregal (e)**
picture	**das Bild (er)**
bedroom	**das Schlafzimmer (-)**
chair	**der Stuhl (¨e)**
wardrobe	**der Schrank (¨e)**
chest of drawers	**die Kommode (n)**
mirror	**der Spiegel (-)**
built-in cupboard	**der Einbauschrank (¨e)**
shelves	**das Regal (e)**
bathroom	**das Badezimmer (-)**
mirror	**der Spiegel (-)**
razor	**der Rasierapparat (e)**
shower	**die Dusche (n)**
wash basin	**das Waschbecken (-)**
toothbrush	**die Zahnbürste (n)**

toothpaste	die Zahnpasta (s)
television	der Fernseher (-)
video recorder	der Videoapparat (e)
DVD player	der DVD-Spieler (-)
remote control	die Fernbedienung (en)
bedding	das Bettzeug (pl)
pillow/pillow case	das Kissen (-)
quilt	die Steppdecke (n), das Federbett (en)
quilt cover	die Bettdecke (n)
sheet	das Laken (-)
fitted sheet	das Spannbetttuch (¨er)
wash basin	das Waschbecken (-)
taps	der Wasserhahn (¨e)
plug	der Stecker (-)
conditioner	die Pflegespülung (en)
hairdryer	der Fön (e)
soap	die Seife (n)
towel	das Handtuch (¨er)
deodorant	das Deodorant (s)
vacuum cleaner	der Staubsauger (-)
duster	das Staubtuch (¨er)
brush	die Bürste (n)
cleaning materials	das Reinigungsmaterial (ien)
scrubbing brush	die Scheuerbürste (n)
floor mop	der Fußbodenwischer (-)
detergent	der Reiniger (-)

Useful words and phrases

Where is the ...?	Wo ist ...?
It's on the table.	Es ist auf dem Tisch.
under the bed	unter dem Bett
in the armchair	auf dem Sessel
in the cupboard/drawer	in dem Schrank/in der Kommode
Can I have a clean ...?	Kann ich ein sauberes ... haben?
How does the (television) work?	Wie funktioniert der Fernseher?

He has to separate the rubbish in the kitchen into separate rubbish bins.	Er muss den Müll in der Küche in getrennte Abfalleimer tun.
She did not clean the stairs properly.	Sie hat die Treppe nicht richtig gereinigt.
The furniture should really be highly polished.	Die Möbel sollten wirklich auf Hochglanz gebracht werden.
She did not iron the tablecloths properly.	Die Tischdecken hat sie nicht richtig gebügelt.
The flat is in immaculate condition.	Die Wohnung befindet sich in einem einwandfreien Zustand.

Useful verbs

to do housework	die Hausarbeit machen
to wash	waschen
to clean	sauber machen
to do the vacuuming	staubsaugen
to make the beds	die Betten machen

5.4 In the kitchen

Core vocabulary

Insight

Look at the following words which are similar or the same in both languages and remember to use the German pronunciation.

washing machine **die Waschmaschine,** *salt* **das Salz,** *pepper* **der Pfeffer,** *glass* **das Glas,** *wine glass* **das Weinglas,** *water glass* **das Wasserglas,** *beer glass* **das Bierglas.**

Look out for the following false friend: *stool* ≠ **der Stuhl.** English *stool* is **der Hocker. Der Stuhl** means *chair*.

in the kitchen	in der Küche
table	der Tisch (e)
chair	der Stuhl (¨e)
stool	der Hocker (-)
drawer	die Schublade (n)
cupboard	der Schrank (¨e)
shelf	das Regal (e)
sink	das Waschbecken (-)
fridge	der Kühlschrank (¨e)
dishwasher	der Geschirrspüler (-)
dryer	der Trockner (-)
mixer	die Rührmaschine (n)
liquidizer	das Mixgerät (e)
plate	der Teller (-)
dinner plate	der Essteller (-)
bowl	die Schüssel (n)
dishes	das Geschirr
cup	die Tasse (n)
saucer	die Untertasse (n)
mug	der Becher (-)
jug	die Kanne (n)
teapot	die Teekanne (n)
sugar bowl	die Zuckerdose (n)
knife	das Messer (-)
fork	die Gabel (n)
spoon	der Löffel (-)
mustard	der Senf
teaspoon	der Teelöffel (-)
soup spoon	der Suppenlöffel (-)
dessert spoon	der Esslöffel (-)
serving spoon	der Vorlegelöffel (-)
carving knife	das Tranchiermesser (-)
bread knife	das Brotmesser (-)
sharp knife	ein scharfes Messer (-)
champagne flute	das Champagnerglas (¨er)
tumbler	der Becher (-)

Some useful phrases

I like/dislike cooking.	**Ich koche gerne/nicht gerne.**
I'll do the washing up.	**Ich mache den Abwasch.**
I'll take the rubbish out.	**Ich bringe den Abfall raus.**

Useful verbs

Insight

When checking through vocabulary lists, it's a good idea to find the verbs which are the same or similar in German and English and highlight or underline them.

Cooking terms **Kochanleitungen**

to mix	**mischen/vermischen**
to beat	**schlagen**
to roast	**rösten**
to toast	**toasten**
to bake	**backen**
to steam	**dämpfen**
to grill	**grillen**
to barbecue	**grillen**
to peel	**pellen**
to cut	**schneiden**
to slice	**in Scheiben schneiden**
to chop	**hacken**

Dealing with waste

Insight

The following words to do with waste are the same or similar: *recycling* **das Recyling**, *paper* **das Papier**, *compost* **der Kompost**.

rubbish	**der Müll**
leftovers	**die Essensreste**
packaging	**die Verpackungen**
plastic bags	**die Plastiktüten**

kitchen bin/waste bin	**der Abfalleimer**
bin liner	**die Abfalltüten**
dustbin	**der Staubbeutel**
recycling	**das Recycling**
bottle bank	**der Glaskontainer**
paper bank	**der Papierkontainer**
compost	**der Küchenabfall/der Kompost**
clothes bank	**die Kleidertonne**

5.5 Outside

Core vocabulary

shed	**der Schuppen (-)**
footpath	**der Gartenweg (e)**
gate	**das Gartentor (e)**
in the garden	**in dem Garten**
flower bed	**das Blumenbeet (e)**
lawn	**der Rasen (-)**
flower	**die Blume (n)**
tree	**der Baum (¨e)**
weed(s)	**das Unkraut (¨er)**
herb	**das Gewürz (e)**
bulb	**die Blumenzwiebel (n)**

Types of tree

beech	**die Buche (n)**
birch	**die Birke (n)**
chestnut	**der Kastanienbaum (¨e)**
oak	**die Eiche (n)**

holly	**die Stechpalme (n)**
lime tree	**der Lindenbaum (¨e)**
oak	**die Eiche (n)**
willow	**die Weide (n)**
pine	**die Tanne (n)**

Types of flower

···

Insight
These flowers are easy to remember:

lily **die Lilie,** *narcissus* **die Narzisse,** *rose* **die Rose,** *tulip* **die Tulpe.**
···

carnation	**die Nelke (n)**
daffodil	**die Osterglocke (n)**
pansy	**das Stiefmütterchen (-) (n)**
sunflower	**die Sonnenblume (n)**

Tools, etc.

garden tools	**das Gartengerät (e)**
rake	**die Harke (n)**
spade	**der Spaten (-)**
lawnmower	**der Rasenmäher (-)**
strimmer	**der Rasentrimmer (-)**
wheelbarrow	**die Schubkarre (n)**
garden tractor	**der Gartentraktor (en)**
hose	**der Gartenschlauch (¨e)**
sprinkler	**der Sprenger (-)**
watering can	**die Gießkanne (n)**
weedkiller	**das Unkrautmittel (-)**
fertilizer	**Dünger (-)**

Insects and pests Insekten und Ungeziefer

···

Insight
When looking through vocabulary lists, look for nouns which
are similar to English and highlight or underline them.
···

ant	die Ameise (n)
bee	die Biene (n)
greenfly	die Blattlaus (¨e)
housefly	die Hausfliege (n)
mosquito	die Stechmücke (n)
spider	die Spinne (n)
wasp	die Wespe (n)

Furniture, etc.

garden furniture	die Gartenmöbel
barbecue	der Gartengrill (s)
table	der Tisch (e)
deckchair	der Gartentisch (e)
lounger	der Liegestuhl (¨e)
bench	die Gartenbank (¨e)
swing	die Schaukel (n)
slide	die Rutsche (n)

Useful phrases

The grass needs to be cut.	Das Grass muss gemäht werden.
They are ripe/not ripe.	Sie sind reif/noch nicht reif.
I like/dislike gardening.	Ich mag Gartenarbeit (nicht).
He/she has green fingers.	Er hat grüne Finger.
I am allergic to ...	Ich bin allergisch gegen ...
I have been stung!	Ich bin gestochen worden!

Useful verbs

to dig	**um**graben
to water	gießen
to plant	pflanzen
to pick	pflücken
to grow	wachsen
to cut the grass	schneiden
to weed	jäten

Special plants and features

mixed woodland	**der Mischwald**
spruce	**die Fichte**
fir (tree)	**die Tanne**

5.6 Tools and DIY

Core vocabulary

> **Insight**
>
> The following words in connection with tools and DIY are the same or similar:
>
> *hammer* **der Hammer**, *sandpaper* **das Sandpapier**, *ladder* **die Leiter.**

drill	**die Bohrmaschine (n)**
pincers	**die Kneifzange (n)**
pliers	**die Zange (n)**
saw	**die Säge (n)**
chain saw	**die Kettensäge (n)**
screwdriver	**der Schraubenzieher (-)**
spanner	**der Schraubenschlüssel (-)**
tape measure	**das Zentimetermaß (e)**
nail	**der Nagel (¨)**
bolt	**der Bolzen (-)**
nut	**die Schraube (-)**
staple	**die Krampe (n)**
brush	**die Bürste (n)**
paint brush	**die Farbbürste (n)**
scissors	**die Schere (n)**
scaffold	**das Gerüst (e)**
tile	**die Fliese (n)**
slate	**der Ziegelstein (e)**
window frame	**der Fensterrahmen (-)**
shutters	**der Fensterladen (¨)**

pipe	das Rohr (e)
tap	der Hahn (¨e)
wire	der Draht (¨e)
fuse	die Sicherung (en)
plug	der Stecker (-)
socket	die Steckdose (n)

Useful words and phrases

Can you fix it?	Können Sie das reparieren?
Yes, I can!	Ja, das kann ich.
It is impossible/easy to fix.	Es ist unmöglich/einfach zu reparieren.
to fix something to a wall	etwas an der Wand befestigen
that does not work	das funktioniert nicht
it is broken	es ist kaputt
pull it up	heben Sie/heb es hoch
put it down	legen Sie/leg es hin
I have to try it out first.	Ich muss das erst ausprobieren.
DIY	das Heimwerken
DIY shop	Heimwerkergeschäft

Useful verbs

Insight

The following verbs are the same or similar:

reparieren to repair, to hammer **hammern**, to nail **nageln**.

to screw	**schrauben**	to rub down	
to unscrew	**<u>ab</u>schrauben**	(use sandpaper)	**schleifen**
to paint	**<u>an</u>streichen**	to glue	**kleben**
to plane	**hobeln**	to solder	**löten**
to drill	**bohren**	to weld	**schweißen**
to fasten	**befestigen**		
to fix/mend	**reparieren**		
to cut	**schneiden**		

TEST YOURSELF

See how many questions you can get right without looking back at the unit.

1 *A terraced house* is:
   a ein Einfamilienhaus
   b ein Reihenhaus
   c ein Zweifamilienhaus

2 *For sale* is:
   a Zu vermieten
   b Zu leihen
   c Zu verkaufen

3 *A tenant* is:
   a ein Mietvertrag
   b eine Miete
   c ein Mieter

4 *A dining room* is:
   a das Wohnzimmer
   b das Schlafzimmer
   c das Esszimmer

5 *To cancel a lease* is:
   a einen Mietvertrag abschließen
   b einen Mietvertrag auflösen
   c einen Mietvertrag schreiben

6 *An estate agent* is:
   a ein Immobilienmakler
   b ein Vermieter
   c ein Mieter

7 What is a *daffodil*?
   a eine Sonnenblume
   b eine Tulpe
   c eine Osterglocke

8 Which of these verbs is *not* a separable verb?
   a staubsaugen
   b umgraben
   c verkaufen

9 What is *an attic*?
   a ein Dachboden
   b ein Untergeschoss
   c eine Etage

10 *Curtains* are:
   a Rollo
   b Rollläden
   c Gardinen

Answers: 1b; 2c; 3c; 4c; 5b; 6a; 7c; 8c; 9a; 10c

6

Entertaining, food and drink

6.1 Parties and celebrations

Core vocabulary

Congratulations!	**Herzlichen Glückwunsch ...**
on your birthday	**zu Ihrem/deinem Geburtstag**
on your anniversary	**zum Jahrestag**
on your engagement	**zu Ihrer/eurer Verlobung**
on your wedding	**zur Hochzeit**
on your silver wedding	**zur Silberhochzeit**
on your golden wedding	**zur Goldenen Hochzeit**
dinner	**das Abendessen**

a party	**eine Party**
a celebration	**eine Feier**

A formal invitation
We are pleased to announce the wedding of our daughter Anna with Mr Klaus Meier. The wedding ceremony takes place on Friday the 20th of October at 12 p.m. at St Magnus Church and afterwards lunch at Hotel Kaiser. We have great pleasure in inviting you.

Wir freuen uns die Hochzeit unserer Tochter Anna mit Herrn Klaus Meier bekannt zu geben. Die kirchliche Trauung findet am Freitag, dem 20.10. um 12 Uhr in der St. Magnus Kirche <u>statt</u>. Anschließend findet das Hochzeitsessen im Hotel Kaiser <u>statt</u>. Wir laden Sie dazu herzlich <u>ein</u>.

The reply
We thank you for your invitation to the marriage of your daughter and have great pleasure in accepting. Regards Mr and Mrs Braun.

Vielen Dank für die Einladung zur Hochzeit Ihrer Tochter. Wir nehmen die Einladung gerne <u>an</u>. Mit freundlichen Grüßen Herr und Frau Braun

We very much regret that we are unable to accept the kind invitation but we will be attending a conference in America at that time.

Es tut uns außerordentlich Leid, dass wir Ihre freundliche Einladung nicht annehmen können, aber wir sind zu diesem Zeitpunkt auf einer Konferenz in Amerika.

An informal invitation
Can you come to a party at our house on Wed evening from 8 to 12?

Am Mittwochabend gebe ich von 8 Uhr bis 12 Uhr eine Party bei mir zuhause. Kannst Du kommen/Können Sie kommen?

We would be delighted to come and are looking forward to it very much.

Wir kommen sehr gerne und freuen uns schon darauf.

Excuses (Entschuldigungen)

Sorry we/I can't make it.	**Es tut uns/mir Leid, wir können/ ich kann da leider nicht.**
Unfortunately I have to go to ...	**Leider muss ich**
to Hamburg.	**nach Hamburg**
to the theatre.	**zum Theater**
to the university.	**zur Universität**
I will be away on business.	**Ich bin auf Geschäftsreise.**
on holiday	**im Urlaub**
I have a meeting that I can't get out of.	**Ich habe eine Besprechung, die ich leider nicht absagen kann.**
My mother is ill.	**Meine Mutter ist krank.**

More words

an invitation	**eine Einladung**
a reply	**eine Antwort**
an acceptance	**eine Annahme**
a refusal	**eine Absage**
an excuse	**eine Entschuldigung**
a thank you letter	**ein Dankesschreiben**
a cake	**ein Kuchen**
champagne	**der Champagner/Sekt**
a toast (e.g to the bride)	**eine Ansprache/ein Trinkspruch**
a present	**ein Geschenk**
cheers!	**Zum Wohl/Prost**

Insight

You use **zum Wohl** when drinking champagne or wine and **Prost** in informal situations, mainly when drinking beer. **Zum Wohl** means *To your well being.*

Useful phrases

Let's have a party.	**Lassen Sie/Lass uns eine Party machen.**
Let's dance.	**Lassen Sie/lass uns tanzen.**
I would like to propose a toast.	**Ich möchte einen Trinkspruch machen.**

I would like to thank our hosts.	**Ich möchte dem/der Gastgeber/in danken.**
I've got a hangover.	**Ich habe einen Kater.**
I can't drink, I am driving.	**Ich kann nicht trinken, ich fahre Auto.**
I don't drink alcohol.	**Ich trinke keinen Alkohol.**

Useful verbs

to party	**feiern**
to eat	**essen**
to drink	**trinken**
to toast (the bride)	**anstoßen auf .../auf jemanden trinken**
to enjoy onseself	**sich amüsieren**
to overindulge/have too much	**es übertreiben, zu viel haben**
to get drunk	**betrunken werden**
to feel sick	**sich schlecht fühlen**
to be sober	**nüchtern sein**
to stay sober	**nüchtern bleiben**

6.2 Eating out

Core vocabulary

Insight

Spend a short while memorizing these similar words before trying to learn the other words on the same topic.

restaurant **das Restaurant**, *café* **das Café**, *beer garden* **der Biergarten**, *pizzeria* **die Pizzeria**, *bistro* **das Bistro**, *bar* **die Bar**, *icecream parlour* **das Eiscafé**.

inn	**das Gasthaus (¨er)**
	die Gaststätte (n)
	die Wirtschaft (en)
cake shop/café	**die Konditorei (en)**
snack bar	**der Imbiss (e)**
snack bar	**die Imbissbude (n)**
pub	**die Kneipe (n)**

menu	**die Speisekarte/die Karte (n)**
wine list	**die Weinkarte (n)**
wine list	**die Getränkekarte (n)**
waiter	**Ober/in**
waiter	**Kellner/in**
service	**die Bedienung**
tip	**das Trinkgeld (er)**
bill	**die Rechnung (en)**
receipt	**die Quittung (en)**

starter	**die Vorspeise (n)**
main course	**die Hauptspeise (n)/das Hauptgericht (e)**
dessert	**der Nachtisch (-)/die Nachspeise (n)**
coffee	**der Kaffee**
tea	**der Tee**

Useful phrases

A beer please	**Ein Bier bitte**
I would like to order ...	**Ich möchte ... bestellen**
I would like to ...	**Ich hätte gerne ...**
The menu/wine list please.	**Die Speisekarte/Getränkekarte bitte.**
I would like to pay.	**Ich möchte bezahlen.**
Is this seat still free?	**Ist dieser Platz noch frei?**
no thanks	**nein, danke**

| for you (leaving a tip) | **für Sie** |
| It tasted very good. | **Es hat gut geschmeckt.** |

Useful verbs

> ## Insight
>
> Similar verbs in both languages: *to serve* **servieren**, *to reserve*
> **reservieren**, *to book* **buchen**.
>
> You can use both these expressions *to book a table*: **einen
> Tisch buchen** or **einen Tisch bestellen**.

to order	**bestellen**
to pay	**bezahlen**
to choose	**auswählen**
to taste	**schmecken**
to try	**kosten/ausprobieren**
to take	**nehmen**
to book	**bestellen**
to take a seat	**Platz nehmen**

Drinks Getränke

> ## Insight
>
> You will find that many words in connection with drinks
> are the same or very similar in both languages. Look out for
> these words and highlight them.

soft drinks	**alkoholfreie Getränke**
orange juice	**der Orangensaft (¨e)**
water	**das Wasser**
mineral water	**das Mineralwasser**
fizzy	**der Sprudel**
still	**ohne Kohlensäure**
aperitif	**der Aperitif (s)**
cocktail	**der Cocktail (s)**
sherry	**der Sherry (s)**
gin and tonic	**Gin und Tonic (s)**
red wine	**der Rotwein (e)**

white wine	**der Weißwein (e)**
champagne	**der Champagner (-)**
brandy	**der Brandy (s)**
liqueur	**der Likör (e)**
beer	**das Bier (-)**

6.3 German specialities

Insight

When you go to a German-speaking country look out for specialities (**Spezialitäten**) of the region and try them out. It is a good way to remember names for food, both the dishes you liked and those you didn't. Many dishes and specialities are named after regions or cities.

hamburger	**Hamburger**
sausage from Frankfurt	**Frankfurter Bockwurst**
meat balls in caper sauce from Königsberg	**Königsberger Klopse**
smoked sprats from Kiel	**Kieler Sprotten**
marinated roast from Rhineland	**Rheinischer Sauerbraten**
grilled sausage from Thuringia	**Thüringer Bratwurst**
marzipan from Lübeck	**Lübecker Marzipan**
traditional German Christmas cake from Dresden	**Dresdener Christstollen**
Blackforest gateau	**Schwarzwälder Kirschtorte**
spiced biscuits from Nuremberg	**Nürnberger Lebkuchen**
Bavarian sauerkraut	**Bayrisches Sauerkraut**

A lot of beers, too, are named after the area they come from:

beer shandy from Berlin	**Berliner Weiße**
beer from Cologne	**Kölsch**
beer from Clausthal	**Clausthaler**
beer from Detmold	**Detmolder**
beer from Flensburg	**Flensburger Weizen**

Germany is known for its sausages:

beer sausage	**Bierwurst**
ham sausage	**Schinkenwurst**
meat sausage	**Fleischwurst**
turkey sausage	**Geflügelwurst**
liver pate	**Leberwurst**
salami	**Salami**
cheese salami	**Käsesalami**
pepper salami	**Pfeffersalami**
onion salami	**Zwiebelsalami**
herb salami	**Kräutersalami**
smoked and air-dried hams	**Rohschinken**
cooked ham	**gekochter Schinken**
grilling sausage	**Bratwurst**
knackwurst	**Knackwurst**
bockwurst	**Bockwurst**
cocktail sausages	**Cocktailwürstchen**
frankfurter	**Frankfurter**

6.4 Fruit, vegetables and desserts

Insight

Look at the many words for fruit, vegetables and desserts which are the same or similar before learning the others. You will be surprised how many you can learn in a short period of time.

sauerkraut **das Sauerkraut,** *salad* **der Salat (e),** *olives* **die Oliven,** *radish* **das Radieschen,** *tomato* **die Tomate (n),** *broccoli* **der Brokkoli,** *carrot* **die Karotte (n),** *spinach* **der Spinat,** *cress* **die Kresse.**

apple **der Apfel ("),** *banana* **die Banane (n),** *grapefruit* **die Grapefruit (s),** *orange* **die Orange (n),** *avocado* **die Avocado (s),** *coconut* **die Kokusnuss("e),** *kiwi fruit* **die Kiwi (s),** *mango* **die Mango (s),** *melon* **die Melone (n).**

nut **die Nuss ("e)**, *cashew* **die Cashewnuss ("e)**, *hazelnut* **die Haselnuss ("e)**, *pistachio* **die Pistazie (n)**, *walnut* **die Walnuss ("e)**, *rice* **der Reis**, *apple strudel* **der Apfelstrudel (-)**.

Vegetables **das Gemüse**

cauliflower	**der Blumenkohl (e)**
Brussels sprouts	**der Rosenkohl (e)**
red cabbage	**der Rotkohl (e)**
white cabbage	**der Weisskohl(e)**
peas	**die Erbse (n)**
green beans	**die grünen Bohnen (-)**
asparagus	**der Spargel (-)**
cucumber	**die Gurke (n)**
lettuce	**der Kopfsalat (e)**
spring onion	**die Zwiebel (n)**
white beans	**die weißen Bohnen**
cabbage	**der Kohl/das Kraut**
courgette	**die Zucchini (s)**
garlic	**der Knoblauch**
leek	**der Lauch**
mushroom	**der Pilz (e)**
onion	**die Zwiebel (n)**
sweetcorn	**der Mais**
turnip	**die Rübe (n)**
shallots	**die Schalotte (n)**

Fruit **das Obst**

cooking apple	**der Kochapfel**
apricot	**die Aprikose (n)**
pineapple	**die Ananas (-)**
grapes	**die Weintrauben**
cherry	**die Kirsche (n)**
peach	**der Pfirsich (e)**
pear	**die Birne (n)**
plum	**die Pflaume (n)**
raspberry	**die Himbeere (n)**
rhubarb	**der Rharbarba (-)**
strawberry	**die Erdbeere (n)**

grapefruit	**die Grapefruit (s), die Pampelmuse(n)**
lemon	**die Zitrone (n)**
lime	**die Limone (n)**
berries	**die Beeren**
blackcurrant	**die schwarze Johannisbeere (n)**
blueberry/bilberry	**die Blaubeere (n)**
cranberry	**die Preiselbeere (n)**
gooseberry	**die Stachelbeere (n)**
redcurrant	**rote Johannesbeere (n)**
date	**die Dattel (n)**
passion fruit	**die Passionsfrucht (¨e)**
almond	**die Mandel (n)**
peanut	**die Erdnuss (¨e)**
lentil	**die Linse (n)**
pumpkin	**der Kürbis (se)**
potato	**die Kartoffel (n)**
pasta	**die Nudeln (pl)**
	die Spaghetti (pl)
	Spätzle *(type of pasta)*
chips	**die Pommes frites (pl)**

Desserts **die Nachspeisen**

fruit sundae	**der Früchtebecher (-)**
chocolate gateau	**die Sachertorte (n)**
black forest gateau	**die Schwarzwälderkirschtorte**
cheesecake	**die Käsetorte (n)**
whipped cream	**die Schlagsahne**
ice cream	**das Eis (-)**

....

Insight
Many words for ice-cream flavours are similar. Find them and highlight them.
....

apricot	**Aprikoseneis**
strawberry	**Erdbeereis**
chocolate	**Schokoladeneis**
vanilla	**Vanilleeis**
coconut	**Kokosnusseis**

pistachio	**Pistazieneis**
lemon	**Zitroneneis**
raspberry	**Himbeereis**
gooseberry	**Stachelbeereis**
stracciatella	**Stracciatella**
vanilla with almonds	**Vanilleeis mit Mandeln**

Insight

Germany is known for its soft cheese (**Quark**), eaten as a dessert with sweet ingredients such as fresh fruit:

cherries	**Kirschquark**
strawberries	**Erdbeerquark**
bananas	**Bananenquark**
apricot	**Aprikosenquark**
mixed fruit	**Früchtequark**

You can also eat **Quark** with savoury ingredients on bread, with garlic (**Knoblauch**) and herbs (**Kräutern**):

| with herbs | **Kräuterquark** |
| with horseradish | **Mererettichquark** |

6.5 Tea and coffee

Core vocabulary

Insight

First look at these words which are the same or similar in English and German, and memorize them.

coffee **der Kaffee**, *tea* **der Tee**, *espresso* **der Expresso**, *cappuccino* **der Cappuccino**, *sugar* **der Zucker**, *milk* **die Milch**, *water* **das Wasser**, *honey* **der Honig**.

latte	**der Milchkaffee**
coffee with milk	**Kaffee mit Milch**
coffee without milk	**schwarzer Kaffee**
with sugar	**mit Zucker**
without sugar	**ohne Zucker**
with sweetener	**mit Süßstoff**
decaffeinated coffee	**entkoffeinierter Kaffee**
Indian tea	**Indischer Tee**
China tea	**Chinesischer Tee**
herbal tea	**Kräutertee**
peppermint tea	**Pfefferminztee**
camomile tea	**Kamillentee**
fruit tea	**Früchtetee**
green tea	**Grüner Tee**
black tea	**schwarzer Tee**
with milk	**mit Milch**
with lemon	**mit Zitrone**
with sugar	**mit Zucker**
with honey	**mit Honig**

Useful phrases

I'm on a diet.	**Ich mache eine Diät.**
I am allergic to …	**Ich bin allergisch gegen …**
I don't eat …	**Ich esse kein/e/n …**
I can't eat …	**Ich kann kein/e/n … essen**
I am a vegan.	**Ich bin Veganer/in.**
I am a vegetarian.	**Ich bin Vegetarier/in.**
I am diabetic.	**Ich bin Diabetiker/in.**

Insight

Did you spot the similarities between the following words?

vegan **Veganer**, *vegetarian* **Vegetarier**, *allergic* **allergisch**.

Useful verbs

to like/dislike	**mögen/nicht mögen**
to eat	**essen**
to drink	**trinken**
to prefer	**vorziehen**
to love	**lieben**
don't like	**nicht mögen**
to hate	**hassen**
to do without	**verzichten**

6.6 Mealtimes

Core vocabulary

mealtimes	**die Mahlzeiten**
breakfast	**das Frühstück**
lunch	**das Mittagessen**
afternoon tea	**Kaffee trinken**
dinner	**das Abendessen/Abendbrot**
a snack	**etwas Kaltes/eine Zwischenmahlzeit**

Insight

Be aware of the following false friend: **die Marmelade** ≠ *marmalade*. **Die Marmelade** means *jam*. **Bittere Marmelade** is *marmalade*.

In Germany it is very common to go to the bakery first thing in the morning to buy **frische Brötchen,** *fresh warm crusty morning rolls.*

Breakfast **das Frühstück**

Insight

Start by looking at the following words to do with breakfast, which are the same or similar in English.

(Contd)

cornflakes **die Kornflakes**, *muesli* **das Müsli**, *milk* **die Milch**, *yoghurt* **der Joghurt (s)**, *tomatoes* **die Tomaten**, *grilled* **gegrillt**, *salami* **die Salami (s)**, *soya milk* **die Soyamilch**.

porridge	**die Haferflockenbrei/der Haferschleim**
wheat	**der Weizen**
oats	**der Hafer**
barley	**die Gerste**
rye	**der Roggen**
bran	**die Kleie**
semi-skimmed milk	**die fettarme Milch**
fat-free milk	**die fettfreie Milch**
soya milk	**die Sojamilch**
goat's milk	**die Ziegenmilch**
cream	**die Sahne**
bacon	**der Speck**
egg	**das Ei (die Eier)**
scrambled eggs	**das Rührei**
poached eggs	**verlorene Eier**
boiled egg	**das gekochte Ei**
hard boiled egg	**das hartgekochte Ei**
fried egg	**das Spiegelei**
sausages	**die Wurst/Würstchen**
mushrooms	**die Pilze**
fried	**gebraten**
tinned	**Dosen...**
baked beans	**gebackene weiße Bohnen**
pancake	**der Eierkuchen (-)/Pfannkuchen (-)**
maple syrup	**der Ahornsirup**
cooked ham	**gekochter Schinken**
cured ham	**roher Schinken**
cheese	**der Käse**

Bread **das Brot**

white	**das Weißbrot**
brown	**das Graubrot**
farm bread	**das Landbrot**
farmer's loaf	**das Bauernbrot (Switzerland)**

granary	das Getreidebrot
wholemeal	das Vollkornbrot
organic	das Biobrot/organisches Brot
rolls (crusty)	das Brötchen
rye bread	das Roggenbrot
sunflower bread	das Sonnenblumenbrot
linseed bread	das Leinsamenbrot
crispbread	das Knäckebrot
full grain rye bread	das Vollkornbrot
dark rye bread	das Schwarzbrot
sliced	geschnitten

Insight

Note the following words to do with bread and breakfast, which are similar to English.

bread **das Brot**, honey **der Honig**, butter **die Butter**, margarine **die Margarine**, toast bread **das Toastbrot**, jam **die Marmelade**, marmalade **bittere Marmelade**, organic bread **organisches Brot/Biobrot**, pumpernickel **der Pumpernickel**, croissants **die Croissants**.

More drinks

cold milk	die kalte Milch
hot milk	die heiße Milch
hot chocolate	die heiße Schokolade
fruit juice	der Fruchtsaft (¨e)
orange juice	der Orangensaft
freshly squeezed orange juice	frisch gepresster Orangensaft

Useful phrases

I don't eat breakfast.	Ich esse kein Frühstück.
I only eat ...	Ich esse nur ...
I don't drink milk.	Ich trinke keine Milch.
I like porridge.	Ich mag Haferschleim.
I don't like meat.	Ich mag kein Fleisch.

6.7 Snacks and fast food

Core vocabulary

green salad	**der grüne Salat**
mixed salad	**der gemischte Salat**
potato salad	**der Kartoffelsalat**
biscuit	**der Keks (e)**
chocolate biscuit	**der Schokoladenkeks (e)**
piece of cake	**ein Stück Kuchen**
sweets	**die Süßigkeiten**
sandwich	**belegtes Brot**
brown bread	**Graubrot**
white bread	**Weißbrot**
in a roll	**in einem Brötchen**
with/without mayonnaise	**mit/ohne Mayonnaise**
salad dressing	**Salatsoße**

curried sausage with mayonnaise	**Currywurst mit Mayo**
curried sausage with ketchup	**Currywurst mit Ketchup**
fried sausage	**Bratwurst**
fried sausage with potato salad	**Bratwurst mit Kartoffelsalat**
meatballs	**Frikadellen**
pancake with apple puree	**Pfannkuchen mit Apfelmus**
pasta	**die Nudeln**

Useful phrases

Can I offer you a cup of coffee?	**Kann ich Ihnen/dir einen Kaffee anbieten?**
How do you take it?	**Wie nehmen Sie/nimmst du ihn?**
With milk or without milk?	**Mit oder ohne Milch?**
Do you take sugar?	**Nehmen Sie/nimmst du Zucker?**
Have you got sweetener?	**Haben Sie/hast du Süßstoff?**
Would you like a biscuit?	**Möchten Sie/möchtest du einen Keks?**
Yes please.	**Ja bitte./Ja gerne.**
No thank you.	**Nein danke./Nein, vielen Dank.**
I am on a diet.	**Ich mache eine Diät.**
I don't take ...	**Ich nehme kein/e/n ...**
It's too hot/cold/spicy.	**Es ist zu heiß/kalt/scharf.**
It isn't cooked properly.	**Es ist nicht richtig gar gekocht.**
It is delicious!	**Es schmeckt ausgezeichnet!**

6.8 Fish, meat and cheese

Core vocabulary

Insight

Look first at the following words which are similar to English and try to memorize them. Make also a list of fish and meat you either like or don't like or make sentences such as: **Ich mag kein Fleisch, aber ich mag Fisch.**

(Contd)

> fish **der Fisch**, *mussels* **die Muscheln**, *oyster* **die Auster**,
> *mackerel* **die Makrele**, *herring* **der Hering**, *sardine* **die Sardine**,
> *crab* **die Krabbe**, *liver* **die Leber**, *langoustine* **die Languste**.

fish der Fisch

anchovy	**die Sardelle (n)**
cod	**der Kabeljau (s)**
haddock	**der Schellfisch (e)**
plaice	**die Scholle (n)**
skate	**der Rochen**
sole	**die Seezunge (n)**
tuna	**der Tunfisch (e)**
lobster	**der Hummer (-)**
prawn	**die Garnele (n)**
trout	**die Forelle (n)**
salmon	**der Lachs (-)**
perch	**der Barsch (e)**
pike	**der Hecht (e)**
eel	**der Aal (e)**
hake	**der Seehecht (e)**
jellyfish	**die Qualle (n)**
octopus	**der Tintenfisch (e)**
squid	**der Kalmar (e)**
whiting	**der Weißfisch (e)**

Meat das Fleisch

beef	**das Rindfleisch**
lamb	**das Lamm**
pork	**das Schweinefleisch**
veal	**das Kalbfleisch**
ham	**der Schinken**
kidneys	**die Nieren**
poultry	**das Geflügel**
chicken	**das Huhn (¨er)/das Hühnchen**
turkey	**der Truthahn (¨e)**
duck	**die Ente (n)**
goose	**die Gans (¨e)**
game	**das Federwild**

grouse	**das Moorhuhn ("er)**
hare	**der Hase (n)**
partridge	**das Rebhuhn ("er)**
pheasant	**der Fasan (e)**
pigeon	**die Taube (n)**
rabbit	**das Kaninchen**
venison	**das Wild**
wild boar	**der Eber**

6.9 Using a recipe

Core vocabulary

Insight
It's a good idea, when reading through vocabulary lists, to highlight words which are the same or similar in English and German.

making a cake	**einen Kuchen machen**
ingredients	**die Zutaten**
flour	**das Mehl**
baking powder	**das Backpulver**
yeast	**die Hefe**
potato flour	**die Kartoffelstärke**
sugar	**der Zucker**
butter	**die Butter**
salt	**das Salz**
melted chocolate	**geschmolzene Schokolade**
grated lemon rind	**geriebene Zitronenschale**
the juice of an orange	**der Saft einer Orange**
chopped nuts	**gehackte Nüsse**
grated chocolate	**geriebene Schokolade**
weighing scale	**die Waage (n)**
mixing bowl	**die Schüssel (n)**
wooden spoon	**der Holzlöffel (-)**
mixer	**der Mixer (-)**

grater	**die Reibe (n)**
sieve	**das Sieb (e)**
baking tin	**die Backform (en)**
oven	**der Ofen (¨)**
oven glove	**der Ofenhandschuh (e)**
silver foil	**die Silberfolie**
cling film	**die Plastikfolie**
plastic bags	**die Plastiktüten**
plastic containers	**die Plastikdosen**
saucepan	**der Kochtopf (¨e)**
casserole	**die Kasserole (n)**
frying pan	**die Pfanne (n)**
lid	**der Deckel (-)**
handle	**der Griff (e)**
making soup	**eine Suppe machen**
prepare the vegetables	**das Gemüse vorbereiten**
peel the carrots	**die Mohrrüben schälen**
chop the leeks	**den Lauch hacken**
melt the butter	**die Butter schmelzen**
add the flour	**das Mehl <u>zu</u>geben**
stir the mixture	**die Mischung verrühren**
pour in the stock	**die Brühe <u>ein</u>gießen**

Useful verbs

to heat	**erwärmen**
to cook	**kochen**
to roast	**rösten**
to fry	**braten**
to boil	**kochen**
to bake	**backen**
to poach	**pochieren**

Bratkartoffeln mit Eiern und Petersilie

1 kg gekochte Pellkartoffeln
60 g Butter
2 große Zwiebeln
Salz
frisch gemahlener weißer Pfeffer
6 Eier
1/8 l Schlagsahne
1 EL gehackte Petersilie
Zubereitung: ca. 30 Minuten

Pellkartoffeln <u>ab</u>ziehen und in Scheiben schneiden. Butter in einer großen Pfanne erhitzen. Kartoffelscheiben darin goldbraun braten. Zwischendurch die geschälten, gewürfelten Zwiebeln zugeben, salzen und pfeffern. Eier mit Schlagsahne verquirlen. Petersilie <u>unter</u>heben. Auf die Bratkartoffeln gießen und stocken lassen.

Guten Appetit!

Insight

Remember to say **Guten Appetit!** before you start eating.

TEST YOURSELF

See how many questions you can get right without looking back at the unit.

1 How would you say *Best wishes for your birthday?*
   a Herzlichen Glückwunsch zum Geburtstag.
   b Herzlichen Glückwunsch zur Hochzeit.
   c Herzlichen Glückwunsch zur Verlobung.

2 How would you say *I would like to order?*
   a Ich möchte bezahlen.
   b Ich möchte bestellen.
   c Ich möchte es ausprobieren.

3 Which expression would you use if you want to choose a soft drink?
   a Die Weinkarte bitte.
   b Die Speisekarte bitte.
   c Die Getränkekarte bitte.

4 Kirschquark is:
   a cherry tart
   b cherry cake
   c soft cheese with cherries

5 You would like to buy a loaf of wholemeal bread. What do you ask for?
   a Graubrot
   b Vollkornbrot
   c Landbrot

6 You would like to eat a fried egg. What do you ask for?
   a Gekochtes Ei
   b Spiegelei
   c Hartgekochtes Ei

7 You would like to order salmon, so you ask for ...
  a Seehecht
  b Lachs
  c Schellfish

8 How do you ask somebody: Would you like a coffee?
  a Trinken Sie gerne Kaffee?
  b Möchten Sie einen Kaffee?
  c Mögen Sie keinen Kaffee?

9 You don't like pork. What do you say?
  a Ich mag kein Kalbfleisch.
  b Ich mag kein Rindfleisch.
  c Ich mag kein Schweinefleisch.

10 You would like to eat scrambled eggs. What do you ask for?
  a verlorene Eier
  b Rührei
  c Spiegelei

Answers: 1a; 2b; 3c; 4c; 5b; 6b; 7b; 8b; 9c; 10b

7

In town

7.1 Town plan and sights

Core vocabulary

> **Insight**
> First look at the nouns which are similar or the same in English and in German and learn their gender. Remember to use the German pronunciation. If you are not sure how to pronounce German vowels and consonants go the pronunciation guide in the introduction or the audio recording at www.teachyourself.com
>
> *bank* **die Bank**, *hotel* **das Hotel (s)**, *market* **der Markt (¨e)**, *post* **die Post**, *cathedral* **die Kathedrale (n)**, *museum* **das Museum (Museen)**, *opera house* **das Opernhaus**, *park* **der Park (s)**, *statue* **die Statue (n)**, *theatre* **das Theater (-)**, *region* **die Region (en)**, *police station* **die Polizeistation (en)**, *monument* **das Monument**, *temple* **der Tempel**, *mosque* **die Moschee**, *kirk (Scottish)* **die Kirche**, *football stadium* **das Fußballstadium**.

bus station	**die Bushaltestelle (n)**
car park	**der Parkplatz (¨e)**
cinema	**das Kino (s)**
football ground	**der Fußballplatz (¨e)**
hospital	**das Krankenhaus (¨er)**
library	**die Bücherei (en)**

post office	**das Postamt ("er)**
station	**der Bahnhof ("e)**
swimming pool	**das Schwimmbad ("er)**
tourist office	**das Verkehrsbüro (s)**
town hall	**das Rathaus ("er)**
bridge	**die Brücke (n)**
castle	**das Schloss ("er)**
church	**die Kirche (n)**
mosque	**die Moschee**
temple	**der Tempel**
fountain	**der Springbrunnen (-)**
monument	**das Denkmal ("er)**
old town	**die Altstadt ("e)**
river	**der Fluss ("e)**
square	**der Platz ("e)**
district	**der Bezirk (e)**
town	**die Stadt ("e)**
suburb	**der Stadtrand ("er)**
town centre	**die Stadtmitte (n)**
industrial zone	**die Industriezone (n)**
council offices	**die Kommunalverwaltung**
law court	**das Gericht (e)**
opening times	**die Öffnungszeiten**
open	**geöffnet**
closed	**geschlossen**
holidays	**die Ferien**
bank holiday	**der Feiertag (e)**
annual holiday	**jährlicher Urlaub**

Useful phrases

Excuse me.	**Entschuldigung.**
I'm lost.	**Ich habe mich verlaufen.**
Where is the town hall?	**Wo ist das Rathaus?**
The town hall is situated on the square.	**Das Rathaus befindet sich auf dem Platz.**
How do I get to ...?	**Wie komme ich ...?**
How do I get to the theatre?	**Wie komme ich zum Theater?**

How do I get to the main street?	**Wie komme ich zur Hauptstraße?**
It is in the centre.	**Es/sie/er ist im Stadtzentrum.**
on the main street	**an der Hauptstraße**
near the post office	**in der Nähe der Post**
opposite the bank	**gegenüber der Bank**
at the marketplace	**auf dem Marktplatz**
beside the river	**neben dem Fluss**
Where shall we meet?	**Wo wollen wir uns treffen?**

Insight

Remember: When asking for places you use **zum** for masculine and neuter nouns and **zur** with feminine nouns.

Wie komme ich zur Post? but: **Wie komme ich zum Bahnhof?** If you are not sure about the article, don't worry: people will still understand where you want to go to.

Useful verbs

to meet	**treffen**
to look for	**suchen**
to be situated	**sich befinden**
to be lost	**sich verlaufen**

Insight

If you ring up to find out when the bank is open, this is the sort of message you might hear:

Unsere Bankfiliale ist montags von 8 Uhr bis 16 Uhr geöffnet. Wir sind samstags und sonntags geschlossen.

The bank is open Mondays from 8 a.m. to 4 p.m. We are closed on Saturdays and Sundays.

At a doctor's surgery.

Hier ist die Gemeindschaftpraxis von Dr. Sauer und
Dr. Blumenstock. Es tut uns Leid, aber die Praxis ist zur
Zeit geschlossen. Unsere Öffnungszeiten sind wie folgt:
montags bis freitags von 9 Uhr bis 18 Uhr. In dringenden
Notfällen rufen Sie bitte die folgende Telefonnummer an ...

*You are connected to the surgery of Dr Sauer and Dr Blumenstock.
We are sorry but our surgery is closed at present. Our opening
hours are as follows: Monday to Friday from 9 a.m. to 6 p.m. In an
emergency please phone the following telephone number ...*

7.2 Getting around town

Core vocabulary

road/street	**die Straße (n)**
avenue	**die Allee (n)**
pavement	**der Bürgersteig (e)**
gutter	**die Gosse (n)**
pedestrian	**der Fußgänger**
pedestrian crossing	**der Zebrastreifen (-)**
pedestrian zone	**die Fußgängerzone (n)**
traffic lights	**die Ampel (n)**
subway (foot passage)	**die Unterführung (en)**
parking disc	**die Parkscheibe**
parking meter	**die Parkuhr**

Insight

Note the following false friend: **die Allee** ≠ *alley*. *Alley* in
German is **eine enge Gasse. Die Allee** is *an avenue* in English.

How do I get into town?	**Wie komme ich in die Stadt?**
by car	**mit dem Auto**
by bus	**mit dem Bus**
by tram	**mit der Straßenbahn**
by subway (metro)	**mit der U-Bahn**
by bike	**mit dem Fahrrad**

Where is ...? **Wo ist ...?**

the bus stop	**die Bushaltestelle**
the subway station	**die U-Bahnstation**
the taxi stop	**der Taxistand**
parking the car	**das Auto parken**
car park	**der Parkplatz (¨e)**
multi-storey car park	**das Parkhaus (¨er)**
underground car park	**die unterirdische Garage**
full	**besetzt**
spaces	**frei**
entrance	**der Eingang (¨e)**
exit	**der Ausgang (¨e)**
ticket machine	**der Parkautomat (en)**
change	**das Wechselgeld**
credit card	**die Kreditkarte (n)**
ticket	**das Ticket(s)/die Karte (n)**
barrier	**die Schranke (n)**
traffic warden	**der/die Verkehrspolizist/in (en) (nen)**
one-way street	**die Einbahnstraße (n)**

Insight

Most car parks will have signs telling you how many spaces are available on each level and some will even indicate which spaces are free:

free spaces	**Plätze frei**
no spaces	**voll**
no spaces	**besetzt**

Useful words and phrases

Cross the road.	**Überqueren Sie/Überquer die Straße!**
Use the crossing!	**Benutzen Sie/Benutz den Übergang!**
Don't cross!	**Nicht überqueren!**
There's a car coming!	**Da kommt ein Auto!**
Wait until it is green.	**Warten Sie/warte bis es grün ist!**

Go	Gehen Sie/geh
Excuse me ...	Entschuldigen Sie?/Entschuldigung
Can you tell me ...	Können Sie mir sagen ...
How do I get to ...?	Wie komme ich zur/zum/nach ...?
Where is the nearest car park?	Wo ist der nächste Parkplatz?
When is the next bus to ...?	Wann fährt der nächste Bus nach ...?

Useful verbs

to walk	gehen
to cross	überqueren
to turn left/right	rechts/links abbiegen
to go straight on	geradeaus gehen
to run	laufen
to drive	fahren
to catch the bus	einen Bus nehmen
to miss the bus	einen Bus verpassen

Insight

Some street signs you might see in pedestrian areas:

No entrance	Kein Eintritt
Emergency exit	Notausgang
Not drinking water	Kein Trinkwasser
Danger!	Vorsicht!
Go to the left	Links gehen
Bus/tram stop	Haltestelle
Careful! Building work	Vorsicht! Bauarbeiten
Careful! Cyclists	Achtung! Fahrradfahrer
... is forbidden	... verboten
no swimming	Schwimmen verboten
no smoking	Rauchen verboten
do not walk on the grass	Rasen betreten verboten
no ballgames	Ball spielen verboten

7.3 Shops and shopping

Core vocabulary

Insight

Start by learning these words which are similar or the same in English. Note that all of them are masculine, which will help you to remember them.

market **der Markt (¨e)**, *bakery* **der Bäcker/die Bäckerei (en)**, *supermarket* **der Supermarkt (¨e)**, *optician* **der Optiker (-)**, *lift* **der Lift**, *price* **der Preis**, *shop* **der Shop**.

shop	**das Geschäft (e)/der Shop**
butcher	**der Fleischer/die Metzgerei (en)**
cake shop	**die Konditorei (en)**
chemist	**die Drogerie (n)**
clothes shop	**das Kleidungsgeschäft (e)**
department store	**das Kaufhaus (¨er)**
flower shop	**das Blumengeschäft (e)**
hairdresser	**der Frisör (e)**
shoe shop	**der Schuhladen (¨)**
sports shop	**das Sportgeschäft (e)**
confectioner	**der Süßwarenladen (¨)**
sweetshop	**das Süßigkeitsgeschäft (e)**
shopping centre	**das Einkaufszentrum (en)**
hypermarket	**der großer Supermarkt (¨e)**
department store	**das Kaufhaus (¨er)**
health food store	**das Reformhaus (¨er)/der Naturkostladen (¨)**
wholefood shop	**der Bioladen (¨)**
newsagent	**das Zeitungsgeschäft (e)**
dry cleaners	**die Reinigung (en)**
travel agent	**das Reisebüro (s)**
escalator	**die Rolltreppe (n)**
lift	**der Lift (s)/der Aufzug (¨e)/der Fahrstuhl (¨e)**

ground floor	**das Erdgeschoss**
first floor	**der erste Stock/die erste Etage**
bedding	**die Bettwaren**
department	**die Abteilung (en)**
fashion	**die Modeabteilung (en)**
sportswear	**die Sportabteilung (en)**
casualwear	**die Freizeitkleidung**
children's wear	**die Kinderabteilung**
leather goods	**Lederwaren**
television and electrical goods	**Elektrobedarf**
salesperson	**der/die Verkäufer/in (-) (nen)**
cash desk	**die Kasse (n)**
changing room	**die Umkleidekabine (n)**
customer, client	**der/die Kunde/in**
deposit	**die Anzahlung (en)**
discount	**die Ermäßigung (en)**

Useful phrases

How much does it cost?	**Wie viel kostet es?**
How are you paying?	**Wie bezahlen Sie/bezahlst du?**
Are you paying cash?	**Bezahlen Sie bar?**
Do you have the right change?	**Haben Sie es passend?**
Will you wrap it as a gift?	**Können Sie es als Geschenk einpacken?**
It is out of stock.	**Wir haben es nicht auf Lager.**

Useful verbs

to buy	**kaufen**	to order	**bestellen**
to sell	**verkaufen**	to deliver	**liefern**
to look for	**suchen**	to window shop	**bummeln**
to pay	**bezahlen**	to choose	**aussuchen/ auswählen**
to prefer	**bevorzugen**	to decide	**entscheiden**
to go shopping	**einkaufen/ shoppen gehen**		

The sales

summer sales	**der Sommerschlussverkauf**
the summer	**der Sommer**
the end	**der Schluss**
the sale	**der Verkauf**
winter sales	**der Winterschlussverkauf**
sales	**der Ausverkauf**
20% reduction	**20% Ermäßigung**
bargain	**das Schnäppchen**

7.4 At the supermarket

Core vocabulary

food department	**die Lebensmittelabteilung (en)**
fruit and vegetables	**Obst- und**
department	**Gemüseabteilung (en)**
dairy goods	**Milchprodukte**
frozen foods	**Tiefkühlkost**
cleaning materials	**Reinigungsmittel**
electrical goods	**Elektroartikel**
household appliances	**Haushaltsgeräte**
wines and spirits	**Wein und Spirituosen**
drinks	**Getränke**
bottle of water	**die Flasche (n) Wasser**
jar of jam	**die Dose (n) Marmelade**

box of paper hankies	die Packung (en) Papiertücher
tin of tomatoes	die Dose Tomaten (n)
packet of biscuits	die Packung (en) Kekse
tube of toothpaste	die Tube (n) Zahnpasta
photographic shop	das Fotogeschäft (e)
dry cleaning	die Kleiderreinigung (en)
flower shop	der Blumenladen (-)
card shop	das Kartengeschäft (e)
shopping list	die Einkaufsliste (n)
coffee	der Kaffee (s)
tea bags	die Teebeutel (-)
yoghurt	der Joghurt (s)
juice	der Saft (¨e)
milk	die Milch
water	das Wasser
sugar	der Zucker
flour	das Mehl
rice	der Reis
pasta	die Nudeln
ready meals	die Fertiggerichte
microwaveable meals	Mikrowellenprodukte
detergent	Waschmittel (-)
for the washing machine	Waschmaschinenpulver (-)
for the dishwasher	der Geschirrspülmaschinen-reiniger (-)
for the washing up	das Geschirrspülmittel (-)
cleaner	der Reiniger (-)
for the kitchen	der Küchenreiniger (-)
for the bathroom	der Badezimmerreiniger (-)
for the toilet	der Toilettenreiniger (-)
for glass	das Glasreinigungsmittel (-)
stain remover	der Fleckenentferner (-)
polish	die Politur (en)
assistant	der/die Verkäufer/in (-) (nen)
basket	der Einkaufskorb (¨e)
trolley	der Einkaufswagen (-)
cash dispenser	der Geldautomat (en)
check out	die Kasse (n)

Where is/are the ...?	**Wo gibt es ...?**
on the ... aisle/shelf	**im Gang/im Regal**
Where is the gardening section?	**Wo ist die Gartenabteilung?**
on the row with the ...	**in dem Gang mit ...**
at the far end	**am hinteren Ende**
on the left/right-hand side	**auf der linken/rechten Seite**
Is there a restaurant?	**Gibt es dort ein Restaurant?**
What time do you shut?	**Um wie viel Uhr schließen Sie?**
Are you open on a Sunday?	**Sind Sie sonntags geöffnet?**

Useful verbs

to weigh	**wiegen**
to look for	**suchen**
to find	**finden**
to deliver	**beliefern/liefern**
to order	**bestellen**
to order in advance	**in Voraus bestellen**

7.5 At the post office and the bank

Core vocabulary

> **Insight**
> When checking through vocabulary lists, it's a good idea
> to start by finding words which are the same or similar in
> English and German and highlighting or underlining them.

letter box	**der Briefkasten (¨)**
post office	**die Post/das Postamt (¨er)**
letter	**der Brief (e)**
packet	**das Paket (e)**
parcel	**das Päckchen**
postcard	**die Postkarte (n)**

writing paper	**das Briefpapier**
envelope	**der Umschlag (¨e)**
pen (ballpoint)	**der Kugelschreiber (-)**
stamp	**die Briefmarke (n)**
postman/woman	**der/die Briefträger/in**
money	**das Geld**
cash	**das Bargeld**
coins	**die Münzen**
notes	**die Scheine**
cheque book	**das Scheckbuch (¨er)**
credit card	**die Kreditkarte (n)**
phone card	**die Telefonkarte (n)**
telephone box	**die Telefonzelle (n)**
printed matter	**die Drucksache (n)**
recorded delivery	**das Einschreiben (n)**
overnight delivery	**die Express-Lieferung (en)**
air mail	**die Luftpost**
email	**die E-Mail**
cash machine	**der Geldautomat (en)**
cash transfer	**die Geldüberweisung (en)**
date	**das Datum (die Daten)**
amount	**der Betrag (¨e)**
signature	**die Unterschrift (en)**
sort code	**die Bankleitzahl (en)**
account number	**die Kontonummer (n)**
credit card number	**die Kreditkartennummer (n)**
expiry date	**das Auslaufdatum (daten)**
balance	**der Kontostand**
loan	**der Kredit (e), das Darlehen (e)**
mortgage	**die Hypothek (en)**

Useful words and phrases

insert your card	**stecken Sie die Karte <u>ein</u>**
type in your number	**tippen Sie die Nummer**
wait	**warten Sie**
remove your card	**entfernen Sie Ihre Karte**
take your money	**nehmen Sie Ihr Geld**

fill in the form	**füllen Sie das Formular <u>aus</u>**
go to the counter/cash desk	**gehen Sie zum Schalter/zur Kasse**
Where do I have to sign?	**Wo muss ich <u>unter</u>schreiben?**
How much does it cost to	**Wie viel kostet es, das**
send this to …?	**nach … zu senden?**
by air mail	**per Luftpost**

Insight

Note the following useful verbs on this topic, which are all separable.

to withdraw cash **Geld <u>ab</u>heben**, *to deposit* **<u>ein</u>zahlen**, *to fill in* **<u>aus</u>füllen**, *to phone* **<u>an</u>rufen**.

These two verbs are inseparable:

to transfer **überweisen**, *to sign* **unterschreiben**.

Extras

letter	**der Brief**
postman/woman	**der/die Briefträger/in**
post box	**der Briefkasten**
stamp machine	**der Briefmarkenautomat**
envelope	**der Briefumschlag**
letterhead	**der Briefkopf**
circular	**die Briefdrucksache**
penfriend	**der/die Brieffreund/in (e) (nen)**
correspondence	**der Briefverkehr**
to correspond with somebody	**mit jemandem brieflich verkehren**
to stick the stamp on the letter	**die Briefmarke auf den Brief kleben**
to put the letter in the letterbox	**den Brief in den Briefkasten stecken**

TEST YOURSELF

See how many questions you can get right without looking back at the unit.

1 Which of these nouns is masculine?
   a Post
   b Briefkasten
   c Telefon

2 Which sentence means that the shop is open?
   a Das Geschäft ist geschlossen.
   b Das Geschäft wird renoviert.
   c Das Geschäft ist geöffnet.

3 Which word means *tram*?
   a der Zug
   b die Straßenbahn
   c die U-Bahn

4 A *one-way street* is:
   a eine Durchgangsstraße
   b eine Sackgasse
   c eine Einbahnstraße

5 What is *an alley* in German?
   a eine Allee
   b eine Gasse
   c eine Gosse

6 **Ausgang** means:
   a entrance
   b exit
   c motorway exit

7 What is the word for *department*?
  a Abteilung
  b Erdgeschoss
  c Appartment

8 *To buy* is:
  a verkaufen
  b vermieten
  c kaufen

9 What is the word for *envelope* in German?
  a Briefumschlag
  b Briefkasten
  c Briefverkehr

10 *The checkout* is:
  a der Scheck
  b die Kasse
  c der Ausschank

Answers: 1b; 2c; 3b; 4c; 5b; 6b; 7a; 8c; 9a; 10b

8

In the country

8.1 The countryside

Core vocabulary

Insight

The following words in connection with the countryside are similar in English and German. Learning them will help you to build up your vocabulary faster.

land **das Land**, field **das Feld (er)**, stream **der Strom ("e)**, compass **der Kompass**, grass **das Gras ("er)**, plant **die Pflanze (n)**, wild flower **die Wildpflanze (n)**, moss **das Moos (e)**, fern **das Farn (e)**, bush **der Busch ("e)**, hedge **die Hecke (n)**, waterfall **der Wasserfall ("e)**, watermill **die Wassermühle (n)**, dam **der Damm ("e)**.

---

in the countryside	**auf dem Land**
meadow	**die Wiese (en)**
footpath	**der Fußweg (e)**
hill	**der Hügel (-)**
mountain	**der Berg (e)**
river	**der Fluss ("e)**
lake	**der See (n)**
valley	**das Tal ("er)**
points of the compass	**die Himmelsrichtungen**

north	der Norden
south	der Süden
east	der Osten
west	der Westen
northeast	der Nordosten
southwest	der Südwesten
northwest	der Nordwesten
southeast	der Südosten
mushroom	der Pilz (e)
tree	der Baum (¨e)
wood, forest	das Wald (¨er)
fence	der Zaun (¨e)
ditch	das Gebüsch (e)
gate	das Tor (e)
spring	die Wasserquelle (n)
pond	der Brunnen (-)
bridge	die Brücke (n)
weir	das Stauwehr (e)
reservoir	das Wasserreservoir (e)
hydroelectric power station	das Elektrizitätswerk(e)
copse	das Wäldchen (-)
beech	die Buche (n)
chestnut	die Kastanie (n)
elm	die Ulme (n)
oak	die Eiche (n)
sycamore	der Bergahorn (e)
willow	die Weide (n)

Useful phrases

Where shall we go?	Wohin sollen wir gehen?
What shall we do?	Was sollen wir tun/machen?
How shall we go?	Wie sollen wir gehen?

Useful verbs

to go for a walk	spazieren gehen
to go swimming	schwimmen gehen

to go hiking	**wandern (gehen)**
to ride a bike	**Fahrrad fahren**
to go fishing	**fischen (gehen)**

8.2 In the mountains

Core vocabulary

> **Insight**
>
> Start by checking the following words which are similar in
> English and German. This will help you to build up your
> vocabulary faster. Remember to use the German pronunciation.
>
> *the weather* **das Wetter**, *sunny* **sonnig**, *windy* **windig**, *extreme*
> **extrem**, *rucksack* **der Rucksack ("e)**.

hill	**der Hügel (-)**
mountain	**der Berg (e)**
mountain range	**die Bergkette (n)**
mountain pass	**der Bergpass ("e)**
mountain path	**der Bergweg (e)**
mountain railway	**die Bergbahn (en)**
elevated railway	**die Schwebebahn (en)**
funicular railway	**die Drahtseilbahn (en)**
mountain hut/refuge	**die Berghütte (n)**
cable car	**die Gondelbahn (en)**
summit	**der Gipfel (-)**
cloudy	**wolkig**
rainy	**regnerisch**
dry	**trocken**
easy	**leicht**
moderately difficult	**ziemlich schwierig**
difficult	**schwierig**
peak	**der Gipfel (-)**
rock face	**die Felswand ("e)**
slope	**der Abhang ("e)/das Gefälle (-)**

gorge	**die Schlucht (en)**
cave	**die Höhle (n)**
equipment	**die Ausrüstung (en)**
rope	**das Seil (e)**
harness	**der Klettergurt (e)**
carabiner	**der Karabiner (-)**
torch	**die Taschenlampe (n)**
stove	**der Kocher (-)**
dried food	**getrocknetes Essen**
waterproofs	**wasserfeste Kleidung**
knife	**das Messer (-)**
water bottle	**die Wasserflasche (n)**
sleeping bag	**der Schlafsack ("e)**
tent	**das Zelt (e)**

Useful phrases

What is the forecast?	**Wie ist die Wettervorhersage?**
How difficult is it?	**Wie schwierig ist es?**
How long does it take?	**Wie lange dauert es?**

Useful verbs

to climb	**klettern**	*to hike*	**wandern**
to abseil	**<u>ab</u>seilen**	*to rock climb*	**klettern**
to bivouac	**biwakieren**		

8.3 At the seaside

Core vocabulary

....

Insight

The following words in connection with the seaside are
similar in English and German. Learning them will help you
to build up your vocabulary faster.

sea **die See**, ocean **der Ozean (e)**, sand **der Sand**, cliff **die Klippe (n)**, wave **die Welle (n)**, harbour **der Hafen (¨)**, island **die Insel (n)**, quay **der Kai (s)**, yacht **die Yacht (en)**, boat **das Boot (e)**, sailing boat **das Segelboot (e)**, navigation **die Navigation**, buoy **die Boje (n)**, mast **der Mast (en)**, anchor **der Anker (-)**, rough **rauh**, sandy **sandig**, dune **die Dühne**

seaside	**an der See**
sand dune	**die Sanddühne (n)**
pebbles	**die Steine**
rock	**der Felsen (-)**
port	**der Fährhafen (¨)**
beach	**der Strand (¨e)**
reef	**das Riff (e)**
jetty	**der Anlegesteg (e)/die Landungsbrücke (en)**
pier	**der Brückenpfeiler (-)**
surf	**die Brandung (en)**
shore	**die Küste (n)/das Ufer (-)**
estuary	**die Mündung (en)**
cape, promontory	**das Kap (s)**
peninsula	**die Halbinsel (n)**
rowing boat	**das Ruderboot (e)**
dinghy	**das Schlauchboot (e)**
ferry boat	**die Fähre (n)**
car ferry	**die Autofähre (n)**
cruiser	**das Kreuzfahrtsschiff (e)**
liner	**das Fahrgastschiff (e)**
pilot	**der Pilot (en)**
port	**der Backbord (-)**
lighthouse	**der Leuchtturm (¨e)**
sail	**das Segel (-)**
rudder	**das Steuer (-)**
paddle	**das Ruder (-)**
satellite positioning	**die Satellitenausrichtung (en)**
automatic pilot	**die automatische Ansteuerung (en)**
ropes	**die Seile**
pedalboat	**das Tretboot (e)**

high tide	die Flut (en)
low tide	die Ebbe (n)
sea-level	der Meeresspiegel
calm	ruhig
choppy	böig
rocky	felsig
smooth	ruhig

Useful phrases

When is high tide?	**Wann ist Flut?**
Where can I moor?	**Wo kann ich mein Schiff <u>fest</u>machen?**
We would like to hire a pedal boat.	**Wir möchten gerne ein Tretboot mieten.**

Useful verbs

to row	**rudern**	to cast off	<u>aus</u>werfen
to sail	**segeln**	to tie up	<u>an</u>binden
to motor	**mit Motor fahren**		

Insight

Be careful: the meaning of the word **See** changes depending on the article. <u>**Der**</u> **See** = *the lake*; <u>**die**</u> **See** = *the sea*. Also be aware of the following false friend: *the lake* ≠ **die Lake**. *The lake* is **der See**, but **die Lake** is *a water paddle*.

8.4 Working in the countryside

Core vocabulary

Insight

The following words in connection with work in the countryside are similar in English and German. Learning them will help you to build up your vocabulary faster.

forestry **das Forstwesen/die Forstwirtschaft,** *tractor* **der Traktor (en),** *plough* **der Pflug (ˆe),** *farm* **die Farm (en),** *market* **der Markt (ˆe),** *garden* **der Garten (ˆ),** *stable/stall* **der Stall (ˆe),** *rice* **der Reis,** *hay* **das Heu,** *wine grower* **der/die Weinbauer/in (-) (en),** *apples* **Äpfel,** *pheasant* **der Fasan (e),** *lamb* **das Lamm (ˆer),** *hen* **die Henne (n),** *to cultivate* **kultivieren,** *to plant* **pflanzen,** *to milk* **melken.**

....

agriculture	**die Landwirtschaft/die Agrarindustrie**
bee keeping	**die Bienenzucht**
game keeping	**die Wildhaltung**
horticulture	**der Gartenbau**
wine growing	**der Weinbau**
trailer	**der Anhänger (-)**
harvester	**die Erntemaschine (n)**
farmhouse	**das Bauernhaus (ˆer)**
barn	**die Scheune (n)**
cattle shed	**der Rinderschuppen (-)**
crops	**die Ernte (n)**
grain	**das Getreide**
barley	**die Gerste**
oats	**der Hafer**
rye	**der Roggen**
wheat	**der Weizen**
straw	**das Stroh**
farmshop	**der Bauernladen (ˆ)**
bee keeper	**der/die Imker/in, Bienenzüchter/in (-) (nen)**
farmer	**der/die Bauer/in (-) (nen)**
farm worker	**der/die Landarbeiter/in (-) (en)**
horticulturalist	**der/die Gärtner/in (-) (en)**
vet	**der/dieTierarzt (ˆe)/in (en)**
vineyard	**der Weinberg (e)**
vine	**die Rebe (-)**
grape	**die Weintraube (n)**
fruit growing	**der Obstbau**
cherries	**Kirschen**
poultry	**das Federvieh**
turkey	**der Truthahn (ˆe)**

Words for families of animals

cow	heifer	bull	calf
die Kuh (¨e)	**die junge Kuh (¨e)**	**der Bulle (n)**	**das Kalb (¨er)**
sheep	ewe	ram	lamb
das Schaf (¨e)	**das Mutterschaf (e)**	**der Bock (¨e)**	**das Lamm (¨er)**
sow	pig	boar	piglet
die Sau	**das Schwein (e)**	**der Eber (-)**	**das Schweinchen**
goat	nanny	billy kid	
die Ziege (-)	**die Zicke (-)**	**der Ziegenbock (¨e)**	
dog	bitch	puppy	
der Hund (e)	**die Hündin (en)**	**kleine(r) Hund (e)/ Hündchen (-)**	
hen	chicken		
die Henne (n)	**das Hühnchen**		
duck	duckling		
die Ente (n)	**das Entlein**		
goose	gosling		
die Gans (¨e)	**das Gänschen**		

Useful phrases

Beware of the dog!	**Vorsicht! Hund**
Please shut the gate	**Tor schließen bitte**
electric fence	**elektrischer Zaun**
No entry/entrance	**kein Eintritt**

Useful verbs

to spread fertilizer	**düngen**
to weed	**Unkraut jäten**
to harvest	**ernten**
to feed	**füttern**
to breed	**züchten**
to sow	**sähen**
to pick	**pflücken**
to take to market	**zum Markt bringen**

TEST YOURSELF

See how many questions you can get right without looking back at the unit.

1 Ein Berg in English is ...
  a a mountain
  b a hill
  c a tree

2 What is the German word for *spring*?
  a Wassermühle
  b Wasserquelle
  c Wasserfall

3 *A mountain railway* is:
  a eine Bergbahn
  b ein Bergpass
  c eine Berghütte

4 *A lake* is:
  a die See
  b der See
  c die Lake

5 *High tide* is:
  a die Ebbe
  b die Hochebene
  c die Flut

6 *A turkey* is:
  a Türkei
  b Truthahn
  c Huhn

7 **Kein Eintritt** means:
    a Entry
    b No entry
    c No exit

8 *To harvest* in German is:
    a melken
    b füttern
    c ernten

9 *A grape* is:
    a eine Weintraube
    b ein Graben
    c ein Weinbau

10 Which of these translates *The sea is rough*?
    a Die See ist ruhig.
    b Die See ist rau.
    c Die See ist felsig.

Answers: 1a; 2b; 3a; 4b; 5c; 6b; 7b; 8c; 9a; 10b

9

Hobbies and sports

Insight

The following words in connection with hobbies are either Anglicisms or similar words in English and German. Learning them will help you to build up your vocabulary faster.

hobby **das Hobby**, *sport* **der Sport**, *to jog* **joggen**, *jazz* **das Jazz**, *dance* **der Tanz**, *to dance* **tanzen**, *gardening* **die Gartenarbeit**, *music* **die Musik**, *to take photographs* **fotografieren**, *tennis* **das Tennis**, *football* **der Fußball**, *to sing* **singen**, *film* **der Film**, *to film* **filmen**, *fishing* **fischen**, *horse riding* **reiten**.

9.1 Hobbies

Core vocabulary

I like ...	**ich ... gerne/ich mag ...**
I like to jog	**ich jogge gerne**
I like jazz dance	**ich mag Jazztanz**
acting	**schauspielern**
cooking	**kochen**
dancing	**tanzen**
modern	**moderne Tänze**
ballroom	**Standardtänze**
DIY	**heimwerkern**
drawing	**zeichnen**

gardening	**die Gartenarbeit**
going out (socially)	**ausgehen**
horse riding	**reiten**
listening to music	**Musik hören**
meeting people	**Leute treffen**
painting	**malen**
photography	**fotografieren**
playing tennis	**Tennis spielen**
playing football	**Fußball spielen**
to do pottery	**töpfern**
reading	**lesen**
sailing	**segeln**
sewing	**schneidern**
singing	**singen**
sport	**Sport treiben/machen**
walking	**spazieren gehen**
watching films	**Filme ansehen**
watching television	**fernsehen**
writing	**schreiben**
birdwatching	**Vögel beobachten**
fishing	**fischen**
hunting	**jagen**
shooting	**schießen**
rambling	**wandern (gehen)**

Useful words

archaeology	**die Archäologie**
astronomy	**die Astronomie**
history	**die Geschichte**
historical sites	**historische Plätze**
touring	**Reisen/Touren machen**
visiting foreign countries	**ferne Länder besuchen**
playing chess/cards/ bridge/party games	**Schach/Karten/Bridge/ Partyspiele spielen**
bingo	**Bingo**
jigsaw puzzle	**Puzzle**
dominoes	**Domino**
draughts	**Dame**

billiards	**Billard**
snooker	**Snooker**
table football	**Tischfußball**
crossword	**Kreuzworträtsel**
making music	**Musik machen**
playing in an orchestra	**im Orchester spielen**
singing in a group	**in einer Gruppe singen**
playing an instrument	**ein Instrument spielen**
piano	**das Klavier**
guitar	**die Gitarre**
violin	**die Violine**
trumpet	**die Trompete**
drums	**die Trommel**

Insight

An easy way to talk about hobbies and interests is to ask: *What do you do in your free time?* **Was machen Sie (machst du) in Ihrer (deiner) Freizeit?** When you answer remember: you use **mögen** with a noun and **gerne** with a verb.

Ich mag Sport/Ich mag Tennis/Ich mag Filme/Ich mag Gartenarbeit.

Use **gerne** with a verb: *I like to read.* **Ich lese gerne. Ich schwimme gerne. Ich jogge gerne.**

But also: *I like to play tennis.* **Ich spiele gerne Tennis.** *I like working in the garden.* **Ich arbeite gerne im Garten.**

For more on **mögen** and **gerne**, see the Toolbox.

Useful phrases

What do you do in your free time?	**Was machen Sie in Ihrer/ deiner Freizeit?**
I like to go for a walk.	**Ich gehe gerne spazieren.**
I like to cycle.	**Ich fahre gerne Fahrrad.**
Are you interested in ...?	**Sind Sie an ... interessiert?**

football/golf/music	Fußball/Golf/Musik
I am interested in ... art/ classical music	Ich interessiere mich für... Kunst/klassische Musik
It's interesting/fantastic.	Es ist interessant/fantastisch.
It's boring.	Es ist langweilig.

Useful verbs

to be keen on	sich begeistern für
to enjoy	genießen
to meet somebody	sich treffen
to spend my time	meine Zeit verbringen mit

Insight

Learn verbs to do with hobbies and interests in context as they need a bit of practice.

I enjoy listening to classical music. **Ich genieße klassische Musik.**

We meet every Friday. **Wir treffen uns jeden Freitag.**

Shall we meet? **Wollen wir uns treffen?**

I spend my time listening to music/reading the newspaper.
Ich verbringe meine Zeit mit Musik hören/Zeitung lesen.

9.2 Sports

Core vocabulary

Insight

German vocabulary in connection with hobbies is very often similar to English or even the same, especially words to do with *sport* **der Sport.** You will be astonished how many words are the same, but remember that the German nouns are all written with capital letters.

ball game	das Ballspiel (e)
football	der Fußball
ball	der Ball (¨e)
team	das Team (s)
goal	das Tor (e)
match	das Spiel (e)
football ground	das Fußballfeld (er)
to score a goal	ein Tor schießen
rugby	das Rugby
player	der Spieler (-)
pitch	das Feld (er)
basketball	das Basketballspiel
basket	der Korb (¨e)
volleyball	das Volleyballspiel
net	das Netz
hockey	das Hockey
hockey stick	der Hockeyschläger
golf	das Golf
golf ball	der Golfball (¨e)
golf clubs	die Schläger
golf course	der Golfplatz (¨e)
green	das Grün (s)
hole	das Loch (¨er)
bunker	der Bunker (-)
clubhouse	das Clubhaus (¨er)
tee	das Tee (s)
to putt	putten
to hole a putt	einlochen
good putt	der gute Schlag (¨e)
tennis	das Tennisspiel (e)
tennis racquet	der Tennisschläger (-)
tennis court	der Tennisplatz (¨e)
tennis ball	der Tennisball (¨e)
tennis player	der Tennisspieler (-)
match	das Tennisspiel
doubles	das Doppel
singles	das Einzel
mixed doubles	das gemischte Doppel

service	**der Aufschlag**
love	**null**
set	**der Satz**
advantage	**Vorteil**
badminton	**das Federballspiel (e)**
net	**das Federballnetz (e)**
shuttlecock	**der Federball (¨e)**
squash	**das Squash**
squash court	**der Squashcourt (s)**
squash racquet	**der Squashschläger (-)**
boxing	**das Boxen**
judo	**das Judo**
karate	**das Karate**
tae-kwando	**das Tae-kwando**
wrestling	**das Ringen**
running	**das Laufen**
cross-country running	**das Querfeldeinrennen**
jumping	**das Springen**
hurdles	**das Hürdenspringen**
track	**die Rennbahn (en)**
aerobics	**das Aerobic**
gymnastics	**die Gymnastik**
jogging	**das Joggen**
weightlifting	**das Gewichtheben**
weight training	**das Gewichtstraining**
yoga	**das Yoga**

Useful phrases

I like ...	**Ich mag/ich ... gerne**
Do you like ...?	**Mögen sie/Magst du ...?**

Useful verbs

to win	**gewinnen**	to box	**boxen**
to lose	**verlieren**	to do	**machen**
to draw	**unentschieden**	to jog	**joggen**
to play	**spielen**	to run	**rennen**

9.3 More sports

Core vocabulary

water sports	**der Wassersport**
canoeing	**Kanu fahren**
canoe	**das Kanu (s)**
paddle	**das Paddel (-)**
to paddle	**paddeln**
diving (deep sea)	**das Tiefseetauchen**
to dive	**tauchen**
wet suit	**der Taucheranzug ("e)**
dry suit	**der Trockenanzug ("e)**
oxygen cylinder	**die Sauerstoffflasche (n)**
mask	**die Tauchermaske (n)**
flippers	**die Schwimmflossen (-)**
snorkel	**der Schnorchel (-)**
to row	**rudern**
boat	**das Boot (e)**
oar	**das Ruder (-)**
to sail	**segeln**
sail	**das Segel (-)**
to surf	**surfen**
surfboard	**das Surfbrett (er)**
wind surfing	**das Windsurfen**
wind surfer	**der Windsurfer (-)**
yachting	**Boot fahren**
yacht	**die Yacht (en)**
dinghy	**das Schlauchboot (e)**
to swim	**schwimmen**
breast stroke	**das Brustschwimmen**
to do front crawl	**kraulen**

butterfly	**der Schmetterlingsstil**
backstroke	**das Rückenschwimmen**
diving	**das Tauchen**
swimming pool	**das Schwimmbecken (-)**
length	**die Länge (n)**
diving board	**das Sprungbrett (er)**
swimming costume	**der Schwimmanzug (¨e)**
swimming trunks	**die Badehose(n)**
goggles	**die Taucherbrille (n)**
archery	**das Bogenschießen**
bow	**der Bogen (-)**
arrow	**der Pfeil (e)**
to cycle	**Rad fahren/Fahrrad fahren**
racing bike	**das Rennrad (¨er)**
mountain bike	**das Mountainbike(s)**
bike	**das Fahrrad (¨er)**
handlebars	**die Lenkstange (n)**
saddle	**der Sattel (-)**
saddle bag	**die Satteltasche (n)**
to fence	**fechten**
foil	**das Florett (s)**
to ride a horse	**Pferde reiten**
saddle	**der Sattel (-)**
bridle	**der Zaum (¨e)**
stirrups	**der Steigbügel (-)**
to roller skate	**Rollschuh laufen**
skates	**die Rollschuhe**
to skateboard	**Skateboard fahren**
skateboard	**das Skateboard (s)**
to climb	**klettern**
mountain walking	**das Bergwandern**
mountaineering	**das Bergsteigen**
to (rock) climb	**im Fels klettern**
climbing boots	**der Kletterschuh (e)**
rope	**das Kletterseil (e)**
carabiner	**der Karabiner (-)**
rucksack	**der Rucksack (¨e)**

to go skiing	**Ski fahren gehen**
skis	**die Skier**
poles	**der Skistock (¨e)**
piste	**die Piste (n)**
to go snowboarding	**Snowboarden gehen**
snowboard	**das Snowboard (s)**
to go sledging	**Schlitten fahren/laufen**
sled	**der Schlitten (-)**
to toboggan	**rodeln**
toboggan	**der Rodelschlitten (-)**
to ice skate	**Eis laufen**
skates	**die Schlittschuhe (-)**
ice rink	**der Eisring (e)**

Insight

Look at the following verbs which are taken from the English language and 'made German' by adding **-en** or **-n** at the end.

to sail **sailen**, *to surf* **surfen**, *to box* **boxen**, *to fish* **fischen**, *to sing* **singen**, *to snowboard* **snowboarden**, *to relax* **relaxen**.

Useful phrases

I enjoy doing ...	**ich genieße ...**
I am good/not good at ...	**ich bin gut im ...**
I play ... well	**ich spiele gut ...**
I play regularly ...	**ich spiele regelmäßig ...**
I play from time to time ...	**ich spiele gelegentlich ...**
whenever I have time I ...	**so oft ich Zeit habe mache ich ...**

TEST YOURSELF

See how many questions you can get right without looking back
at the unit.

1 You use **mögen** in connection with:
   a nouns
   b verbs
   c adjectives

2 In German there are Anglicisms or similar words to English in
connection with sport/hobbies.
   a only a few
   b many
   c hardly any

3 The verb **segeln** means:
   a to sew
   b to sail
   c to shoot

4 *To be interested in* German is:
   a interessant sein
   b sich interessieren für
   c Interessanter Weise

5 Which of the following words is not the same in German?
   a golf
   b tennis
   c drums

6 *To take photographs* in German is:
   a einen Fotoapparat mitnehmen
   b ein Foto ansehen
   c fotografieren

7 *A gym* is:
- **a** ein Gymnasium
- **b** ein Fitness Center
- **c** Gymnastik

8 *I play tennis regularly* translates as:
- **a** Ich spiele oft Tennis.
- **b** Ich spiele regelmäßig Tennis.
- **c** Ich spiele kaum Tennis.

9 *Visiting foreign countries* in German is:
- **a** fremde Länder sehen
- **b** fremde Länder besetzen
- **c** fremde Länder besuchen

10 Ich begeistere mich für ... means:
- **a** I am keen on ...
- **b** I am bewildered about ...
- **c** I am enjoying ...

Answers: 1a; 2b; 3b; 4b; 5c; 6c; 7b; 8b; 9c; 10a

10

Clothing

> ### Insight
>
> Nouns which have been adapted from English in connection with clothing are:
>
> **der Pullover, das T-shirt, die Jeans, die Shorts, der Pyjama, das Neglige, der Blazer, das Sweatshirt, die Boxershorts, die Trainer, das Jersey, der Satin, der Tweed.** Try to memorize them first and learn the article with the noun at the same time.
>
> After you have familiarized yourself with the above nouns, look at the following words which are very similar in English and German.
>
> *socks* **die Socken,** *hat* **der Hut,** *to reduce* **reduzieren,** *length* **die Länge,** *width* **die Weite,** *shoulder* **die Schulter,** *material* **das Material,** *leather* **das Leder,** *linen* **das Leinen,** *wool* **die Wolle,** *striped* **gestreift,** *needle* **die Nadel,** *powder* **das Pulver,** *to wash* **waschen.**

10.1 Garments and styles

Core vocabulary

clothes	**die Kleidung**
ladies' fashion	**die Damenbekleidung**
blouse	**die Bluse (n)**
cardigan	**die Strickjacke (n)**
dress	**das Kleid (er)**
evening dress	**das Abendkleid (er)**
summer dress	**das Sommerkleid (er)**
jacket	**die Jacke (n)**
long jacket	**die lange Jacke (n)**
short jacket	**die kurze Jacke (n)**
jumper/sweater	**der Pulli (s)**
skirt	**der Rock (¨e)**
suit	**der Anzug (¨e)**
suit (jacket and skirt)	**das Kostüm (e)**
trouser suit	**der Hosenanzug (¨e)**
trousers	**die Hose (n)**
lingerie	**die Damenunterwäsche**
bra	**der BH (s) (Büstenhalter)**
knickers	**die Unterhose (n)**
stocking/s	**der Strumpf (¨)e**
tights	**die Strumpfhose (n)**
nightie	**das Nachthemd (en)**
negligee	**das Neglige (s)/das Hauskleid (er)/der Morgenanzug (¨e)**
men's fashion	**die Herrenmode**
jacket	**das Jackett (s)**
dinner jacket	**der Smoking (s)**
shirt	**das Hemd (en)**
suit	**der Anzug (¨e)**
tie	**die Krawatte (n)**
trousers	**die Hose (n)**
belt	**der Gürtel (-)**

braces	**die Hosenträger**
waistcoat	**die Weste (n)**
vest	**das Unterhemd (en)**
pyjamas	**der Pyjama (s)/der Schlafanzug (ˮe)**
changing room	**die Umkleidekabine**
fitting room	**der Anproberaum**

Insight

Remember that in German **der Pyjama**, **die Hose** and **die Brille** are all singular. In English these words are plural.

My pyjamas <u>are</u> warm. **Mein Pyjama <u>ist</u> warm.**

My trousers <u>are</u> new. **Meine Hose <u>ist</u> neu.**

Where <u>are</u> my glasses? **Wo <u>ist</u> meine Brille?**

coat	**der Mantel (ˮ)**
raincoat	**der Regenmantel (ˮ)**
hat	**der Hut (ˮe)**
scarf	**der Schal (s)**
gloves	**die Handschuhe (-)**

Useful phrases

The blue dress fits me.	**Das blaue Kleid passt mir.**
The hat suits me well.	**Der Hut steht mir gut.**
I will be wearing …	**Ich werde eine/n … tragen**
a dark suit	**einen dunklen Anzug**
a coat and hat	**einen Mantel und einen Hut**
a sweatshirt, jeans and trainers	**ein Sweatshirt, Jeans und Turnschuhe**
What will you be wearing?	**Was werden Sie/wirst du tragen?**
What size are you?	**Welche Größe haben Sie/hast du?**
I wear size 10.	**Ich trage Größe 10.**
it is too short	**es ist zu kurz**

too wide	zu weit
too long	zu lang
too tight	zu eng
Have you got anything bigger/smaller?	Haben Sie es/ihn/sie etwas größer/kleiner?
in a different colour?	in einer anderen Farbe?
It suits you/It doesn't suit you.	Es steht Ihnen/dir gut/es steht Ihnen/dir nicht gut.
I am going to wear a brown coat.	Ich ziehe einen braunen Mantel an.
Are you going to wear a dress or a skirt?	Ziehen Sie ein Kleid oder einen Rock an?

Insight

Retail in Germany uses a lot of Anglicisms. Nowadays you will find many shop windows using the sign *sale* instead of **Ausverkauf**. Look out for marketing slogans and adverts which use Anglicisms.

Young people also tend to use more and more Anglicisms in connection with shopping. English words are added to a German sentence, e.g. **Ich gehe heute shoppen und kaufe mir Jeans im Sale.**

Some useful vocabulary you might find in a clothes shop

clothing department	die Kleiderabteilung
ladies' clothing	die Damenbekleidung
gents' clothing	die Herrenbekleidung
children's clothing	die Kinderbekleidung
the till	die Kasse
sizes 10–16	die Größen 10–16
changing room	die Umkleidekabine/der Umkleideraum

Useful verbs

to wear	tragen
to fit	passen

to suit	**gut stehen**
to get dressed	**anziehen**
to take off	**ausziehen**
to take off	**ablegen**
to get dressed	**sich <u>an</u>ziehen**
to get undressed	**sich <u>aus</u>ziehen**
to put on	**<u>über</u>ziehen**
to get changed	**sich <u>um</u>ziehen/<u>um</u>kleiden**
to try on	**<u>an</u>probieren**

10.2 Measurements and materials

Core vocabulary

measurements	**die Maße**
tape measure	**das Zentimetermaß (e)**
length	**die Länge (n)**
width	**die Weite (n)**
size	**die Größe (n)**
collar	**der Kragen (-)**
neck	**der Hals (¨e)**
shoulders	**die Schultern**
sleeves	**der Ärmel (-)**
chest	**der Brustumfang (¨e)**
waist	**die Taillenweite (n)**
cuffs	**die Manschette (-)**
material	**das Material (ien)**
fabric	**der Stoff (e)**
It is made out of …	**Es ist aus … gemacht**
cotton	**die Baumwolle**
fur	**der Pelz (-e)**
artificial fur	**künstlicher Pelz**
jersey	**der Jersey**
leather	**das Leder**
linen	**das Leinen**
satin	**der Satin**

silk	die Seide
suede	das Wildleder
synthetic fibre	die Kunstfaser/die Chemiefaser
tweed	der Tweed
velvet	der Samt
wool	die Wolle
floral	geblümt
pleated	gefaltet
multi-coloured	mehrfarbig
patterned	gemustert
plain (one colour)	einfarbig
spotted	gepunktet
striped	gestreift
tartan	kariert
button	der Knopf (¨e)
thread	der Faden (¨)
snap fastener	der Druckknopf (¨e)
needle	die Nadel (-n)
ribbon	die Schleife (n)
scissors	die Schere (n)
sewing machine	die Nähmaschine (n)
velcro	der Klettverschluss (¨e)
zip	der Reißverschluss (¨e)
detergent	das Waschmittel (-)
detergent for wool	Feinwaschmittel für Wolle
fabric softener	das Weichspülmittel (-)
soap powder	das Waschpulver (-)

Useful phrases

I have lost a button.	Ich habe einen Knopf verloren.
Can I get this dry cleaned/ pressed (ironed)?	Kann ich das gereinigt/gebügelt bekommen?
How long will it take?	Wie lange dauert es?
Can you remove this stain?	Können Sie den Fleck entfernen?
Can you sew this button on?	Können Sie den Knopf annähen?

When do you need it back?	**Wann möchten Sie es zurück haben?**
Can you shorten it?	**Können Sie es kürzen?**
This garment must be dry cleaned.	**Das Teil muss gereinigt werden.**
This garment can be machine washed.	**Das Teil ist waschmaschinenfest.**
handwash only	**nur Handwäsche**
Don't use bleach.	**Nicht bleichen.**

Useful verbs

to wash	**waschen**
to dry	**trocken**
to dry clean	**reinigen**
to iron	**bügeln**
to mend	**ändern**

10.3 Special occasions

Core vocabulary

> **Insight**
>
> Some words are used in German which sound English but do not have the same meaning. For example, in German the word **der Smoking** is a *dinner jacket* (tuxedo).
>
> When tackling a new topic, remember to look out for words which are similar to English. Try to learn the German words with the correct article.

going to work	**zur Arbeit gehen**
uniform	**die Uniform (en)**
apron	**die Schürze (n)**
overall	**der Kittel (-)**
raincoat	**der Regenmantel (¨)**

rainhat	der Regenhut (¨e)
waterproof trousers	die wasserdichte Hose
rubber boots	die Gummistiefel
umbrella	der Schirm (e)/der Regenschirm (e)
anorak	der Anorak (s)
walking boots	die Wanderschuhe
thick socks	dicke Socken
woolly hat	die Wollmütze (n)
gloves	die Handschuhe
hard hat	der Schutzhelm (-e)
blue overalls	der blaue Overall
swimming costume	der Schwimmanzug (¨e)/der Badeanzug (¨e)
bikini	der Bikini (s)
trunks	die Badehose (n)
flippers	die Schwimmflossen
goggles	die Schwimmbrille (n)
snorkel	der Schnorchel (-)
flip flops	die Badelatschen/schuhe
suntan cream	die Sonnencreme (s)
evening wear	die Abendkleidung
evening dress	das Abendkleid (er)
high heels	die Stöckelschuhe
smart clothes	schicke Kleidung
polo shirt	das Polohemd (en)
shorts	die Shorts
socks	die Socken
trainers	die Turnschuhe/die Trainers
sweatshirt	das Sweatshirt (s)
T-shirt	das T-Shirt (s)
formal dress	die Gesellschaftskleidung
casual dress	die Freizeitkleidung
sports clothes	die Sportkleidung
school clothes	die Schulkleidung
jewellery	der Schmuck
bracelet	das Armband (¨er)
brooch	die Brosche (n)
earring	der Ohrring (e)

necklace	**die Halskette (n)**
ring	**der Ring (e)**
watch	**die Uhr (en)**
silver	**das Silber**
gold	**das Gold**
platinum	**das Platin**
diamond	**der Diamant (en)**
emerald	**der Smaragd (e)**
ruby	**der Rubin (e)**
sapphire	**der Saphir (e)**
semi-precious stone	**der Halbedelstein (e)**

Useful phrases

he/she always looks …	**er/sie sieht immer … aus**
casual	**leger**
elegant	**elegant/vornehm**
fashionable	**modisch**
smart	**schick**
unfashionable	**altmodisch**
untidy	**unordentlich**
stylish	**stilvoll**
to go out in	**zum Ausgehen**
smart clothes to go out with	**die Ausgehkleidung**
clothes	**die Kleidung**
cupboard	**der Kleiderschrank (¨e)**
to dress	**sich kleiden**
coathanger	**der Kleiderbügel (-)**
flattering	**schmeichelhaft**
clothes on offer	**das Kleidungsangebot (e)**
clothes department	**die Kleidungsabteilung (en)**
dress regulations	**die Kleiderordnung/zwang**

Useful verbs

to wear	**tragen**
to take off	**<u>ab</u>legen**
to get dressed	**sich <u>an</u>ziehen**

to get undressed	**sich <u>aus</u>ziehen**
to put around	**<u>um</u>legen**
to put on	**<u>auf</u>setzen**

10.4 Footwear

Core vocabulary

the shoe shop	**das Schuhgeschäft (e)**
hosiery	**die Strumpfwaren**
socks	**die Socken**
stockings	**die Strümpfe**
tights	**die Strumpfhosen**
leggings	**die Leggings**
I would like a pair of ...	**Ich hätte gerne ein Paar ...**
boots	**Stiefel**
clogs	**Clogs**
flip flops	**Badelatschen/Flip flops**
high heels	**Stöckelschuhe**
flat shoes	**flache Schuhe**
sandals	**Sandalen**
shoes	**Schuhe**
slip-ons	**Schlipper**
slippers	**Pantoffeln/Hausschuhe**
trainers	**Turnschuhe/Trainer**
wellingtons/rubber boots	**Gummistiefel**
sport shoes	**Sportschuhe**
ballet shoes	**Ballettschuhe**
climbing boots	**Kletterschuhe**
cycling shoes	**Fahrradschuhe**
dancing shoes	**Tanzschuhe**
diving boots	**Taucherflossen**
flippers	**Schwimmflossen**
football boots	**Fußballschuhe**
golf shoes	**Golfschuhe**
ski boots	**Skistiefel**

tennis shoes	**Tennisschuhe**
walking boots	**Wanderschuhe**
leather	**das Leder**
rubber	**das Gummi**
synthetics	**die Kunstfaser**
shoe polish	**die Schuhcreme**
shoe cleaner	**der Schuhreiniger (-)**
shoe protector	**der Schuhschoner (-)**
shoe stretcher	**der Schuhspanner (-)**
chiropody	**die Fußpflege**
massage	**die Massage (n)**
reflexology	**die Reflexologie**
foot	**der Fuß ("e)**
toe	**der Zeh (en)**
ankle	**das Fußgelenk (e)**
sole	**die Fußsohle (n)**
toe nails	**der Fußnagel (")**
arch of the foot	**der Spann**

Useful words and phrases

barefoot	**barfuß**
I have got sore feet.	**Mir tun die Füße weh.**
I have got blisters.	**Ich habe Blasen.**
Have you got a plaster?	**Haben Sie/hast du ein Pflaster?**
What shoe size are you?	**Was ist Ihre/deine Schuhgröße?**
These shoes are comfortable/ uncomfortable.	**Diese Schuhe sind bequem/ unbequem.**

Useful verbs

to try shoes on	**Schuhe <u>an</u>probieren**
to put on your shoes	**Schuhe <u>an</u>ziehen**
to take off your shoes	**Schuhe <u>aus</u>ziehen**
to get blisters	**Blasen bekommen**

TEST YOURSELF

See how many questions you can get right without looking back
at the unit.

1 *A dress* is:
   a die Kleidung
   b das Kleid
   c die Kleider

2 *Socks* are:
   a die Strumpfhose
   b der Strumpf
   c die Socken

3 **Bitte mit Smoking** would mean:
   a Smoking is allowed.
   b Dinner jackets please.
   c Please smoke.

4 Which verb is *not* separable?
   a anziehen
   b umziehen
   c tragen

5 *To get dressed* is:
   a sich ausziehen
   b sich anziehen
   c anprobieren

6 You would like to get your clothes dry cleaned. Which verb
should you use?
   a bügeln
   b trocknen
   c reinigen

7 The word for *umbrella* is:
- **a** Regenbogen
- **b** Regenschirm
- **c** Regenmantel

8 The word for *evening wear* is:
- **a** Abendkleid
- **b** Freizeitkleidung
- **c** Abendkleidung

9 A *watch* is:
- **a** eine Uhr
- **b** eine Weste
- **c** eine Stunde

10 A *suit* is:
- **a** ein Zug
- **b** ein Anzug
- **c** ein Auszug

Answers: 1b; 2c; 3b; 4c; 5b; 6c; 7b; 8c; 9a; 10b

11

Travel

11.1 Travel

Core vocabulary

Insight

Memorize the following words in connection with travel which are either similar or the same in English and German.

ticket **das Ticket**, *boat* **das Boot**, *route* **die Route**, *ferry* **die Fähre**, *on foot* **zu Fuß**, *reservation* **die Reservation**, *online booking* **die Online Buchung**.

journey	**die Reise (n)**
itinerary	**der Reiseplan (¨e)**
route	**die Reiseroute (n)**
map	**die Landkarte (n)**
overland	**auf dem Landweg**
by air	**auf dem Luftweg**
by sea	**auf dem Seeweg**
by public transport	**mit öffentlichen Verkehrsmitteln**
by train	**mit dem Zug**
by plane	**mit dem Flugzeug**
by coach	**mit dem Bus**
by car	**mit dem Auto**
by hire car	**mit dem gemieteten Auto**

by boat	**mit dem Boot**
by ferry	**mit der Fähre**
by bike	**mit dem Fahrrad**
on horseback	**zu Pferd**
on foot	**zu Fuß**
timetable	**der Fahrplan ("e)**
ticket (train, bus, tram)	**das Ticket (s)/die Fahrkarte (n)**
ticket (plane)	**der Flugschein (e)/das Ticket(s)**
booking, reservation	**die Buchung (en)/die Reservierung (en)**
online booking	**die Online-Buchung (en)**
arrival	**die Ankunft ("e)**
departure (train, bus)	**die Abfahrt (en)**
departure (plane)	**der Abflug ("e)**

Useful phrases

Can you help me please?	**Können Sie mir bitte helfen?**
I'm lost …	**Ich habe mich verlaufen …**
How do I get to …?	**Wie komme ich zum/zur …**
Is it far (to …)?	**Ist es weit (zum/zur …)?**
How far is it?	**Wie weit ist es?**
How long does it take?	**Wie lange dauert das?**
Where is the next bus stop?	**Wo ist die nächste Bushaltestelle?**
What is the best way to go to …?	**Wie komme ich am besten zum/zur …?**

Useful verbs

to travel	**reisen**
to go	**fahren**
to sail	**segeln**
to fly	**fliegen**
to drive	**fahren**
to tour	**touren**
to arrive	**<u>an</u>kommen**
to leave	**<u>ab</u>fahren**

Words and phrases with *fahren*

to go to	<u>hin</u>fahren
to go back	<u>zurück</u>fahren
to go up the hill	den Berg <u>hoch</u>fahren
to go down the hill	den Berg <u>runter</u>fahren
to go straight on	geradeaus fahren
to go into a one-way street	in die Einbahnstraße fahren
to continue driving	<u>weiter</u>fahren
Keep on driving!	Fahren Sie weiter!

Compound nouns with *Fahrrad*

the bicycle	das Fahrrad (¨er)/das Rad
cycle path	der Fahrradweg (e)

cyclist	der/die Fahrradfahrer/in (nen)
cycle route	die Fahrradroute (n)
cycle stand	der Fahrradständer (-)
cycle insurance	die Fahrradversicherung (en)
cycle test	die Fahrradprüfung (en)

Other useful words/phrases

ticket price	der Fahrpreis (e)
reduction	die Ermäßigung (en)
ticket reduction	die Fahrpreisermäßigung (en)
driving ban	das Fahrverbot (e)

11.2 Travel by train

Core vocabulary

train station	der Bahnhof ("e)
station master	der Bahnhofsbeamte (n)
booking office	der Fahrkartenschalter (-)
timetable	der Zugfahrplan ("e)
ticket	die Fahrkarte(n)/das Ticket(s)
single ticket	Hinfahrkarte/Einfache Fahrt
return ticket	Hin- und Rückfahrkarte
arrival	die Ankunft ("e)
departure	die Abfahrt (en)
indicator board	der Fahrplananzeiger (-)
information	die Information (en)
platform	das Gleis (e)
subway	die Unterführung (en)
stairs	die Treppe (n)
escalator	die Rolltreppe (n)
trains	die Züge
international long-distance trains	EC (Euro-City)
high-speed train	ICE (InterCity Express)
fast train	IC (InterCity)
limited-stop fast train	D (Schnellzug)
local train stopping at all stations	RE (Regional Express)

limited-stop local train	**SE (Städte Express)**
suburban railway	**S-Bahn (Schnellbahn)**
underground railway	**U-Bahn**
non-smoking	**Nichtraucher**
smoker	**Raucher**
first class	**Erste Klasse/First class**
second class	**Zweite Klasse/Second class**
trolley service	**der Essens- und Getränkewagen**
train restaurant	**das Zugrestaurant (s)**
train personnel	**das Zugpersonal (-)**
guard	**der Schaffner (-)**
ticket inspector	**der Fahrkartenkontrolleur (e)**
train driver	**der/die Zugführer/in (-) (en)**
passenger	**der Passagier (e)**
level crossing	**der Bahnübergang**
railway track	**die Schiene (-)**
train signal	**das Zugsignal (e)**
luggage	**das Gepäck**
suitcase	**der Koffer (-)**
left luggage	**die Gepäckaufbewahrung**

Insight

Memorize the following words in connection with travel, which are either the same or similar in English and German.

signal **das Signal**, personnel **das Personal**, waiting room **die Wartehalle/der Warteraum**, restaurant **das Restaurant**, bus **der Bus**, ticket **das Ticket**.

Useful phrases

Insight

There are many verbs in connection with travel which are separable verbs. Look out for them. Remember that separable verbs are all marked very clearly throughout this book. The prefix is underlined, e.g. **aussteigen** to get off a bus/train, so you will remember to split it off and add it to the end of the sentence. **Ich steige in Berlin aus**.

Do I have to change?	**Muss ich umsteigen?**
Where do I have to change?	**Wo muss ich umsteigen?**
Is the train on time?	**Fährt der Zug fahrplanmäßig?**
How late is the train?	**Wie viel Verspätung hat der Zug?**
Do we arrive in time?	**Kommen wir fahrplanmäßig an?**
Which platform does it leave from?	**Von welchem Gleis fährt der Zug ab?**
Which platform does the train arrive?	**Auf welchem Gleis kommt der Zug an?**
Is this the train for ...?	**Ist das der Zug nach ...?**
What time does the train leave?	**Um wie viel Uhr fährt der Zug ab?**
I have a reservation.	**Ich habe einen Platz reserviert.**
Sorry, but this is my seat.	**Entschuldigen Sie, das ist mein Platz**
How often does the train/ tram/bus run?	**Wie oft fährt der Zug/die Straßenbahn/der Bus?**
Which line do I need for ...?	**Welche Linie muss ich zum/zur ... nehmen?**

Useful verbs

to book a ticket	**eine Fahrkarte buchen**
to reserve a seat	**einen Platz reservieren**
to leave luggage	**Gepäck aufbewahren**

Extras

to get on	**einsteigen**
Get on board please!	**Alle einsteigen bitte!**
to change	**umsteigen**
Where do I have to change?	**Wo muss ich umsteigen?**
to get off	**aussteigen**
You have to get off at the next stop.	**Sie müssen an der nächsten Haltestelle aussteigen.**
the train	**der Zug (¨e)**
the connection	**die Verbindung (en)**
late	**spät**
delay	**die Verspätung (en)**
to be late	**sich verspäten**
Are we late?	**Gibt es eine Verspätung?**

11.3 Travel by plane

Core vocabulary

airport	**der Flughafen (¨)**
car park	**der Parkplatz (¨e)**
departures	**der Abflug (¨e)**
arrival	**die Ankunft (¨e)**
booking in	**die Flugabfertigung (en)**
desk	**der Schalter (-)**
luggage search	**die Gepäckdurchsuchung**
security check	**die Sicherheitskontrolle (n)**
which class?	**welche Klasse?**
economy	**die Touristenklasse/Zweiter Klasse/**
	Economy Class
first	**Erster Klasse**
ticket	**die Flugkarte (n)/das Ticket (s)**
departure lounge	**die Abflughalle (n)**
information	**der Informationsschalter (-)**
announcements	**die Ansage (n)**
flight	**der Flug (¨e)**
gate	**der Flugsteig (e)**
delay	**die Verspätung (en)**
plane	**das Flugzeug (e)**
row	**die Reihe (n)**

seat	der Sitz (e)
window seat	der Fensterplatz (¨e)
aisle seat	der Gang (¨e)
seat belt	der Gurt (e)
life jacket	die Schwimmweste (n)
emergency exit	der Notausgang (¨e)
overhead locker	das Handgepäckfach (¨er)
Can I have ...?	Könnte ich bitte ... haben?
earphones	Kopfhörer
a blanket	eine Decke
a pillow	ein Kopfkissen
a drink of water	einen Schluck Wasser
baggage reclaim	die Gepäckrückgabe (n)
baggage processing	die Gepäckabfertigung (en)
customs	der Zoll (¨e)
duty-free	Zollfrei
emergency landing	die Notlandung (en)
emergency exit	der Notausgang (¨e)
steward	der Flugbegleiter/Steward (s)
stewardess	die Flugbegleiterin/die Stewardess (en)
ticket	der Flugschein (e)

Useful phrases

The plane is delayed.	Das Flugzeug hat Verspätung.
Your flight leaves from gate ...	Ihr Flug fliegt vom Flugsteig ... ab.
Please will you return to your seats and fasten your seat belts.	Bitte kehren Sie zu Ihrem Sitz zurück und schnallen Sie sich an.
We are flying at an altitude of ...	Wir fliegen auf einer Höhe von ...
and a speed of ...	und einer Geschwindigkeit von ...
My luggage is missing.	Mein Gepäck ist nicht da.
I missed my connection flight.	Ich habe meinen Anschlussflug verpasst.
I can't find my boarding card.	Ich kann meine Bordkarte nicht finden.

Useful verbs

to leave/depart	**ab**fliegen
to fly	**fliegen**
to arrive	**an**kommen
to land	**landen**
to navigate	**steuern**
to put the seat back	**den Sitz** zurück**stellen**
to put the seat upright	**den Sitz** auf**stellen**
to miss	**verpassen**
to take off	**starten**

11.4 Travel by car

Core vocabulary

car	**das Auto (s)**
estate car	**der Kombiwagen (-)**
camper	**der Campingbus (se)**
sports car	**das Sportauto (s)**
convertible	**das Cabrio (s)**
automatic	**automatisch**
2/4 doors	**2/4 Türen**
accelerator	**das Gaspedal (e)**
brake	**die Bremse (n)**
clutch	**die Kupplung (en)**
windscreen	**die Windschutzscheibe (n)**
gears	**der Gang ("e)**
gear lever	**die Gangschaltung (en)**

steering wheel	das Lenkrad ("er)
handbrake	die Handbremse (n)
indicator	der Blinker (-)
headlamp	der Scheinwerfer (-)
side light	das Seitenlicht (er)
speedometer	das Geschwindigkeitsmesser (-)
milometer	der Kilometerzähler (-)
petrol gauge	die Benzinuhr (en)
interior	die Innenausstattung (en)
seat	der Sitz (e)
safety belt	der Sicherheitsgurt (e)
leg room	der Beinbereich (e)
glove compartment	das Handschuhfach ("er)
visor/sunshield	die Sonnenblende (n)
wing mirror	der Seitenspiegel (-)
rear mirror	der Rückspiegel (-)
heating	die Heizung (en)
air conditioning	die Klimaanlage (en)
wheel	das Rad ("er)
tyre	der Reifen (-)
valve	das Ventil (e)
tyre pressure	der Luftdruck
jack	der Wagenheber (-)
spare wheel	der Ersatzreifen (-)
boot	der Kofferraum ("e)
bonnet	die Motorhaube (n)
bumper	die Stoßstange (n)
number plate	das Nummernschild (er)
foglights	die Nebelleuchte (n)
rear lights	das Rücklicht (er)
exhaust	der Auspuff (e)
radiator	die Heizung (en)
ignition	die Zündung (en)
spark plug	die Zündkerze (n)
water hose	der Wasserschlauch ("e)
oil pressure	der Öldruck
fan belt	der Gebläseriemen (-)
windscreen wiper	der Scheibenwischer (-)

Useful phrases

You have left your lights on.	**Sie haben/du hast Ihr/dein Licht angelassen.**
How do I move the seat?	**Wie kann ich den Sitz verstellen?**
How do I open the boot?	**Wie öffne ich den Kofferraum?**
Does the car have an airbag?	**Hat das Auto eine Airbag?**

Useful verbs

to exchange	<u>aus</u>wechseln
to put your lights on	das Licht <u>an</u>schalten
to turn your lights off	das Licht <u>aus</u>schalten
to put your indicator on	blinken
to shut	schließen
to check	prüfen
to repair	reparieren

Insight

It is a good idea to make sentences with seperable verbs used in connection with travel in order to practise them. If you are not sure how to form sentences with separable verbs, go to the Toolbox section.

11.5 The road

Core vocabulary

country road	die Landstraße (n)
main road	die Hauptstraße (n)
one-way road	die Einbahnstraße (n)
carriageway	die Fahrbahn (en)
motorway	die Autobahn (en)
motorway lane	die Autospur (en)
inside lane	die Innenbahn (en)
outside lane	die Außenbahn (en)

access road	**die Zugangsstraße (n)**
road surface	**die Straßenoberfläche (n)**
good/bad	**gut/schlecht**
smooth/uneven	**glatt/uneben**
bumpy	**holprig**
potholes	**das Schlagloch (¨er)**
crossroads	**die Kreuzung (en)**
dead end	**die Sackgasse (n)**
roundabout	**der Kreisverkehr**
pedestrian crossing	**der Zebrastreifen (-)**
bridge	**die Brücke (n)**
toll bridge	**die gebührenpflichtige Brücke (n)**
traffic lights	**die Ampel (n)**
road works	**die Straßenarbeiten**
emergency traffic lights	**das Warnlicht (er)**
diversion	**die Umleitung (en)**
road sign	**das Verkehrszeichen (-)**
road work	**die Bauarbeiten (-)/Baustelle (n)**
road narrows	**die Fahrbahnverengung (en)**
speed limit	**die Geschwindigkeitsbegrenzung (en)**
speed trap	**die Radarfalle (n)**
traffic police	**die Verkehrspolizei**
driving licence	**der Führerschein (e)**
insurance	**die Versicherung (en)**
fine	**die Geldbuße (n)**
penalty ticket	**der Strafzettel (-)**
services	**die Dienstleistung (en)**
garage	**die Werkstatt (¨en)**
petrol station	**die Tankstelle (n)**
petrol	**das Benzin**
diesel	**der Diesel**
air	**die Luft**
water	**das Wasser**
oil	**das Öl**
oil change	**der Ölwechsel**
emergency services	**der Notfalldienst (e)**
breakdown	**die Autopanne (n)**

Useful phrases

I have broken down.	**Ich habe eine Panne.**
The car is overheating.	**Das Auto ist überhitzt.**
The engine does not start.	**Der Motor geht nicht an.**
I have a puncture.	**Ich habe eine Reifenpanne.**
The light does not work.	**Das Licht funktioniert nicht.**

Useful verbs

to speed	**rasen**
to accelerate	**beschleunigen**
to slow down	**drosseln**
to brake	**bremsen**
to give way	**Vorfahrt gewähren**
to overtake	**überholen**

Typical German road signs

Abstand halten!	*Keep your distance*
Achtung, Achtung!	*Watch! Look out!*
Bauarbeiten	*roadworks*
Durchfahrt verboten	*No through traffic*
Einbahnstraße	*one-way street*
Glatteisgefahr	*icy road*
Keine Einfahrt	*No entry*
Links abbiegen verboten	*No left turn*
Radweg kreuzt	*Cycle path crossing*
Rechts fahren	*Keep right*
Rechts einbiegen	*Turn right*
Sackgasse	*cul-de-sac*
Umleitung	*diversion*
Vorsicht!	*Be careful!*
Vorfahrt beachten	*Give way*

TEST YOURSELF

See how many questions you can get right without looking back at the unit.

1 The German verb *to travel* is:
   a reisen
   b gehen
   c fliegen

2 Which verb is *not* a separable verb?
   a abfliegen
   b ankommen
   c verpassen

3 To *switch your lights on* in German is:
   a das Licht reparieren
   b das Licht ausschalten
   c das Licht einschalten

4 What is the English word for **Abflug**?
   a arrival
   b timetable
   c departure

5 What is *a cycle path*?
   a ein Fahrradweg
   b eine Fahrradversicherung
   c ein Fahrradständer

6 When asking for directions you use **zur** for:
   a masculine nouns
   b neuter nouns
   c feminine nouns

7 Which of the following sentences means: *When does the train leave?*
  a Wann kommt der Zug an?
  b Wann hält der Zug?
  c Wann fährt der Zug ab?

8 The word **Verspätung** means:
  a arrival
  b delay
  c departure

9 *To get off the bus* is:
  a in den Bus einsteigen
  b aus dem Bus aussteigen
  c umsteigen

10 *To go by ferry* in German is:
  a zu Fuss gehen
  b mit dem Fahrrad fahren
  c mit der Fähre fahren

Answers: 1a; 2c; 3c; 4c; 5a; 6c; 7c; 8b; 9b; 10c

12

Tourism

12.1 Where to go

Core vocabulary

> **Insight**
>
> It is a good exercise to memorize German compound words
> which are based on the same stem. Look at these examples:
>
> **der Tourismus** *tourism*, **die Touristen** *tourists*, **die
> Tourismusindustrie** *tourist industry*, **die Touristenklasse** *tourist
> class*, **das Touristenverkehrsamt** *tourist information office*, **die
> Touristenorte** *places for tourists*, **touristische Attraktionen**
> *tourist attractions*.
>
> The following words are similar in both languages:
>
> *tour* **die Tour (en)**, *to tour* **touren**, *brochure* **die Broschüre**.

tourist industry	**die Tourismusindustrie (en)/die Fremdenverkehrsindustrie (n)**
travel agent	**das Reisebüro (s)**
travel brochure	**der Reiseprospekt (e)/die Reisebroschüre (n)**
excursion	**der Ausflug (¨e)**

tour by bus, car	**die Reise (n), die Tour (en), die Fahrt (en)**
guided tour by bus	**die Rundfahrt(en)**
coach trip	**die Busfahrt (en)**
guided visit	**die Führung (en)**
cruise	**die Kreuzfahrt (en)**
adventure holiday	**der Abenteuerurlaub (e)**
activity holiday	**der Aktivitätsurlaub**
farm holiday	**der Bauernhofurlaub**
family holidays	**der Familienurlaub**
golfing holiday	**der Golfurlaub**
alternative holidays	**die Alternativurlaube**
bike holiday	**der Fahrradurlaub**
sea, sand and sun	**Meer, Sand und Sonne**
mountains and lakes	**Berge und Seen**
in the countryside	**auf dem Land**
to go on holiday	**in Urlaub fahren**
peak holiday time	**die Haupturlaubszeit**
national holiday	**der Feiertag (e)**
to go on a tour	**auf Tour gehen**
to go for a drive/walk/climb	**eine Tour machen**
long-distance driver	**der/die Tourenfahrer/in (¨) (nen)**

12.2 What to take

Core vocabulary

....

Insight

Familiarize yourself with the following words which are the same or similar in English and German. Remember to use the German pronunciation.

rucksack **der Rucksack (¨e)**, *visa* **das Visum/das Visa (s)**, *passport* **der Pass (¨e)**, *credit card* **die Kreditkarte (n)**, *laptop* **der Laptop (s)**, *shampoo* **das Shampoo (s)**, *comb* **der**

(Contd)

Kamm (¨e), *hand cream* **die Handcreme (s),** *sun cream* **die Sonnencreme (-),** *factor 10* **der Faktor 10,** *mobile phone* **das Mobiltelefon/Handy.**

Although the German equivilant for *mobile phone* is **das Mobiltelefon,** most people call it **das Handy.**

luggage	**das Gepäck**
suitcase	**der Koffer (-)**
travel bag	**die Reisetasche (n)**
hand luggage	**das Handgepäck**
passport	**der Reisepass (¨e)/der Personalausweis (e)**
cash	**das Bargeld**
insurance	**die Versicherung (en)**
driving licence	**der Führerschein (e)**
currency	**die Währung (en)**
traveller's cheques	**die Reiseschecks**
emergency phone number	**die Notfallnummer (n)**
sponge bag/toilet bag	**das Reiseetui (s)**
soap	**die Seife (n)**
toothbrush	**die Zahnbürste (n)**
toothpaste	**die Zahnpasta (s)**
razor	**der Rasierapparat (e)**
nail scissors	**die Nagelschere (n)**
tweezers	**die Pinzette (n)**
conditioner	**die Pflegespülung**
hairbrush	**die Haarbürste (n)**
face creams	**die Gesichtscreme (-)**
cleanser	**der Gesichtsreiniger (-)**
moisturizer	**die Feuchtigkeitscreme**
waterproof sun cream	**die wasserabweisende Creme (-)**
after-sun cream	**die Sonnenbrandcreme (s)**
wardrobe	**der Schrank (¨e)**
coat hanger	**der Bügel (-)**
iron	**das Bügeleisen (-)**

Useful phrases

I have lost my luggage.	Ich habe mein Gepäck verloren.
I can't find …	Ich kann … nicht finden.
Have you got a …?	Haben Sie ein/e …?
Where can I get a …?	Wo kann ich ein/e/en … bekommen?
Where is the nearest …?	Wo ist der/die nächste …?

Useful verbs

to pack	**ein**packen
to unpack	**aus**packen
to fold	**falten**
to hang	**hängen**
to hang up	**auf**hängen
to wash	**waschen**
to clean	**reinigen**
to put on (make up)	**auf**tragen
to take along	**mit**nehmen

12.3 Where to stay

Core vocabulary

accommodation	die Unterkunft ("e)
two-star hotel	Zwei-Sterne-Hotel
three-star hotel	Drei-Sterne-Hotel
luxury hotel	das Luxushotel
inn	der Gasthof ("e)
bed and breakfast	die Pension (en), das Gasthaus("er)
holiday house	das Ferienhaus ("er)
youth hostel	die Jugendherberge (n)
campsite	der Campingplatz ("e)
caravan site	der Campingplatz für Wohnwagen
self-catering holiday	die Ferienwohnung (en) apartment
holiday bungalow	der Ferienbungalow (s)
holiday home	das Ferienhaus ("er)

entrance	**der Eingang (¨e)**
reception	**die Rezeption/der Empfang**
night porter	**der Nachtportier (s)**
manager	**der/die Manager/in (-) (nen)**
staff	**die Angestellten**
porter	**der Portier (s)**
single room	**das Einzelzimmer (-)**
double room	**das Doppelzimmer (-)**
twin-bedded room	**das Zweibettzimmer (-)**
family room	**das Familienzimmer (-)**
with shower	**mit Dusche**
with bathroom	**mit Bad**
with toilet	**mit Toilette**
with phone	**mit Telefon**
with television (TV)	**mit Fernsehen/TV**
with internet connection	**mit Internetanschluss**
with a balcony	**mit Balkon**
with a sea view	**mit Seeblick**
with air conditioning	**mit Klimaanlage**
stairs	**die Treppe (n)**
lift	**der Lift (e), der Aufzug (¨e), der Fahrstuhl (¨e)**
restaurant	**das Restaurant (s)**
fitness room	**der Fitnessraum (¨e)**
swimming pool	**das Schwimmbad (¨er)**
whirlpool	**der Whirlpool**
bill	**die Rechnung (en)**

Insight

Did you notice the large number of words to do with holiday
accommodation which are the same or similar in English and
German?

hotel **das Hotel,** *luxury hotel* **das Luxushotel,** *bungalow* **der Bungalow (s),** *reception* **die Rezeption,** *night porter* **der Nachtportier,** *manager* **der Manager,** *porter* **der Portier,** *toilet* **die Toilette,** *phone* **das Telefon,** *TV* **TV,** *internet* **das Internet,** *balcony* **der Balkon,** *whirlpool* **der Whirlpool,** *swimming pool* **das Schwimmbad,** *lift* **der Lift.**

Useful phrases

Have you got anything ...?	**Haben Sie etwas ...?**
bigger/smaller	**größeres/kleineres**
cheaper/better	**billigeres/besseres**
quieter	**ruhigeres**
a non-smoking room	**ein Nichtraucherzimmer**
It is too noisy.	**Es ist zu laut.**
The shower doesn't work.	**Die Dusche geht nicht.**
There is no hot water.	**Es gibt kein heißes Wasser.**
There is no plug in the sink.	**Es gibt keinen Stöpsel in dem Waschbecken.**

12.4 Camping and caravanning

Core vocabulary

Insight

The following words in connection with camping and caravanning are similar in English and German.

camping **das Camping,** *toilets* **die Toiletten,** *gas* **das Gas,** *electricity* **die Elektrizität,** *restaurant* **das Restaurant,** *bar* **die Bar(s),** *to park* **parken,** *to wash* **waschen,** *washroom* **der Waschraum,** *shopping* **shoppen,** *shop* **der Shop.**

campsite	**der Zeltplatz (¨e)**
caravan site	**der Campingplatz (¨e)**
caravan	**der Wohnwagen (-)**

camper van	das Wohnmobil (e)
trailer	der Anhänger (-)
tent	das Zelt (e)
site	der Platz/die Lage
shady site	die Schattenlage
sunny site	die Sonnenlage
sea view	der Ausblick auf das Meer
mountain view	der Ausblick auf die Berge
facilities	die Einrichtungen
connection	der Anschluss (¨e)
electricity connection	der Elektrizitätsanschluss (¨e)
water connection	der Wasseranschluss (¨e)
running water	fließendes Wasser
drinking water	das Trinkwasser
water tap	der Wasserhahn (¨e)
hook-up	die Schaltung (en)
showers	die Duschen
wash basins	die Waschbecken
hairdryers	der Haartrockner/Haarföne
cooking area	die Kochecke
washing-up sinks	die Abwaschbecken
washing machines	die Waschmaschinen
dryers	die Wäschetrockner
drying area	der Trockenraum (¨e)
shop	das Geschäft(e)/der Laden/der Shop
swimming pool	das Schwimmbad (¨er)
paddling pool	das Planschbecken (-)
children's playground	der Kinderspielplatz (¨e)
swings	die Schaukel (n)
slide	die Rutsche (n)
roundabout	das Karussel (s)
tent	das Zelt (e)
tent pegs	die Zeltpflöcke
guy ropes	das Spannseil (e)
groundsheet	die Unterlegeplane (n)
sleeping bag	der Schlafsack (¨e)
torch	die Taschenlampe (n)
blanket	die Decke (n)

gas cooker	**der Gaskocher (-)**
gas bottle	**die Gasflasche (n)**

Useful phrases

Can you help me?	**Können Sie mir helfen?**
I don't understand how the ...	**Ich verstehe nicht, wie ...**
works.	**funktioniert.**
Where is the ...?	**Wo ist der/die/das ...?**
Is there electricity/water?	**Gibt es hier Elektrizität/Wasser?**
Do you have ...?	**Haben Sie ...?**
When is the shop open?	**Wann ist das Geschäft geöffnet?**
Where can I get ...?	**Wo kann ich ... bekommen?**

Useful verbs

to tow	**ziehen**
to put up (tent)	**das Zelt <u>auf</u>bauen**
to take down (tent)	**das Zelt <u>ab</u>bauen**
to get wet	**nass werden**
to do the washing	**die Wäsche waschen**
to dry	**trocknen**

12.5 What are you going to do?

Core vocabulary

activity holiday	**der Aktivitätsurlaub**
We want to go ...	**Wir wollen ...**
swimming	**schwimmen gehen**
diving	**tauchen**
water skiing	**Wasserski fahren**
surfing	**surfen**
sailing	**segeln**
walking	**spazieren gehen**
hiking	**wandern**

climbing	**klettern**
gliding	**Segelfliegen**
paragliding	**Paragliding**
hanggliding	**Drachenfliegen**
to play tennis	**Tennis spielen**
to play volleyball	**Volleyball spielen**
to go bike riding	**Fahrrad fahren gehen**
sights	**die Sehenswürdigkeiten**
monuments	**die Monumente, die Denkmäler**
castles	**die Schlösser/Burgen**
archeological sites	**die archäologischen Stätten**
ancient monuments	**uralte Monumente**
historic buildings	**geschichtliche Gebäude**
scenery	**die Landschaft**
animals	**die Tiere**

Useful phrases

What is there to see/do?	**Was gibt es dort ... zu sehen/tun?**
Is it suitable for ...?	**Ist es für ... geeignet?**
older people	**ältere Leute**
younger people	**jüngere Leute**
children	**Kinder**

Useful verbs

to have a good time	**sich vergnügen**
to have a rest	**sich <u>aus</u>ruhen**
to relax	**sich entspannen/relaxen**
to do nothing	**nichts tun**
to laze about	**faulenzen/gammeln**
to go skiing	**Skifahren**
to go snowboarding	**Snowboard fahren**
to go sledging	**Schlitten fahren/rodeln**
to go ice skating	**Schlittschuh laufen/skaten**
to sun oneself	**sich sonnen**
to surf	**surfen**
to fish	**fischen**

12.6 On the beach

Core vocabulary

sea	**das Meer/die See**
beach	**der Strand (¨e)**
bay	**die Bucht (en)**
shore	**das Ufer (-)**
rocks	**die Felsen**
high tide	**die Flut (-)**
low tide	**die Ebbe (-)**
waves	**die Wellen**

beach bar	die Strandbar (s)
windbreak	der Windschutz
shelter	der Schutz
parasol	der Sonnenschirm (e)
lounger	die Sonneliege (n)
deckchair	der Liegestuhl (¨e)
air mattress	die Luftmatratze (n)
shower	die Dusche (n)
towel	das Handtuch (¨er)
swimming costume	der Schwimmanzug (¨e)
trunks	die Badhose (n)
sun cream	die Sonnencreme (s)
sunglasses	die Sonnenbrille (n)
rubber ring	der Gummiring (e)
swimming cap	die Bademütze (n)
sandcastle	die Sandburg (en)
bucket	der Eimer (-)
kite	der Drachen (-)
flippers	die Schwimmflossen/die Flippers
inflatable	aufblasbar
surfboard	das Surfbrett (er)
shells	die Muscheln
octopus	die Kraken
squid	die Tintenfische
scallops	die Jakobsmuscheln
shrimps	die Garnelen
jellyfish	die Qualle (n)

Useful phrases

The tide is in.	Es ist Flut.
The tide is out.	Es ist Ebbe.
It is safe for bathing/swimming.	Es ist sicher zu baden/ schwimmen.
I have been stung by a jellyfish.	Ich bin von einer Qualle gestochen worden.
The water is too deep.	Das Wasser ist zu tief.

He/she can't swim.	**Er/sie kann nicht schwimmen.**
He/she needs help.	**Er/sie braucht Hilfe.**
Help!	**Hilfe!**
Attention!	**Achtung!**

Useful verbs

to snorkel	**schnorcheln**
to sunbathe	**sonnenbaden**
to relax	**entspannen/relaxen**
to play	**spielen**
to dig	**buddeln**
to dive	**tauchen**
to sting	**stechen**
to splash around	**planschen**
to fish	**fischen**
to surf	**surfen**

12.7 At sea

Core vocabulary

canoe	**das Kanu (s)**
motor boat	**das Motorboot (e)**
rubber dinghy	**das Schlauchboot (e)**
rowing boat	**das Ruderboot (e)**
sailing boat	**das Segelboot (e)**
sailing ship	**das Segelschiff (e)**
surfboard	**das Surfbrett (er)**
waterski	**der Wasserski (er)**
wind surfer	**der/die Windsurfer/in (-) (nen)**
yacht	**die Yacht (en)**
MAYDAY	**MAYDAY**
SOS	**SOS**
lifeboat	**das Rettungsboot (e)**

lifejacket	**die Lebensrettungsjacke (n)**
lifeguard	**der/die Bademeister/in (-) (nen)**
	Strandmeister/in (-) (nen)
flare	**die Leuchtkugel (n)/das Leuchtsignal (e)**
weather forecast	**die Wettervorhersage (n)**
the sea is …	**die See ist …**
calm	**ruhig**
rough	**rauh**
windforce	**die Windstärke**
galeforce	**die Orkanstärke**
rain	**der Regen**
visibility	**die Sicht**
foggy	**neblig**
equipment	**die Ausrüstung (en)**
compass	**der Kompass (e)**
sail	**das Segel (-)**
hull	**der Rumpf**
cabin	**die Kabine (n)**
berth	**die Koje (n)**
wheel	**das Steuerrad (¨er)**
starboard	**das Steuerbord**
harbour, port	**der Hafen (¨)**
lighthouse	**der Leuchtturm (¨e)**
the coast	**die Küste (n)**
cliffy coast	**die Kliffküste (n)**
the coastguard	**die Küstenwache**
sea coast	**die Seeküste (n)**
west coast	**die Westküste**

Useful verbs

to moor	**fest**machen
to chain	**an**ketten
to anchor	**Anker legen**
to sail	**segeln**
to navigate	**navigieren**
to steer	**steuern**
to tie up/moor	**fest**binden

to anchor	**verankern**
to rescue	**retten**
to be rescued	**gerettet sein**

12.8 The great outdoors

Core vocabulary

··

Insight
Start by learning the following words which are the same or
similar in English and German.

rucksack **der Rucksack**, *compass* **der Kompass**, *chocolate* **die
Schokolade**, *nuts* **die Nüsse**, *batteries* **die Batterien**.

··

sleeping bag	**der Schlafsack (¨e)**
ground mat/mattress	**die Bodenmatratze (n)**
torch	**die Taschenlampe (n)**
penknife	**das Taschenmesser (-)**
map	**die Karte (n)**
water bottle	**die Wasserflasche (n)**
camping stove	**der Campingkocher (-)**
matches	**die Streichhölzer**
lighter	**das Feuerzeug (e)**
gas container	**die Gasflasche (n)**
billy can	**der Wasserkessel (-)**
bowl	**die Schüssel (n)**
knife	**das Messer**
fork	**die Gabel**
spoon	**der Löffel (n)**
plate	**der Teller (-)**
mug	**der Becher (-)**
emergency rations	**die Notfallrationen**
dried food	**getrocknetes Essen**
dried fruit	**das Trockenobst**
transceiver (for snow rescue)	**das Verschüttungsgerät**

mobile phone	das Handy (s)
charger	das Aufladegerät (e)
plug	der Stecker (-)
waterproofs	wasserdichte Kleidung
spare clothing	Kleidung zum Umziehen
rope	das Seil (e)
climbing harness	der Klettergurt (e)
climbing gear	die Kletterausrüstung (en)
crampons	das Steigeisen (-)
boots	die Stiefel (-)
ice axe	der Eispickel (-)

Useful phrases

My feet are sore.	Meine Füße tun weh.
My back is sore.	Mein Rücken tut weh.
I need extra socks.	Ich brauche extra Socken.
I have blisters.	Ich habe Blasen.
Do you have plasters?	Haben Sie Pflaster?
antiseptic cream	antiseptische Creme
insect repellent	Insektenschutzmittel
antihistamine cream (for insect bites)	das Antihistaminikum
Have you got something for ...?	Haben Sie etwas gegen ...?
I have been stung by a wasp/ bee/mosquito.	Ich bin von einer Wespe/Biene/ Mücke gestochen worden.
I have been bitten by ...	Ich bin von ... gebissen worden.
by a snake	von einer Schlange
by a dog	von einem Hund

TEST YOURSELF

See how many questions you can get right without looking back
at the unit.

1 What is the word for *an adventure holiday*?
- **a** ein Aktivitätsurlaub
- **b** ein Abenteuerurlaub
- **c** ein Alternativurlaub

2 *Sun, sea and sand* in German is:
- **a** der See, der Sand und die Sonne
- **b** die See, der Sand und die Sonne
- **c** die See, die Sandale und die Sonne

3 Which word means *shore*?
- **a** Ufer
- **b** Flut
- **c** Ebbe

4 In German *to have a rest* is:
- **a** sich vergnügen
- **b** tauchen
- **c** sich ausruhen

5 Which verb is *not* a separable verb?
- **a** faulenzen
- **b** ausruhen
- **c** festbinden

6 *A fork* is:
- **a** ein Messer
- **b** ein Löffel
- **c** eine Gabel

7 **Ein Schlauchboot** is:
  a a sailing boot
  b a surfboard
  c rubber dinghy

8 *A tent* is:
  a eine Taschenlampe
  b ein Zelt
  c eine Treppe

9 The German word **Handy** means:
  a handy
  b mobile phone
  c hand

10 The German word for *castle* is:
  a Kaufhaus
  b Schloss
  c Kastanie

Answers: 1b; 2b; 3a; 4c; 5a; 6c; 7c; 8b; 9b; 10b

13

···

The body and health

13.1 The face

Core vocabulary

head	**der Kopf (¨e)**
face	**das Gesicht (er)**
hair	**das Haar (e)**
forehead	**die Stirn (en)**
ears	**die Ohren**
eyes	**die Augen**
eyebrows	**die Augenbrauen**
eyelashes	**die Augenwimpern**
nose	**die Nase (n)**
nostrils	**der Nasenflügel (-)**
cheeks	**die Wangen**
chin	**das Kinn (e)**
mouth	**der Mund (¨er)**
lips	**die Lippen**
tongue	**die Zunge (n)**
tooth	**der Zahn (¨e)**
neck	**der Hals (¨e)**

Useful phrases

He has	**Er hat**
a beard	**einen Bart**
a moustache	**einen Schnurrbart**

He/she wears glasses.	**Er/sie trägt eine Brille.**
contact lenses	**Kontaktlinsen**
I am short sighted/long sighted.	**Ich bin kurzsichtig/langsichtig.**

Insight

Remember that **die Brille** (*glasses*) is singular in German whereas glasses are plural in English.

Die runde Brille ist schön. *The round glasses are nice.*

Useful verbs

to hear	**hören**
to see	**sehen**
to smell	**riechen**
to taste	**schmecken**
to feel	**fühlen**
to sleep	**schlafen**
to smile	**lächeln**
to laugh	**lachen**
to talk	**sprechen**
to shout	**schimpfen**
to cry	**weinen**
to snore	**schnarchen**
to hiccup	**aufstoßen**
to cough	**husten**
to touch	**berühren**

Extras

Insight

The word **Schmerzen** means *pain*. To describe that you are *in pain* you just add the word **Schmerzen** to the particular part of your body where the pain is, e.g. *pain in your stomach* **Bauchschmerzen**, *pain in your foot* **Fussschmerzen** etc. Remember to pronounce the **z** in **Schmerzen** clearly.

It hurts/it is sore translates as **Es tut weh.** For example:
My arm is hurting **Mein Arm tut weh.**

My leg is hurting **Mein Bein tut weh.** Pay attention to the
plural: *My legs are hurting* **Meine Beine tun weh.**

I have ... a headache	**Ich habe ... Kopfschmerzen**
toothache	**Zahnschmerzen**
earache	**Ohrenschmerzen**
a nose bleed	**Nasenbluten**
My eyes are sore.	**Meine Augen tun weh.**
to have a facial	**eine Gesichtsbehandlung haben**
to have your hair done	**das Haar gemacht bekommen**
to have a nose job	**eine Nasenoperation haben**
to have plastic surgery	**eine Schönheitsoperation haben**
to have wrinkles	**Falten haben**
to have a nice smile	**ein nettes Lächeln haben**

Kosmetik die Kosmetik

Insight

Have a look at cosmetic items or product descriptions, as
many are written in both languages. The following words are
the same or similar in English and German.

mascara **das Mascara,** *make-up* **das Make-up,** *shampoo*
das Shampoo, *lipstick* **der Lippenstift.** Sometimes you
see a combination of German and English in the product
description such as: **schwarzer Eye Liner.** *Powder* is sometimes
used instead of **Puder.**

shampoo	**das Haarwaschmittel (-)/Shampoo (s)**
conditioner	**das Haarpflegemittel (-)**
face cream	**die Gesichtscreme (s)**
moisturizer	**die Feuchtigkeitscreme (s)**
face pack	**die Gesichtspackung (en)**
lip salve	**die Lippencreme (s)**
shaving cream	**der Rasierschaum**

shaving brush	der Rasierpinsel (-)
razor	die Rasierklinge (n)
after-shave lotion	die Aftershave-Lotion/das Rasierwasser
make-up	das Make-up
mascara	die Wimperntusche (n)/Mascara (n)
lipstick	der Lippenstift (e)
eye shadow	der Lidschatten (-)
powder	das Puder (-)

13.2 The body

Core vocabulary

....

Insight

The following words in connection with the body are similar in English and German. Learning them will help you to build up your vocabulary faster. It is a good idea to learn the right article for each noun.

arm **der Arm,** *hand* **die Hand,** *finger* **der Finger,** *shoulder* **die Schulter,** *elbow* **der Ellenbogen,** *skeleton* **das Skelett,** *veins* **die Venen,** *arteries* **die Arterien,** *blood* **das Blut,** *lung* **die Lunge,** *knee* **das Knie,** *foot* **der Fuß,** *sexual organs* **die Sexualorgane,** *penis* **der Penis,** *vagina* **die Vagina,** *circulation* **die Zirkulation,** *nervous system* **das Nervensystem,** *nerve* **der Nerv.**

....

wrist	das Armgelenk (e)
thumb	der Daumen (-)
fingernail	die Fingernagel (¨)
body	der Körper
chest	die Brust
breasts	der Busen
nipple	die Brustwarze (n)

waist	**dieTaille (n)**
hips	**die Hüfte (n)**
abdomen	**der Unterleib (e)**
bottom	**der Hintern (-)/der Po (s)**
testicles	**die Hoden**
vagina	**die Vagina/die Scheide**
leg	**das Bein (e)**
thigh	**der Oberschenkel (-)**
ankle	**der Fußknöchel**
toe	**der Zeh (en)**
heel	**die Fersen/die Hacke (n)**
back	**der Rücken**
front	**die Vorderseite (n)**
side	**die Seite (n)**
internal organs	**die inneren Organe**
brain	**das Gehirn**
stomach	**der Magen (¨)**
throat	**der Hals (¨e)**
kidney	**die Niere (n)**
heart	**das Herz (en)**
blood transfusion	**die Bluttransfusion (en)**
blood donor	**die Blutspende**
blood type	**die Blutgruppe**
intestines	**die Innereien**
bone	**der Knochen (-)**
joint	**das Gelenk (e)**
breathing	**die Atmung**
digestion	**die Verdauung**

Useful phrases

I have …	**Ich habe …**
stomach ache	**Magenschmerzen**
heart burn	**Sodbrennen**
indigestion	**Magenverstimmung**
high/low blood pressure	**hohen/niedrigen Blutdruck**
My feet/hands/legs hurt.	**Meine Füße/Hände/Beine tun weh.**

Useful verbs

to feel	**fühlen**
to touch	**berühren**
to stroke	**streicheln**
to massage	**massieren**
to hold	**halten**
to embrace	**umarmen**
to kiss	**küssen**
to kick	**treten**
to walk	**gehen**
to run	**rennen**
to jump	**springen**

13.3 I need a doctor

Core vocabulary

> **Insight**
> Remember to address a male doctor with **Herr Doktor** and
> a female doctor with **Frau Doktor**. For more on addressing
> people of different professions, look back at Unit 1.

doctor	**der Doktor/die Doktorin, der Arzt (¨e)/die Ärztin (nen)**
specialist	**Facharzt/-¨in für ...**
internist	**Facharzt/-¨in für Innere Medizin (Internist)**
eye specialist	**Augenarzt/-¨in**
paediatrician	**Kinderarzt/-¨in**
ear, nose and throat specialist	**Halsnasenohrenarzt/-¨in**
gynaecologist	**der/die Gynäkologe, der/die Frauenarzt/-¨in**
orthopaedic specialist	**Arzt/-¨in für Orthopädie**
heart specialist	**der/die Herzspezialist/in**
general practitioner (GP)	**Praktischer Arzt**

dentist	**Zahnarzt/-¨in**
appointment	**der Termin (e)**
surgery	**die Arztpraxis (praxen)**

Useful phrases

I would like to make an appointment.	**Ich möchte gerne einen Termin vereinbaren.**
I have a pain ...	**Ich habe Schmerzen ...**
It hurts.	**Es tut weh.**
I don't feel well.	**Mir geht es nicht gut.**
I can't sleep/eat/walk ...	**Ich kann nicht schlafen, essen/gehen.**
I am pregnant.	**Ich bin schwanger.**
I am in the menopause.	**Ich bin in den Wechseljahren.**
I feel sick.	**Mir ist schlecht.**
I feel dizzy.	**Mir ist schwindlig.**
I have got spots.	**Ich habe Pickel.**
I have been bitten/stung.	**Ich bin gebissen/gestochen worden.**

Ailments

cold	**die Erkältung (en)**
flu (influenza)	**die Grippe (n)**
measles	**Masern**
mumps	**Mumps**
German measles	**Röteln**
tonsillitis	**die Mandelentzündung (en)**
cough	**der Husten**
sore throat	**das Halsweh**
indigestion	**die Magenverstimmung (en)**
hypertension	**der Hypertonie/der erhöhte Blutdruck**
constipation	**die Verstopfung**
diarrhoea	**der Durchfall**
Aids	**das Aids**
HIV	**das HIV**
polio	**die Kinderlähmung/die Polio**

hepatitis	**die Hepatitis**
rabies	**die Tollwut**
typhoid fever	**der Typhus**
typhus	**das Fleckfieber**
cholera	**die Cholera**
yellow fever	**das Gelbfieber**
malaria	**die Malaria**
cancer	**der Krebs**
multiple sclerosis	**die Multiple Sklerose (MS)**

Useful words and phrases

I am ill.	**Ich bin krank.**
I am allergic to ...	**Ich bin allergisch gegen ...**
penicillin	**Penizillin**
nuts	**Nüsse**
animals	**Tiere**
I have hay fever.	**Ich habe Heuschnupfen.**
asthma	**Asthma**
He needs an inhaler.	**Er braucht ein Inhalationsgerät.**
She is handicapped.	**Sie ist behindert.**
She is paraplegic.	**Sie ist gelähmt.**
She has her period.	**Sie hat ihre Periode.**
He is in puberty.	**Er ist in der Pubertät.**
an injection/a jab for	**eine Injektion/Spritze gegen**
immunization	**die Immunisierung**
inoculation	**die Impfung (en)**
health certificate	**der Gesundheitspass**
examination	**die Untersuchung**
x-ray	**die Röntgenaufnahme**
I have broken my leg/	**Ich habe mein Bein/mein**
ankle/wrist	**Fußgelenk/mein Handgelenk gebrochen.**
plaster	**das Pflaster (-)**
crutches	**die Krücken**
walking stick	**der Krückstock (¨e)**
wheelchair	**der Rollstuhl (¨e)**

Useful verbs

to go to bed	**zu Bett gehen**
to sleep	**schlafen**
to take more exercise	**sich mehr bewegen**
to eat less	**weniger essen**
to avoid	**vermeiden**

Extras

medicine	**die Medizin**
conventional medicine	**die Schulmedizin**
alternative medicine	**die alternative Medizin**
pills	**die Pillen**
pain killers	**Schmerztabletten**
vitamin supplements	**Vitamintabletten**
injection	**die Spritze (n)**
cure	**die Heilung**
homeopathic remedy	**homöopathische Mittel**
physiotherapy	**die Physiotherapie**
aromatherapy	**die Aromatherapie**
reflexology	**die Reflexologie**
yoga	**das Yoga**
meditation	**die Meditation**
sleep	**der Schlaf**
to rest	**sich ausruhen**
to recover	**sich erholen**

13.4 At the hospital

Core vocabulary

hospital	**das Krankenhaus (¨er)**
department	**die Abteilung (en)**
emergency	**der Notfall (¨e)**
doctor	**der/die Arzt/¨in (¨e) (nen)**
nurse	**der/die Krankenpfleger/in (-) (nen)**

ward	die Station (en)
bed	das Bett (en)
anaesthetic	die Anästhesie (n)/die Narkose (n)
surgery	die Chirurgie
operation	die Operation (en)
operating theatre	der Operationssaal (¨e)

Health resorts

spa	die Kur (en)
health resort	der Kurort (e)
assembly rooms at health resort	das Kurhaus (¨er)
visitor to a spa	der Kurgast (¨e)
spa park	der Kurpark (s)
spa water	das Kurwasser
spa concert	das Kurkonzert (e)
to take a cure, take the spa water	kuren
thermal bath	das Thermalbad (¨er)
mud bath	der Fango
massage	die Massage (n)

Insight

The emergency doctor service is called **Ärztlicher Notfalldienst:**

a house call **Ärztlicher Hausbesuch**
dental emergencies **Zahnärztlicher Notfalldienst**
chemist **die Apotheke** (n)
chemist **die Drogerie** (n)

There are two types of chemist: **Apotheke** and **Drogerie**. If you have a prescription from your doctor you have to go to the **Apotheke.**

TEST YOURSELF

See how many questions you can get right without looking back at the unit.

1 Which word means *dentist*?
   a Augenarzt
   b Zahnarzt
   c Halsnasenohrenarzt

2 What is the word for *pain*?
   a der Schmerz
   b die Periode
   c das Fieber

3 Which of the following words is *not* the same in German?
   a operation
   b yoga
   c cold

4 *It hurts* in German is:
   a Es tut weh.
   b Mir ist es schlecht.
   c Mir geht es nicht gut.

5 The word *spa* is translated as:
   a das Krankenhaus
   b der Kurort
   c die Kur

6 *To rest* in German is:
   a sich erholen
   b sich ausruhen
   c sich massieren

7 Which word is the same in German?
   a lung
   b heart
   c finger

8 *Swine flu* in German is:
   a die Schweinezucht
   b die Schweinehaltung
   c die Schweinegrippe

9 *To eat less* is:
   a weniger essen
   b mehr essen
   c alles essen

10 *German measles* are:
   a Deutsche Muscheln
   b Masern
   c Röteln

Answers: 1b; 2a; 3c; 4a; 5c; 6b; 7c; 8c; 9a; 10c

14

The world

14.1 Geography and regions

Core vocabulary

> **Insight**
>
> Most words in connection with *geography* **die Geographie**
> look very similar in both languages, but remember to
> use the German pronunciation. If necessary look at the
> pronunciation guide in the introduction. It's a good idea to
> start your work on the vocabulary lists by highlighting or
> underlining words which are the same or similar and then
> memorizing them.

world	**die Welt**
earth	**die Erde**
globe	**der Globus**
atlas	**der Atlas**
continents	**die Kontinente**
Africa	**Afrika**
America	**Amerika**
North America	**Nordamerika**
South America	**Südamerika**
Asia	**Asien**
Australia	**Australien**
Europe	**Europa**

the Arctic	**die Arktis**
the Antarctic	**die Antarktis**
the Middle East	**der Nahe Osten**
the Far East	**der Ferne Osten**
India	**Indien**
China	**China**
Japan	**Japan**
Indonesia	**Indonesien**
New Zealand	**Neuseeland**
Pacific Islands	**die Pazifischen Inseln**

14.2 Some European countries

Austria	**Österreich**
Belgium	**Belgien**
Bulgaria	**Bulgarien**
Bosnia	**Bosnien**
Croatia	**Kroatien**
Cyprus	**Zypern**
Czech Republic	**die Tschechische Republik**
Denmark	**Dänemark**
Estonia	**Estland**
Finland	**Finnland**
France	**Frankreich**
Germany	**Deutschland**
Greece	**Griechenland**
Hungary	**Ungarn**
Iceland	**Island**
Italy	**Italien**
Ireland	**Irland**
Latvia	**Lettland**
Lithuania	**Litauen**
Luxembourg	**Luxemburg**
Malta	**Malta**
Netherlands	**die Niederlande**
Norway	**Norwegen**

Poland	**Polen**
Portugal	**Portugal**
Romania	**Rumänien**
Russia	**Russland**
Scotland	**Schottland**
Spain	**Spanien**
Sweden	**Schweden**
Slovakia	**Slowakei**
Slovenia	**Slowenien**
Switzerland	**die Schweiz**
Turkey	**die Türkei**
Ukraine	**Ukraine**
United Kingdom	**Großbritannien**
England	**England**
Ireland	**Irland**
Northern Ireland	**Nordirland**
Wales	**Wales**
European Union	**die Europäische Union**
European Parliament	**das Europäische Parlament**
Common Market	**der gemeinsamer Markt**
member of the European parliament	**Mitglieder des Europäischen Parlaments**
common agricultural policy	**die gemeinsame Landwirtschaftspolitik**
euro	**der Euro**
dollar	**der Dollar**
pound	**das Pfund**
European institutions	**die Europäischen Institutionen**
European Bank	**die Europäische Bank**

14.3 The high seas!

Core vocabulary

points of the compass	**die Kompassrichtungen**
north	**der Norden**
south	**der Süden**

east	der Osten
west	der Westen
northeast	der Nordosten
southwest	der Südwesten
ocean	der Ozean (e)
Atlantic	der Atlantische Ozean
Indian	der Indische Ozean
Pacific	der Pazifische Ozean
Arctic	das Nordpolarmeer
Antarctic	das Südpolarmeer
Mediterranean	das Mittelmeer
North Sea	die Nordsee
Baltic	die Ostsee
Red Sea	das Rote Meer
English Channel	der Ärmelkanal
navigation	die Navigation
longitude	das Längengrad
latitude	das Breitengrad
equator	der Äquator
northern hemisphere	die Nordhalbkugel
southern hemisphere	die Südhalbkugel
tropics	die Tropen
bay	die Bucht (en)
island	die Insel (n)
peninsula	die Halbinsel (n)
canal	der Kanal (¨e)
Suez Canal	der Sueskanal
Panama Canal	der Panamakanal
straits	die Meerenge (n)
currents	die Strömungen
tides	die Gezeiten
ferry	die Fähre (n)
liner	das Passagierschiff (e)
cruise ship	das Kreuzfahrtschiff (e)
tanker	der Tanker (-)
container ship	das Containerschiff (e)
hazards	Gefahren
icebergs	der Eisberg (e)

shipping	**die Schifffahrt**
shipping line	**die Schifffahrtslinie**
storm, gale	**der Sturm (¨e)**
galeforce	**die Sturmstärke**
rough seas	**rauhe See**
calm seas	**ruhige See**

Useful verbs

to board	**besteigen**
to embark	**<u>ein</u>schiffen**
to disembark	**<u>aus</u>schiffen**
to disembark	**von Bord gehen**

14.4 The weather forecast

Core vocabulary

Insight

Familarize yourself with the core vocabulary in connection with weather and highlight words which are the same or similar to English. For practice go to a German internet site such as http://www.de.weather.yahoo.com to listen to or read the weather report.

weather report	**der Wetterbericht (e)**
snow	**der Schnee**
wind	**der Wind**
cloud	**die Wolke (n)**
fog	**der Nebel**
sun	**die Sonne**
hail	**der Hagel**
sleet	**der Schneeregen**
thunder	**der Donner (-)**
lightning	**der Blitz (e)**

rain	**der Regen**
it is raining	**es regnet**
it is rainy	**es ist regnerisch**
the rainy season	**die Regenzeit**
shower of rain	**der Regenschauer (-)**
light rain	**leichter Regen**
umbrella	**der Regenschirm (e)**
rainwear	**die Regenkleidung**
sun	**die Sonne**
sunbeam	**der Sonnenstrahl (en)**
sunrise	**der Sonnenaufgang (¨e)**
sunset	**der Sonnenuntergang (¨e)**
solar eclipse	**die Sonnenfinsternis**
position of the sun	**der Sonnenstand**
the sun is shining	**die Sonne scheint**
it is sunny	**es ist sonnig**
the heat	**die Hitze**
heat stroke	**der Hitzschlag (¨e)**
heatwave	**die Hitzewelle (n)**

Degrees of temperature

warmth	**die Wärme**
it is warm	**es ist warm**
cold	**die Kälte**
cold weather front	**die Kaltwetterfront**
cold spell	**der Kälteeinbruch**
5 degrees	**5 Grad**
it is cold	**es ist kalt**
it is freezing	**es ist eiskalt**

Insight

Be aware of the following false friends: *I am cold (I feel cold)* ≠ **Ich bin kalt.**

Don't mix it up because **Ich bin kalt** means *I have a cold personality.*

I feel cold in German is **Mir ist (es) kalt.** You can drop the **es.**
The same applies to:

I am warm ≠ **Ich bin warm. Ich bin warm** means *I am a warm person.* I feel warm is **Mir ist (es) warm.**

Useful words and phrases

I'm shivering with cold.	**Ich zittere vor Kälte.**
The cold is getting to me.	**Die Kälte macht mir zu schaffen.**
it is snowing	**es schneit**
snowstorm	**der Schneesturm (¨e)**
frost	**der Frost**
it is frosty	**es ist frostig**
it is cloudy	**es ist bewölkt**
clear sky	**wolkenlos**
sky	**der Himmel (-)**
dryness	**die Trockenheit**
dry	**trocken**
wetness	**die Feuchtigkeit**
it is wet	**es ist feucht**
humidity	**die Luftfeuchtigkeit**
humid	**feucht**
dampness	**die Nässe**
it is damp	**es ist nass**
The constant wetness is getting to my bones.	**Die ewige Nässe fährt mir in die Knochen.**
today	**heute**
tomorrow	**morgen**
over the next few days	**für die nächsten Tage**
the weather is getting worse	**das Wetter wird schlimmer**
is improving	**das Wetter verbessert sich**
stays the same	**das Wetter bleibt so**
dangerous driving conditions	**gefährliche Fahrbedingungen**
risk of flooding	**Überflutungsgefahr**
danger of black ice	**Glatteisgefahr**
the temperature is ...	**die Temperatur beträgt ...**

degrees	**das Grad**
Centigrade	**das Grad Celsius**
Fahrenheit	**das Grad Fahrenheit**
the temperature is rising/falling	**die Temperatur steigt/fällt**
maximum temperature	**die Höchsttemperatur**
minimum temperature	**die Mindesttemperatur**
cloudy	**bedeckt/bewölkt**
ice	**das Eis**
light rain at times	**zeitweise leichter Regen**
becoming less cloudy	**zurückgehende Bewölkung**
light	**schwach**
lowest temperature	**die niedrigste Temperatur**

TEST YOURSELF

See how many questions you can get right without looking back at the unit.

1 How do you spell the word for *Europe* in German?
   a Europe
   b Europa
   c Euro

2 How do you spell the word for *India* in German?
   a Indien
   b India
   c Indianer

3 How do you say *Italy* in German?
   a Italienisch
   b Italien
   c Italy

4 The word for *today* is:
   a morgen
   b heute
   c gestern

5 The word for *island* in German is:
   a Irland
   b Island
   c Insel

6 The word for *lightning* in German is:
   a Licht
   b Blitz
   c Donner

7 If you feel cold, you say:
    a Mir ist kalt.
    b Ich bin kalt.
    c Es ist kalt.

8 The word for *tomorrow* is:
    a übermorgen
    b morgen
    c morgens

9 *An umbrella* is:
    a ein Regenmantel
    b ein Regenschauer
    c ein Regenschirm

10 **Es ist bewölkt** means:
    a It is cloudy.
    b It is frosty.
    c It is damp.

Answers: 1b; 2a; 3b; 4b; 5c; 6b; 7a; 8b; 9c; 10a

15

Government and society

15.1 Politics and government

Core vocabulary

politics	**die Politik**
government	**die Regierung (en)**
democracy	**die Demokratie (en)**
dictatorship	**die Diktatur (en)**
monarchy	**die Monarchie (n)**
federal president	**der Bundespräsident (en)**
prime minister	**der Premierminister (-)**
federal chancellor	**der/die Bundeskanzler/in**
member of parliament	**der/die Abgeordnete (n)**
head of state	**das Staatsoberhaupt (¨er)**
party leader	**der/die Partievorsitzende (n)**
members of parliament	**die Parlamentsmitglieder**
constituency	**die Konstitution (en)**
election	**die Wahl (en)**
vote	**die Stimme (n)**
parliament	**das Parlament (e)**
foreign minister	**der Außenminister (-)**
home secretary	**der Innenminister (-)**
minister of defence	**der Verteidigungsminister (-)**
minister of agriculture	**der Landwirtschaftsminister (-)**
finance minister	**der Finanzminister (-)**

local government	die Kommunalverwaltung (en)
town hall	das Rathaus ("er)
town council	der Stadtrat ("e)
town councillors	die Stadträte
local taxes	die Gemeindesteuer (n)
job centre	das Arbeitsamt ("er)
social services	die Sozialeinrichtungen
social welfare office	das Sozialamt ("er)

Useful verbs

to make a speech	eine Ansprache halten
to debate	debattieren
to vote	wählen
to pass a bill	ein Gesetz verabschieden
to pay taxes	Steuern bezahlen

More vocabulary

....

Insight

The following words in connection with politics and government are similar in English and German. Learning them will help you to build up your vocabulary faster.

politics **die Politik,** *democracy* **die Demokratie,** *dictatorship* **die Diktatur,** *minister* **der Minister,** *parliament* **das Parlament,** *social* **sozial,** *army* **die Armee,** *soldier* **der/die Soldat/in,** *to fly* **fliegen,** *police* **die Polizei,** *terrorism* **der Terrorismus,** *to hijack* **hijacken,** *bomb* **die Bombe,** *conference* **die Konferenz,** *Nobel Prize* **der Nobelpreis,** *pilot* **der/die Pilot/in,** *crisis* **die Krise,** *conflict* **der Konflikt.**

....

army	die Armee/das Militär
German Army	die Bundeswehr
navy	die Marine
sailor	der Matrose (n)
to sail	segeln
warship	das Kriegsschiff (e)

airforce	**die Luftwaffe**
jet fighter	**Düsenjäger (-)**
police officer	**der/die Polizist/in (en)(nen)**
police car	**das Polizeiauto (s)**

Useful verbs

to arrest	**verhaften**
to invade	**einmarschieren**
to withdraw troops	**Truppen abziehen**
to agree on something	**etwas vereinbaren**
to avoid war	**den Krieg vermeiden**
to defend	**verteidigen**
to fight	**kämpfen**
to guard/protect	**beschützen**
to spy	**spionieren**
to attack	**angreifen**
to occupy	**besetzen**
to wound	**verletzen**

Useful phrases

the war against terrorism	**der Krieg gegen den Terrorismus**
to carry out an attack	**einen Anschlag verüben**
to plan a terrorist attack	**einen terroristichen Anschlag planen**
to hijack a plane	**ein Flugzeug entführen/hijacken**
to take a hostage	**Geiseln nehmen**
to carry out a suicide bombing	**Selbstmordattentat verüben**

Vocabulary for peace

Insight

Look at the word **Frieden** and the following compound words containing **Frieden**. It's a good way of building up your vocabulary.

(Contd)

der Frieden *peace*
Frieden schließen *to make one's peace*
die Friedensbewegung *peace movement*
die Friedenstruppe (n) *peacekeeping force*
der Friedensnobelpreis *Nobel Peace Prize*
die Friedenskonferenz *peace conference*
die Friendensgespräche *peace talks*
der Friedensvertrag *peace treaty*
die Friedensverhandlungen *peace negotiations*
friedlich leben *to live peacefully*
friedliebend *peace-loving*

15.2 Local government and services

Core vocabulary

police	die Polizei
emergency services	Notfalldienste
ambulance	der Krankenwagen (-)
fire brigade	die Feuerwehr (en)
telephone	das Telefon (e)
electricity	die Elektrizität
gas	das Gas
water	das Wasser
mayor	der Bürgermeister (-)
town hall	das Rathaus (¨er)
local council	die Kommunalverwaltung (en)
roads	die Straßen
transport	der Verkehr
tourist office	das Touristeninformationsbüro
council offices	die Stadtverwaltung (en)
taxes	die Steuern
council tax	die Gemeindesteuer (n)
bureaucracy	die Bürokratie (n)
small print	das Kleingedruckte
civil servant	der Beamte (n)/die Beamtin (nen)

paperwork	**die Papierarbeit**
pass	**der Pass ("e)**
permit	**die Genehmigung (en)**
resident's permit	**die Aufenthaltsgenehmigung (en)**
receipt	**der Beleg (e)**
driving licence	**der Führerschein (e)**
insurance	**die Versicherung (en)**
medical insurance	**die Krankenversicherung (en)**
medical check	**die ärztliche (n) Untersuchung (en)**
solicitor	**der/die Rechtsanwalt/"in ("e) (nen)**
criminal lawyer	**der/die Anwalt/in ("e) (nen)**
criminal offence	**die Straftat (en)**
court	**das Gericht (e)**
sentence	**das Urteil (e)**
fine	**die Buße (n)**
imprisonment	**die Inhaftierung (en)**
local taxes	**die Gemeindesteuern**

Useful phrases

I don't understand that.	**Ich verstehe das nicht.**
I don't understand you.	**Ich verstehe Sie nicht.**
I didn't know.	**Ich wusste das nicht.**
I have already supplied you with this document.	**Ich habe Ihnen das Dokument schon gegeben.**
I need help.	**Ich brauche Hilfe.**
Is there anyone who can help me?	**Gibt es jemanden, der mir helfen kann?**
When are the offices open?	**Wann ist das Büro geöffnet?**
Where do I need to go to get ...?	**Wohin muss ich gehen, um ... zu bekommen?**
What do I need?	**Was brauche ich?**
Where can I get it?	**Wo kann ich es bekommen?**

15.3 Money

Core vocabulary

currency	**die Währung (en)**
cash	**das Bargeld**
bank account	**das Bankkonto (konten)**

current account	**das Girokonto (konten)**
savings account	**das Sparkonto (konten)**
deposit	**die Anzahlung (en)**
account number	**die Kontonummer (n)**
bank sort code	**die Bankleitzahl (en)**
signature	**die Unterschrift (en)**
PIN number	**die Geheimnummer (n)**
loan	**das Darlehen (-)**
overdraft	**der Überziehungskredit (e)**
bank transfer	**die Banküberweisung (en)**
in credit	**im Haben**
in the red	**im Soll**
mortgage	**die Hypothek (en)**
household insurance	**die Hausratversicherung (en)**
stocks and shares	**Börse und Aktien**
stock market	**der Börsenmarkt ("e)**
loss	**der Verlust (e)**

Useful verbs

to apply	**beantragen**
to be accepted	**angenommen sein**
to be refused	**verweigert sein**
to win	**gewinnen**
to lose	**verlieren**
to make a gain	**einen Gewinn machen**
to make a loss	**einen Verlust machen**
to buy/sell shares	**Aktien kaufen/verkaufen**
to save	**sparen**

Allowances and taxes

accounts	**die Buchhaltung**
accountant	**der Buchhalter/in (-) (nen)/**
	Steuerberater/in (-) (nen)
annual accounts	**jährliche Buchführung**
income tax	**die Lohnsteuer/Einkommenssteuer**
tax class	**die Steuerklasse**

church tax	**die Kirchensteuer**
child allowance	**der Kinderfreibetrag**
employee expenses	**der Arbeitnehmer-Pauschalbetrag**
threshold level	**der Grundfreibetrag**
income tax table	**die Einkommensteuertabelle**
inheritance tax	**die Erbschaftssteuer**

15.4 National holidays

Public and state holidays

Note: Not everything is closed on all of these days.

24 December *Christmas Eve* **Weihnachtsabend**

25 December **1. Weihnachtstag**

26 December **2. Weihnachtstag**

31 December *New Year's Eve* **Sylvester**

1 January *New Year's Day* **Neujahr**

March or April *Good Friday* **Karfreitag**

Easter Monday **Ostermontag**

1 May *May Day* or *Labour Day* **1. Mai** oder **Tag der Arbeit**

3 October *Day of Unification* **Tag der Deutschen Einheit**
  (not throughout Germany)

For the exact dates of holiday, check the internet.

Individual **Land** holidays

6 January *Epiphany* **Heilige Drei Könige**

May or June *Ascension Day* **Himmelfahrtstag**

  June *Pentecost* or *Whitsun* **Pfingsten, Pfingstmontag**

    Corpus Christi **Fronleichnam**

1 November *All Saints Day* **Allerheiligen**

Germany is known for its **Karneval** (*carnival*) which is celebrated
  in cities like Mainz, Cologne and Bonn but recently Berlin started
  to have some **Karnevalsumzüge** on **Rosenmontag** (*Rose Monday
  Parade*) as well.

The *crazy days* **Verrückten Tage** are on **Rosenmontag**, the 42nd day
  before Easter.

Core vocabulary

village fete	**das Dorffest**
circus	**der Zirkus**
concert	**das Konzert (e)**
band	**die Band (s)**
gig	**der Gig (s)**
competition	**der Wettbewerb (e)**
music competition	**der Musikwettbewerb (e)**

Insight

There are many festivals held throughout Germany. All federal states have their own. It is worthwhile looking up the festival calendar on the internet for exact dates before you go to a certain region. Here are some examples:

Internationaler Karneval in Berlin
The Love Parade in Berlin, mainly for young people
Potsdam Bachtage
Chiemsee Reggae Summer Festival
Dresden Music Festival
Salzburger Festspiele
Potsdamer Jazz Festival
Wagner Festspiele in Bayreuth
Händel Festspiele in Halle

Munich has its famous beer festival, the **Oktoberfest**, which begins at the end of September. Wine festivals (**Weinfeste**) take place along the Rhine and Moselle rivers.

Depending upon which area of Germany you visit, you may find people wearing their various traditional costumes (**Trachtenkleidung**) to their local festival. In Bavaria, for example, they wear **das Dirndl** and **die Lederhose**, and in the Black Forest they wear a traditional hat called a **Schwarzwaldhut** or **Bollenhut**.

15.5 Environmental issues

> **Insight**
>
> Don't shy away from talking about technical subjects, such as
> environmental issues, as many words are the same or similar
> in German and English. I suggest you highlight or underline
> these words in the vocabulary list as this will help you build
> up your vocabulary faster. It also helps to learn compound
> words, such as these with **Umwelt** environment:
>
> **die Umwelt** *environment*
> **die Umweltfragen** *environmental issues*
> **der/die Umweltschützer/in (-) (nen)** *environmentalist*
> **die Umweltbelastung (en)** *environmental health*
> **die Umweltverschmutzung** *environmental pollution*
> **umweltbewusst** *environment-conscious*

public health	**das Gesundheitswesen**
housing	**das Wohnungswesen**
architect	**der/die Architekt/in (en) (nen)**
builder	**der Bauherr (en)/Baumeister (-)**
planner	**der/die Stadtplaner/in (-) (nen)**
planning permission	**die Baugenehmigung (en)**
building regulations	**die Bauauflage (n)**
water	**das Wasser**
electricity	**die Elektrizität**
sewage	**das Abwasser**
water level	**der Wasserstand**
drinking water	**das Trinkwasser**
water supply	**die Wasserversorgung**
well	**der Brunnen (-)**
irrigation	**die Bewässerung**
ecology	**die Ökologie**
ecosystem	**das Ökosystem (e)**

erosion	**die Erosion (en)**
GM	**manipulierte Nahrungsmittel**
organic	**organisch**
artificial fertilizer	**der künstliche Dünger**
nitrates	**die Nitrate**
pesticides	**die Pestizide**
poison	**das Gift**
weedkiller	**die Unkrautvernichter (-)**
pollution	**die Verschmutzung**
acid rain	**saurer Regen**
air pollution	**die Luftverschmutzung**
car exhaust	**die Autoabgase**
detergent	**die Reinigungsmittel**
biodegradable detergent	**biologisch abbaubare Reinigungsmittel**
global warming	**die globale Erwärmung (der Erdatmosphäre)**
greenhouse gas	**das Treibhausgas**
nuclear testing	**nukleare Tests**
hole in the ozone layer	**das Ozonloch**
radiation	**die radioaktive Strahlung**
radioactive waste	**der radioaktive Abfall**
water pollution	**die Wasserverschmutzung**
energy	**die Energie**
nuclear power	**die Atomenergie**
electric power	**die elektrische Energie**
solar power	**die Solarenergie/Sonnenenergie**
wind power	**die Windenergie**
power station	**das Kraftwerk/das Elektrizitätswerk**
national park	**der Nationalpark (s)**
regions of special scientific interest	**Gebiete von besonderem wissenschaftlichem Interesse**
protected area	**geschützte Gegenden**
conservation area	**das Landschaftsschutzgebiet (e)**
listed building	**denkmalgeschütztes Gebäude**
ancient monument	**die Denkmalpflege**
archaeological site	**das archäologische Gebiet**

Recycling

rubbish	**der Müll**
glass	**das Glas**
bottle	**die Flasche (n)**
white/clear	**weiß**
green	**grün**
brown	**braun**
white paper	**weißes Papier**
coloured paper	**das Buntpapier**
plastic articles	**der Plastikmüll**
plastic bags	**die Plastiktüten**
linen bags	**die Leinentaschen**
non-organic waste	**der Restmüll**
organic waste	**der Biomüll**
paper collection	**die Papierabfuhr**
yellow bags	**die gelben Säcke**

Insight

Remember this false friend: *gift* ≠ **das Gift**. **Das Gift** in German means *poison* in English. *The gift* in English is **das Geschenk** in German.

Greenpeace

protection of the environment	**der Umweltschutz**
of animals	**der Tierschutz**
of plants	**der Pflanzenschutz**
of oceans	**der Schutz der Ozeane**
of forests	**der Schutz der Wälder**

Useful phrases

to draw attention to	**die Aufmerksamkeit lenken auf**
global environmental problems	**globale Umweltprobleme**
threat to the natural environment	**die Bedrohung der natürlichen Umwelt**

Useful verbs

to protect	**beschützen**
to conserve	**erhalten, schonen**
to destroy	**zerstören**
to dispose of	**beseitigen**
to throw away	<u>**weg**</u>**werfen**

15.6 Religion

Core vocabulary

> **Insight**
>
> Vocabulary in connection with religion is very similar in English and German, as you will see in the list below.

religion	**die Religion (en)**
belief	**der Glaube (n)**
Buddhism	**der Buddhismus**
Christianity	**das Christentum**
Hinduism	**der Hinduismus**
Islam	**der Islam**
Judaism	**das Judentum**
agnostic	**agnostisch**
atheist	**der/die Atheist/in (en) (nen)**
Buddhist	**der/die Buddhist/in (en) (nen)**
Catholic	**der/die Katholik/in (en) (nen)**
Christian	**der/die Christ/in (en) (nen)**
Hindu	**der/die Hinduist/in (en) (nen)**
Jew	**der/die Jude/Jüdin (en) (nen)**
Moslem	**der/die Moslem (en) (nen)**
Quaker	**der/die Quaker/in (-) (nen)**
Jehovah's witness	**die Zeugen Jehovas**
God	**Gott**

the Buddha	**Buddha**
Christ	**Christus**
Mohammed	**Mohammed**
the prophet	**der Prophet (en)**
Allah	**Allah**
cathedral	**die Kathedrale (n)**
chapel	**die Kapelle (n)**
church	**die Kirche (n)**
mosque	**die Moschee (n)**
temple	**der Tempel (-)**
synagogue	**die Synagoge (n)**
religious leader	**das Religionsoberhaupt (¨er)**
bishop	**der Bischof (¨e)**
pope	**der Papst**
Dalai Lama	**der Dalai Lama**
imam	**der Imam (s)**
monk	**der Mönch (e)**
nun	**die Nonne (n)**
priest	**der Priester (-)**
rabbi	**der Rabbi (s)**
prayer	**das Gebet (e)**
mass	**die Messe (n)**
baptism	**die Taufe (n)**
christening	**die Taufe (n)**
to take refuge	**Zuflucht nehmen**
communion	**die Kommunion (en)**
wedding	**die Hochzeit (en)**
funeral	**die Beerdigung (en)**
religious	**religiös**
religion	**die Religion (en)**
affiliation	**die Zugehörigkeit**
religious affiliation	**die Religionszugehörigkeit**
religiousness	**die Religiösität**
religious community	**die Religionsgemeinschaft**

15.7 Social issues

Insight

The following is a list of words in connection with social issues which are similar or the same as English, in order to build up your vocabulary quickly. Remember however to use the German pronunciation. If you are not sure about the correct pronunciation, check the introduction or listen to the audio pronunciation guide at www.teachyourself.com

social **sozial**, problems **die Probleme**, financial **finanziell**, psychological **psychologisch**, depression **die Depression**, emotional **emotional**, drug problems **die Drogenprobleme**, emotional deprivation **die emotionale Deprivation**, alcohol problems **die Alkoholprobleme**, racial **rassistisch**, stress **der Stress**, family problems **die Familienprobleme**, to meditate **meditieren**, help **die Hilfe**, to help **helfen**, to sing **singen**, job **der Job**, to work **jobben**, fundamental **fundamental**.

community	**die Gemeinschaft**
charities	**die Wohlfahrtsverbände**
social services	**die Sozialdienste**
social work	**die Sozialarbeit**
fundamental problems	**fundamentale Probleme**
financial problems	**finanzielle Probleme**
poverty	**die Armut**
debt	**die Schulden**
psychological problems	**die psychologischen Probleme**
insecurity	**die Unsicherheit (en)**
loneliness	**die Einsamkeit**
mental health	**die geistige/mentale Gesundheit**
neglect	**vernachlässigen**
racial tension	**die rassistischen Spannungen**
unemployment	**die Arbeitslosigkeit**
homelessness	**die Obdachlosigkeit**
environmental problems	**die Umweltprobleme**
bad housing	**die schlechten Wohnverhältnisse**

lack of food/water	die Lebensmittelknappheit/ Wasserknappheit
overpopulation	die Überbevölkerung
poverty	die Armut
unhealthy living conditions	ungesunde Lebensbedingungen
bad environment	das schlechte Umfeld
social worker	der/die Sozialarbeiter/in (-) (nen)

Useful verbs

to attend church	zur Kirche gehen
to believe	glauben
to pray	beten
to preach	predigen
to kneel	knien
to sing, chant	singen
to worship	anbeten
to meditate	meditieren
to do charity work	freiwilligen Dienst in sozialen Einrichtungen machen
to counsel	beraten
to assist/help	helfen

Insight

Don't be afraid of long German (compound) nouns; think of them as a combination of separate nouns joined together as one. My tip is to take a little breath in between the elements. Look at the following examples:

die Arbeitslosenzahlen *unemployment figures*
die Arbeit *work*
los *without*
die Zahlen *figures*
die Arbeitsbeschaffungsmaßnahmen *job creation scheme*
die Arbeit *job/work*
die Beschaffung *creation*
die Maßnahmen *measure/action/scheme*

TEST YOURSELF

See how many questions you can get right without looking back at the unit.

1 *To debate* in German is:
- **a** Debatte
- **b** debattieren
- **c** debate

2 The meaning of the noun **die Wahl** is:
- **a** a whale
- **b** an election
- **c** a vote

3 The word for *peace* in German is:
- **a** Frieden
- **b** Krieg
- **c** ein Stück

4 Which verb is a separable verb?
- **a** verteidigen
- **b** verletzen
- **c** angreifen

5 **Die Hypothek** means
- **a** mortgage
- **b** rent
- **c** household insurance

6 Which word is spelt exactly the same way in both languages?
- **a** Religion
- **b** Priest
- **c** Temple

7 The German word for *bank transfer* is:
   a Bankangestellte
   b Bankleitzahl
   c Banküberweisung

8 Die Arbeitslosigkeit is:
   a employment
   b unemployment
   c contract

9 What is the word for *christening*?
   a das Christentum
   b das Trinkwasser
   c die Taufe

10 The word for *competition* is
   a der Wetterbericht
   b die Bundeswehr
   c der Wettbewerb

Answers: 1b; 2b; 3a; 4c; 5a; 6a; 7c; 8b; 9c; 10c

16

The media

16.1 The press

Core vocabulary

....

Insight

Familiarize yourself first with these words, which are the same or similar in English and German.

media **die Medien**, *press* **die Presse**, *journalist* **der/die Journalist/in**, *journalism* **der Journalismus**, *reporter* **der/die Reporter/in**, *correspondent* **der/die Korrespondent/in**, *criticism/critics* **die Kritik**, *column* **die Kolumne**, *article* **der Artikel**, *terrorist* **der/die Terrorist/in**, *volcano* **der Vulkan**, *to demonstrate* **demonstrieren**, *to hijack* **hijacken**, *political* **politisch**, *strike* **der Streik**, *fire* **das Feuer**.

....

newspaper	**die Zeitung (en)**
national newspaper	**die überregionale Zeitung (en)**
magazine	**die Zeitschrift (en)/die Illustrierte (en)**
review	**der Überblick (e)**
tabloid paper	**die Boulevardzeitung (en)**
trash magazines	**die Regenbogenpresse**
daily	**täglich**
weekly	**wöchentlich**
bi-weekly	**14-täglich**

monthly	monatlich
annual	jährlich
publisher	der/die Verleger/in (-) (nen)
editor	der/die Redakteur/in (-) (nen)/ Herausgeber/in (-) (nen)/Lektor/in (-)
leading article	der Leitartikel (-)
current events	aktuelle Ereignisse (-)
headline	die Schlagzeile (n)
advertisement	die Anzeige (n)
notices	die Bekanntmachungen
obituaries	der Nachruf (e), die Todesanzeige(n)
small ads	die Kleinanzeigen/die Inserate
local news	die Lokalnachrichten
news items	die Nachrichten/die News
natural disasters	die Naturkatastrophen
floods	die Überflutungen
drought	die Dürre
famine	die Hungersnot (¨e)
earthquake	das Erdbeben (-)
epidemic	die Seuche (n)
volcanic eruption	der Vulkanausbruch (¨e)
storm/hurricane	der Wirbelsturm (¨e)/der Orkan (e)
car crash	der Autounfall (¨e)
plane crash	das Flugzeugunglück (e)
collision at sea	der Schiffzusammenstoß (¨e)
terrorist attack	das terroristische Attentat (-e)
bomb attack	der Bombenanschlag (¨e)
to hijack a plane	ein Flugzeug entführen/hijacken
taking a hostage	die Geiselnahme (n)
political demonstration	die politische Demonstration (en)
fire	das Feuer (-)/der Brand (¨e)
forest fire	der Waldbrand (¨e)

Useful verbs

to give one's view on	sich darüber äußern
to complain	beklagen
to remind	mahnen

to enter into negotiations	**in Verhandlungen treten**
to appoint	**beauftragen**
to demand	**verlangen**
to publish	**veröffentlichen/publizieren**
explain/to say	**erklären**
to announce	**bekannt geben**
to gain	**erzielen**
to announce	**verkünden**
to consult	**beraten/konsultieren**
to announce	**ankündigen**

Insight

Newspaper reports are written mainly in the imperfect tense:

Alle politischen Parteien **trafen** sich zu einer Versammlung.
All political parties met for a meeting.

Mehrere Einbrüche **wurden** in der Innenstadt gemeldet.
Several burglaries were reported in the city centre.

Ein Jugendlicher **ertrank** in dem Dorfsee.
One youngster drowned in the village lake.

Der Zusammenstoß zweier Autos auf der A5 **resultierte** in
5 verletzten Personen.
*The collision of two cars on the A5 resulted in 5 people
being injured.*

Insight

Reading German newspapers and magazines not only
helps you to learn more German but also to find out what
is happening in Germany. In order to get used to reading
newspapers in German I suggest you start off by reading
tabloid newspapers or magazines, as they are easier to
understand for learners of the German language. To find out
which level is best for you I recommend going to a newsagent's
(**Zeitungsgeschäft**) or library and flicking through the papers.

Different types of paper
Some daily German newspapers

Bild Zeitung; shortened to **Bild**
Westdeutsche Allgemeine Zeitung
Hannoversche Allgemeine Zeitung
Süddeutsche Zeitung
Frankfurter Allgemeine Zeitung
Die Welt
Berliner Morgenpost
Der Tagesspiegel

Some weekly and Sunday newspapers
Bild am Sonntag
Die Zeit
Welt am Sonntag
Bayernkurier

Some news magazines	*Periodicals*
Der Spiegel	**Die Bunte**
Der Stern	**Brigitte**
Focus	**Cosmopolitan**
	Freundin

16.2 Books

Core vocabulary

> **Insight**
>
> Here is a list of words in connection with books which are the same or similar in English and German. Take some time to learn and memorize them, as it will help you to communicate faster by knowing which words the two languages have in common.

title **der Titel,** *author* **der/die Autor/in,** *illustrator* **der/die Illustrator/in,** *cartoonist* **der/die Cartoonist/in,** *biography* **die Biografie,** *autobiography* **die Autobiografie,** *atlas* **der Atlas,** *literature* **die Literatur,** *paragraph* **der Paragraf,** *comma* **das Komma,** *to publish* **publizieren.**

author	**der/die Schriftsteller/in (-) (nen)/ Autor/in (nen)**
artist	**der/die Künstler/in (-) (nen)**
novel	**der Roman (e)**
romantic novel	**der Liebesroman (e)**
poetry	**die Poesie (-)**
short story	**die Kurzgeschichte (n)**
narrative	**die Erzählung (en)**
paperback	**das Taschenbuch (¨er)**
dictionary	**das Wörterbuch (¨er)**
encyclopedia	**das Lexikon (Lexika)**
guide book	**das Sachbuch (¨er)**
light fiction	**die Unterhaltungsliteratur**
literature for women	**die Frauenliteratur**
literature for children	**die Kinderliteratur**
punctuation	**die Zeichensetzung (en)**
paragraph	**der Absatz (¨e)/der Paragraf**
sentence	**der Satz (¨e)**
line	**die Zeile (n)**
capital letter	**der Großbuchstabe (n)**
full stop	**der Punkt (e)**
dash	**der Gedankenstrich (e)**
hyphen	**der Bindestrich (e)**
upper case	**der Großbuchstabe (n)**
lower case (letters)	**der Kleinbuchstabe (n)**

Useful verbs

to write	**schreiben**	*to describe*	**beschreiben**
to develop	**entwickeln**	*to portray*	**dar̲stellen/ schildern**
to publish	**veröffent- lichen/publizieren**	*to quote*	**zitieren**
to write poems	**dichten**	*to express*	**au̲sdrücken**

16.3 Cinema and television

Core vocabulary

cinema	**das Kino (s)**
auditorium	**das Auditorium/der Zuschauerraum (¨e)**
screen	**die Leinwand (¨e)**
seat	**der Platz (¨e)**
foyer	**die Eingangshalle (n)**
ticket	**die Kinokarte (n)/das Ticket (s)**
booking office	**die Kinokasse (n)**
thriller	**der Krimi(s), der Thriller**
romance	**der romantische Film**
love story	**der Liebesfilm/die Love Story**
historical film	**der histori sche Film**
war film	**der Kriegsfilm**

crime	der Kriminalfilm (e)
adverts	die Werbung
actor/actress	der/die Schauspieler/in (-) (nen)
leading role	die Hauptrolle (n)
supporting role	die Nebenrolle (n)
singer	der/die Sänger/in (-) (nen)
dancer	der/die Tänzer/in (-) (nen)
the crew	die Filmbesatzung/die Crew
the film is dubbed	der Film ist synchronisiert
subtitled	der Film hat Untertitel
television (set)	der Fernseher (-)/das TV
cable TV	das Kabelfernsehen
satellite	der Satellit (en)
dish	der Satellitenempfänger
aerial	die Antenne (n)
video recorder	der Videoapparat (e)
DVD recorder	der DVD-Spieler
remote control	die Fernbedienung (en)
channel	der Kanal ("e)
commercials (adverts)	die Werbung (en)
cartoons	der Zeichentrickfilm (e)
children's programmes	das Kinderprogramm (e)
chat show	die Talkshow (s)
documentary	die Dokumentation (en)
feature film	der Spielfilm (e)
game show	die Spielshow (s)
light entertainment	leichte Unterhaltung
news programmes	die Nachrichtensendung (en)
opinion	die Meinung (en)
soap	die Seifenoper (n)
weather forecast	der Wetterbericht (e)
repeats	die Wiederholungen
news reporter	der/die Nachrichtenjournalist/in (en) (nen)
news reader	der/die Nachrichtensprecher/in (en) (nen)
presenter	der/die Moderator/in (en) (nen)
game show host	der/die Gastgeber/in (en) (nen) der Spielshow
viewer	der/die Zuschauer/in (-) (nen)

| frequency | die Frequenz (en) |
| disc jockey/DJ | der Discjockey (s)/DJ |

Useful phrases

What is your favourite programme?	Was ist Ihr/dein Lieblingsprogramm?
Do you like documentaries?	Mögen Sie/magst du Dokumentarsendungen?
Who is your favourite presenter?	Wer ist Ihr(e)/dein(e) Lieblingsmoderator/in?

Insight

A good way of getting used to understanding spoken German is to watch a film in German. While some people prefer to watch it with subtitles others feel distracted by them. Find out what works best for you.

Useful verbs

to change channels	auf einen anderen Sender umschalten
to turn on/off the TV	den Fernseher einschalten/ausschalten
to turn the sound up/down	die Lautstärke aufdrehen/runterdrehen
to broadcast	berichten
to record	aufnehmen, aufzeichnen

Insight

There are a few expressions for watching TV. It is worth knowing them as people talk about it in different ways.

to watch TV **fernsehen**, I am watching TV **Ich sehe fern/Ich schaue Fernsehen.**

Or: **Ich gucke TV/Ich schaue TV.** Some young people use the slang expression **glotzen** to watch instead of **gucken** or **schauen. Ich glotze TV. Stelle die Glotze an** means Switch the TV on.

TEST YOURSELF

See how many questions you can get right without looking back at the unit.

1 What is the German word for *dictionary*?
   a Wort
   b Wortschatz
   c Wörterbuch

2 The word for *daily* in German is:
   a tagsüber
   b täglich
   c während des Tages

3 The German word for *news* is:
   a die Anzeigen
   b die Nachrichten
   c der Nachruf

4 The word for *earthquake* is:
   a Erdbeben
   b Erde
   c Erdatmosphäre

5 A *newspaper* is:
   a ein Papier
   b eine Zeitschrift
   c eine Zeitung

6 Which of the following words is written differently in German?
   a Band
   b Gig
   c Concert

7 Which of these words is different in German?
   a film
   b quiz
   c soap

8 Which verb is *not* a separable verb?
   a beschreiben
   b ankündigen
   c ausdrücken

9 Which verb means *to write poetry*?
   a beschreiben
   b dichten
   c zitieren

10 A *capital letter* translates into German as:
   a eine Kapitalanlage
   b eine Großbuchstabe
   c ein Kapitel

Answers: 1c; 2b; 3b; 4a; 5c; 6c; 7c; 8a; 9b; 10b

Ich hoffe, es hat Ihnen Spaß gemacht deutsche Vokabeln zu lernen.
I hope you enjoyed learning German vocabulary.

Lisa Kahlen